Insights into Non-native Vocabulary Teaching and Learning

SECOND LANGUAGE ACQUISITION
Series Editor: Professor David Singleton, *Trinity College, Dublin, Ireland*

This series brings together titles dealing with a variety of aspects of language acquisition and processing in situations where a language or languages other than the native language is involved. Second language is thus interpreted in its broadest possible sense. The volumes included in the series all offer in their different ways, on the one hand, exposition and discussion of empirical findings and, on the other, some degree of theoretical reflection. In this latter connection, no particular theoretical stance is privileged in the series; nor is any relevant perspective – sociolinguistic, psycholinguistic, neurolinguistic and so on – deemed out of place. The intended readership of the series includes final-year undergraduates working on second language acquisition projects, postgraduate students involved in second language acquisition research, and researchers and teachers in general whose interests include a second language acquisition component.

Full details of all the books in this series and of all our other publications can be found on http://www.multilingual-matters.com, or by writing to Multilingual Matters, St Nicholas House, 31-34 High Street, Bristol BS1 2AW, UK.

SECOND LANGUAGE ACQUISITION
Series Editor: Professor David Singleton

Insights into Non-native Vocabulary Teaching and Learning

Edited by
Rubén Chacón-Beltrán, Christián Abello-Contesse and María del Mar Torreblanca-López

MULTILINGUAL MATTERS
Bristol • Buffalo • Toronto

Library of Congress Cataloging in Publication Data
A catalog record for this book is available from the Library of Congress.
Insights into Non-native Vocabulary Teaching and Learning/Edited by Rubén Chacón-Beltrán...[et al.].
Second Language Acquisition: 52
Includes bibliographical references and index.
1. Vocabulary--Study and teaching. 2. Language and languages--Study and teaching. 3. Second language acquisition. I. Chacón Beltrán, Rubén
PE1449.I57 2010
418--dc22 2010021278

British Library Cataloguing in Publication Data
A catalogue entry for this book is available from the British Library.

ISBN-13: 978-1-84769-289-4 (hbk)
ISBN-13: 978-1-84769-288-7 (pbk)

Multilingual Matters
UK: St Nicholas House, 31–34 High Street, Bristol, BS1 2AW, UK.
USA: UTP, 2250 Military Road, Tonawanda, NY 14150, USA.
Canada: UTP, 5201 Dufferin Street, North York, Ontario M3H 5T8, Canada.

Copyright © 2010 Rubén Chacón-Beltrán, Christián Abello-Contesse, María del Mar Torreblanca-López and the authors of individual chapters.

All rights reserved. No part of this work may be reproduced in any form or by any means without permission in writing from the publisher.

The policy of Multilingual Matters/Channel View Publications is to use papers that are natural, renewable and recyclable products, made from wood grown in sustainable forests. In the manufacturing process of our books, and to further support our policy, preference is given to printers that have FSC and PEFC Chain of Custody certification.TheFSCand/orPEFClogoswillappearonthosebookswher   e full certificationhasbeengrantedtotheprinterconcerned.

Typeset by Techset Composition Ltd., Salisbury, UK.

Contents

Contributors... vii

1 Vocabulary Teaching and Learning: Introduction and
  Overview.. 1
  *Rubén Chacón-Beltrán, Christián Abello-Contesse and
  M. Mar Torreblanca-López*

Part 1: Development of a Model for Vocabulary Teaching and Learning

2 Form-focused Instruction in Second Language Vocabulary
  Learning 15
  Batia Laufer

3 Key Issues in Teaching and Learning Vocabulary 28
  Norbert Schmitt

4 A Dynamic Perspective on L2 Lexical Development in
  Academic English 41
  Tal Caspi and Wander Lowie

Part 2: Empirical Studies on Lexical Processing in English and Spanish

5 The Effect of Lexicalization in the Native Language on Second
  Language Lexical Inferencing: A Cross-Linguistic Study 61
  T. Sima Paribakht

6 Aural Word Recognition and Oral Competence in English as a
  Foreign Language 83
  James Milton, Jo Wade and Nicola Hopkins

7 A Cascade Model of Lexical Access to Explain the Phonological
  Activation of Recently Practiced Lexical Items.................. 99
  Teresa López-Soto

8 Concordances versus Dictionaries: Evaluating
  Approaches to Word Learning in ESOL......................... 112
  Rachel Allan

9   Evidence of Incremental Vocabulary Learning in Advanced L2
    Spanish Learners 126
    Diana Frantzen

**Part 3: Materials Design and Strategies for Vocabulary Teaching
and Learning**

10 Conspicuous by Their Absence: The Infrequency of Very
    Frequent Words in some English as a Foreign Language
    Textbooks 145
    Jim Lawley

11 The Treatment of Lexical Aspects in Commercial Textbooks
    for L2 Teaching and Learning 156
    María Dolores López-Jiménez

12 A Second-generation CALL Vocabulary-learning Program
    ADELEX: In Search of a Psychopedagogic Model 175
    Carmen Pérez Basanta

13 Word Associations as a Vocabulary Teaching Strategy in an
    Advanced L2 Reading Class 186
    Zorana Vasiljevic

References 206

Index 227

Contributors

Editors

Rubén Chacón-Beltrán is currently Assistant Professor at the UNED (Universidad Nacional de Educación a Distancia), Madrid, Spain, where he teaches undergraduate courses in English as a foreign language, English sociolinguistics and bilingualism, and a graduate course in vocabulary teaching and learning. He holds a PhD in English Applied Linguistics and has taught in various universities in Spain.

Christián Abello-Contesse is currently Associate Professor at the University of Seville, Spain, where he teaches undergraduate and graduate courses in foreign-language teaching methodology, second language acquisition, and bilingualism. He has published journal articles and book chapters on issues in language learning and teaching. He holds degrees in education, English, Spanish and applied linguistics, and has taught English and Spanish as foreign/second languages at several universities in Chile, Spain and the United States.

M. Mar Torreblanca-López is currently Associate Professor at the University of Seville, Spain, where she teaches undergraduate courses in English as a foreign language and discourse analysis and graduate courses in pragmatics and discourse analysis. She holds a PhD in English language and linguistics and has taught in various universities around the world including Spain, the United States and Argentina.

Authors

Rachel Allan has worked as an English language teacher, and more recently, as a teacher trainer, in Asia and Europe for many years; she also holds a CELTA and H.Dip.TEFL. Research for the Masters in Applied Linguistics further developed her long-held interest in vocabulary acquisition, and the research reported here was carried out as part of her current work on the Daedalus Vocabulary Acquisition Project at the Applied Language Centre,

University College Dublin, a University-funded project investigating the effects of different approaches to vocabulary learning.

Carmen Pérez Basanta is Senior Lecturer in Applied Linguistics (University of Granada, Spain). She is the coordinator of a R&D project entitled: 'ADELEX: Assessing and Developing Lexical Competence through New Technologies'. She has been awarded the 'European Label for Innovation' and also 'The International Award for Excellence' for the paper 'Using Techonology for Preservice Second Language Teacher Education Through WebCT' (*International Journal of Technology, Knowledge and Society* 2: 101–117, 2007). Her main interests are vocabulary acquisition, CALL, testing and corpus linguistics.

Tal Caspi completed her MA in Applied Linguistics in Groningen in 2005 and is currently working on her PhD involving a longitudinal investigation of development and variation in non-native English writing and lexicon, using a dynamic systems perspective. She compiled a large item database for testing vocabulary knowledge development, and initiated five ongoing case studies that combine vocabulary testing with multiple indexes of writing complexity and accuracy.

Diana Frantzen is an Associate Professor of Spanish and the Director of the Spanish Language Program in the Department of Spanish and Portuguese at the University of Wisconsin-Madison. She is also a core member of UW-Madison's interdisciplinary Doctoral Program in Second Language Acquisition and served as its co-director (2006–2009). She has published articles on issues in FL lexical and grammatical acquisition and teaching, error correction, culture and FL anxiety. Her textbook, *Lazos: Gramática y vocabulario a través de la literatura* (Pearson/Prentice Hall, 2009), is an intermediate/advanced college Spanish text which combines a selection of 15 Hispanic short stories and an intensive review of selected Spanish grammar and lexical topics. Much of her recent research focuses on linguistic analysis of literature.

Nicola Hopkins is a tutor in the Centre for Applied Language Studies at Swansea University. She has used her expertise in foreign language software and programmes to design and create the software package which allows estimates of phonological vocabulary knowledge to be made.

Batia Laufer (PhD, University of Edinburgh) is Professor in the Department of English Language and Literature at the University of Haifa, Israel. Her research interests are in second language acquisition, particularly vocabulary acquisition, lexicography, cross linguistic influence, reading and testing. She has published several books and numerous articles in various professional journals, and lectured on these subjects extensively in and outside of Israel.

Jim Lawley is a graduate of Oxford University (Modern Languages). He holds an MA in Applied English Linguistics from Birmingham University and a doctorate from the Universidad Nacional de Educación a Distancia (UNED), Spain. He has taught at the UNED since 1996 where he is now a tenured lecturer, teaching English for undergraduate courses, and corpus linguistics and materials design on the UNED's Master en Lingüística Inglesa Aplicada. He specializes in course and syllabus design and is the author and coauthor of books published by HarperCollins, Thomas Nelson, Pearson and Richmond.

María Dolores López-Jiménez is Assistant Professor at Pablo de Olavide University, Seville, Spain, where she teaches undergraduate courses in English as a foreign language. She holds degrees in education, English, Spanish and applied linguistics and has taught English and Spanish as foreign/second languages in Spain and the United States. Her current research focuses on L2 vocabulary teaching.

Teresa López-Soto is currently a Tenure Professor and Researcher at the English Language Department, University of Seville, Spain. Her main areas of research are related to the teaching and learning of EFL and Speech Technologies. In the former area, Dr López-Soto has investigated mainly on the phonological acquisition of EFL and on the integration of listening and vocabulary learning to facilitate the improvement of both skills on a parallel basis. Dr López-Soto has also a deep interest in integrating technologies in the classroom and pays special attention to the spoken input in her English teaching practice.

Wander Lowie studied English and Speech Science at the University of Amsterdam, specializing in second language acquisition. He finished his PhD on the acquisition of L2 morphology in Groningen in 1998 and has worked on the acquisition of phonology and on the multilingual mental lexicon since then. Over the past five years he has focused on L2 developmental processes from a dynamic systems perspective. In 2005 he co-authored a Routledge textbook on *Second Language Acquisition* with Marjolijn Verspoor and Kees de Bot and has recently published in *Language Learning*, *The International Journal of Applied Linguistics*, *Bilingualism* and the *Modern Language Journal*.

James Milton worked formerly as head of English in both Tudun Wada Teachers College, Nigeria and the University of Sebha, Libya and has been head of Applied Linguistics at Swansea University since 1986. In addition to research in vocabulary learning and testing, he also publishes ELT learning materials with Express Publishing.

T. Sima Paribakht is Professor at the Official Languages and Bilingualism Institute of the University of Ottawa. She is currently the Director of the Academic Programs of the Institute. Dr Paribakht's main areas of research interest include second language acquisition, more specifically L2 vocabulary acquisition, teaching and testing, as well as L2 communication strategies, L2 program development and L2 teaching methodology. She has authored and edited several books and has published a number of book chapters and articles in these areas.

Norbert Schmitt is Professor of Applied Linguistics at the University of Nottingham. He is interested in all aspects of second language vocabulary studies. He has published widely in this area, including the books *Vocabulary: Description, Acquisition, and Pedagogy*, *Vocabulary in Language Teaching* and *Formulaic Sequences*, as well as articles in *Studies in Second Language Acquisition*, *Language Learning*, *Applied Linguistics*, *TESOL Quarterly*, *System* and *Language Testing*. His forthcoming publications include an overview of instructed second language vocabulary learning in *Language Teaching Research*, and a vocabulary research manual with Palgrave Press.

Zorana Vasiljevic (PhD, University of Queensland) is an Associate Professor at the Faculty of Language and Literature of Bunkyo University, Japan, where she teaches undergraduate courses in English as a foreign language, L2 teaching methodology and material development. Her research interests include L2 vocabulary acquisition, discourse analysis and EFL methodologies.

Jo Wade has worked at Swansea University since 1993 and is currently head of EFL in the English Language Teaching Unit. She has also worked extensively overseas and spent eight years teaching in Japan, Hungary, Turkey and Barbados. She completed her masters in TEFL in 2006 with a dissertation investigating the relationship between orthographic and phonological vocabulary knowledge.

Chapter 1
Vocabulary Teaching and Learning: Introduction and Overview

RUBÉN CHACÓN-BELTRÁN, CHRISTIÁN ABELLO-CONTESSE
and M. MAR TORREBLANCA-LÓPEZ

Introduction

Traditionally, research in language teaching and learning methods devoted less attention to vocabulary than to other aspects of language as a communication system. Other language elements took precedence, and vocabulary tended to be presented in a way that favored the introduction of grammatical elements (O'Dell, 1997). There was a general consent that grammar should be taught and that in due time learners would 'acquire' the vocabulary necessary to deal with specific communicative situations through their exposure to the target language. In addition, under the influence of structuralism, L2 teaching approaches and methods often preferred to conceive language as a 'closed' and manageable system with a limited number of communication options to be taught, that is, a series of grammar rules rather than an 'open' and unlimited subsystem, such as vocabulary. Grammar teaching tended to receive more attention than processes related to vocabulary teaching (O'Dell, 1997; Pérez Basanta, 1996; Wotjak, 1999; Zimmerman, 1997). Vocabulary is sometimes not so easily controlled by the language teacher who may have more difficulty dealing with it than with grammar rules. During the 1980s, however, interest in vocabulary teaching and learning grew, and during the 1990s, a great deal of attention was given to vocabulary as a key component in L2 learning for successful communication. Laufer (1986) pointed out:

> Until very recently vocabulary has suffered from step-child status in language acquisition research. The reasons for this plight might have been the linguists' preference for closed systems describable by rules, the reaction of psycholinguists against the associative and the stimulus–response theories of learning and the interest of the methodologists in the beginning stages of language learning. (Laufer, 1986: 73)

In fact, the treatment of vocabulary as a 'second class' issue that learners will deal with in due course is not justifiable. Vermeer (1992) and Laufer (1998) emphasized the importance of the lexical component in order to acquire full competence in various registers and contexts. Vermeer (1992) pointed out that the main concern, if a high level of proficiency in the L2 is to be acquired, should be vocabulary, and Laufer (1998) affirmed that the main difference between language learners and native speakers of the target language was precisely their lexical competence.

Some studies comparing native and non-native speaker interaction (Braidi, 2002; Burt, 1975; Khalil, 1985; Sheorey, 1986; Tomiyana, 1980) show that vocabulary knowledge and use play an important role in successful communication and that it is one of the domains where non-native speakers can equal native speakers and, on some occasions, surpass them.

Toward a Model of Lexical Acquisition in an L2

The lack of a general theory explaining the processes involved in lexical acquisition – and later vocabulary retrieval in both its receptive and productive dimensions – seems to be one of the common concerns in language teaching and learning. In Paul Nation's words:

> There isn't an overall theory of how vocabulary is acquired. Our knowledge has mainly been built up from fragmentary studies, and *at the moment we have only the broadest idea of how acquisition might occur.* We certainly have no knowledge of the acquisition stages that particular words might move through. (Schmitt, 1995: 5) (emphasis added).

Several attempts have been made – without much success – to provide a theory or model that can explain vocabulary learning. However, the acquisition of the lexicon involves highly complex neurobiological processes that are still to be described and require the coordinated work of linguists, SLA researchers, psychologists and neurobiologists. This whole process becomes even more complex if we think of distinctions between young or adult learners and monolingual or bilingual subjects. The fragmentary nature of the studies that were carried out up to the mid-1990s (Schmitt, 1995) as well as the complexity of the systems SLA researchers are trying to decode – human language ability and the functioning of the human brain – make it extremely difficult to provide conclusive evidence of underlying lexical processing in our brains. Unfortunately this situation has not changed much over the last decade. In this respect, Meara argued that:

> The L2 research literature contains lots of examples of what might be broadly described as descriptive research on vocabulary acquisition, but very few examples of explanatory, model-based research, which attempts to account for this learning. (Meara, 1997: 109)

Meara (1990, 1997) proposed a multidimensional model in which vocabulary acquisition is to be understood as a cumulative activity, that is 'unknown words' would be those that lack any connection to the language learner's lexicon, whereas 'known words' would have different connections both in number and nature. Thus, degrees of depth of knowledge would be determined by the quantity and type of connections of a given word to others, and this should have an impact on lexical availability both in receptive and productive terms.

Singleton (1999) offered some guidelines for future research in the field of lexical acquisition and he postulated that a coherent model of lexical acquisition should emerge from a coherent model of lexical learning based on linguistic theory, computational linguistics, psycholinguistics, second language teaching and language assessment. In fact, lexis seems to be at crossroads of the aforementioned disciplines and a good model should also embrace both quantitative and qualitative research methodologies. Singleton (1999) added that most research conducted in the area of the lexical component included cross-sectional studies and that more longitudinal, or at least long-term, studies were needed.

Another aspect to be taken into consideration when developing a theory for lexical acquisition and mental processing is that it probably involves different operations both in L1 and L2, so L1 lexical processing does not necessarily match L2 lexical processing. Conceptualization, that is the creation of new concepts, is one of the main developments in child lexical acquisition whereas in non-native language acquisition, the relabeling of already known concepts and words seems to be the most common procedure, and as Jiang (2004) indicates, adult L2 learners often rely on their preexisting semantic system. In this latter case, the mother tongue also plays an important role as cognate languages are presumably easier to acquire even if deceptive cognate words come up (Chacón Beltrán, 2001).

Implicit and Explicit Vocabulary Learning

Nick Ellis (1994) distinguished two possibilities in relation to the processing of new vocabulary, the implicit vocabulary learning hypothesis and the explicit vocabulary learning hypothesis. The former would be related to behaviorist approaches and would argue that new vocabulary is acquired without the language learner being aware of it, especially when reading or due to oral input arising during interaction. This hypothesis refers to an unconscious process where the lack of intentionality is the main feature:

> An *implicit vocabulary learning hypothesis* would hold that the meaning of a new word is acquired totally unconsciously as a result of abstraction from repeated exposures in a range of activated contexts. (Ellis, 1994: 219)

The latter hypothesis, meanwhile, would support the relevance of explicit attention to new words by means of a number of conscious and planned strategies:

> An *explicit vocabulary learning hypothesis* would hold that there is some benefit to vocabulary acquisition from the learner noticing novel vocabulary, selectively attending to it, and using a variety of strategies to try to infer its meaning from the context. Furthermore there may also be advantage from applying metacognitive strategies to remember new vocabulary, to consolidate a new understanding by repetition [...]. (Ellis, 1994: 219)

Even if the two hypotheses presented above embody opposing views of vocabulary learning, at the moment most SLA researchers would probably agree that, as far as L2 learners learning vocabulary are concerned, a combination of the two processes is needed (Schmitt, 2000), resulting in a combination of incidental and explicit learning. The latter has always been perceived as a way to enhance and contribute to the learning process, especially in a foreign language context. A great deal of recent research into second language vocabulary teaching and learning has been devoted to the comparison of explicit and implicit approaches to vocabulary learning and the identification of techniques that can favor and enhance the learning process; these trends continue to be explored nowadays.

As a rule, vocabulary teaching and learning research has been especially prolific in two areas: (1) the teaching of vocabulary through extensive reading, that is exposure to contextualized and real samples of the language containing relevant vocabulary; and (2) an approach based on the teaching of vocabulary carefully selected for the language learner according to criteria such as relevance, frequency and usefulness in accomplishing certain tasks.

The implicit approach based on reading has traditionally been one of the main ways to learn languages, especially before the arrival of new technologies, which now offer an array of possibilities for language learning and easy exposure to samples of real language. Learning vocabulary through reading often implies a cognitive process in which hypotheses about the meaning of unknown words are formed and subsequently checked. This is an unconscious and automatic process, which proves to be a very useful strategy if the number of unknown words is not too high. From a pedagogical point of view this strategy for vocabulary learning can be very convenient: the cognitive process of reading is not interrupted as it is not necessary to check the dictionary for the exact meaning. Some empirical studies within this approach to vocabulary teaching are Elley (1991), Krashen (1989, 1993), Maruyama (1995), Na and Nation (1985). Lao and Krashen (2000) seem to have found new evidence to support the effectiveness of extensive reading tasks. Huckin and Coady (1999) supported the idea that most vocabulary known to any person, either in the L1 or the

L2, has been acquired incidentally through reading and the inference of meaning through context. Huckin and Coady (1999) also emphasized three main advantages in incidental approaches to vocabulary acquisition based on reading, as opposed to explicit approaches to vocabulary learning.

(1) Words are contextualized and the language learner receives a higher amount of information (meaning and use) on each lexical unit. Along the same lines, Ooi and Lee Kim-Seoh (1996) observed that 'Vocabulary taught through reading would give the learner more opportunities to process language use at a deeper level and to develop semantic networks and other kinds of associative links that will ultimately enhance learning' (Ooi & Lee Kim-Seoh, 1996: 57).
(2) It stimulates reading at the same time that new vocabulary is presented and previous vocabulary is fixed with more contextualized information on it.
(3) It favors autonomy in language learning and stimulates individualized language learning at the students' own pace. Qian (2004) shows that guessing new vocabulary from context is one of the most common strategies for L2 learners when dealing with the meaning of unknown words, even more frequent than dictionary use.

Knowing a word is not an easy task; Paribakht and Wesche (1998) pointed out that the complexity and the amount of information needed to have perfectfull knowledge of a word is very large. The lexical learning process requires various forms and levels of mental processing that cannot be attained spontaneously by occasional exposure through reading. A reading-only approach, and an incidental approach to vocabulary learning, may be useful for a syllabus that only aims at developing reading comprehension skills, but that does not seem enough if the aim is to develop a deep processing of vocabulary and the development of productive skills.

> Learning a new word involves establishing relationships between its form, meaning(s) and function(s) in utterances and texts, the elaboration of knowledge about individual words so that they can be used in appropriate contexts, the linking of the word with other words through various kinds of associational networks, and the gradual automaticity of this knowledge leading to fluency in use [...]. This outcome implies the need for diversity and level of mental processing over time, which cannot necessarily be expected from multiple exposures through reading. A reading-based, incidental learning approach may be adequate for an L2 teaching program, which has the development of reading proficiency and related receptive vocabulary as primary objectives. However, *for programs which aim at rapid vocabulary expansion and development of learners' production skills, and which also seek to maintain a measure of influence over what vocabulary is learned, more is needed.* (Paribakht & Wesche, 1998: 205) (emphasis added)

An Explicit Approach Based on Explicit Teaching

Nation (1990) considered that once an L2 learner has acquired a certain amount of basic vocabulary, there is a threshold in which word frequency decreases and extensive reading becomes an unproductive way to learn vocabulary. Rather, he proposed that classroom time be devoted to the development of strategies for L2 learners to learn vocabulary on their own.

Paribakht and Wesche (1997, 1998) compared two teaching techniques for vocabulary learning, one based on extensive reading, and another based on reading together with explicit teaching. Results showed that both teaching techniques were useful and students in both groups increased their vocabulary knowledge considerably, although the group combining reading and related exercises outperformed the extensive reading group.

> [...] although reading for meaning appears to produce significant results in vocabulary acquisition, such reading supplemented with specific vocabulary exercises produces greater gains for the targeted words. This suggests that although instruction makes a difference, *more focused instruction is desirable when the learning period is limited and specific vocabulary outcomes are sought*. (Paribakht & Wesche, 1998: 197) (emphasis added)

Most researchers today seem to agree that a combination of explicit and implicit techniques for vocabulary learning is desirable, although further research is needed to discover the ways in which such a combination can be put into practice most effectively considering class-time limitations and classroom resources that L2 teachers and learners have at their disposal. As Schmitt points out (Chapter 3: 33), both approaches are necessary; each compensating the shortcomings of the other: 'In short, intentional learning is focused and effective, but limited in terms of the number of words (and word knowledge types) it can address. Incidental learning is slow and untargeted, but can fill in the "contextual" types of word knowledge, and provide recycling for words already partially learned'.

Over the last three decades, a great deal of research has been carried out in the field of vocabulary teaching and learning, but the truth is that there has not been a clear focus either on classroom materials or on the analysis of classroom language related to vocabulary learning; there continues to be a gap between research and its application to teaching materials.

Contributions in this Volume

This volume is organized into three sections. The first part focuses on the 'Development of a model for vocabulary teaching and learning', and deals with some general concerns and core aspects in vocabulary development. The second part presents some 'Empirical studies on lexical processing in English and Spanish' that tries to throw light on the complex nature of mental lexical processing and performance. Finally, the third part focuses on 'Materials design and strategies for vocabulary teaching and learning' in various contexts.

Communicative approaches have been criticized for producing greater fluency but less accuracy than traditional approaches. In 'Form-focused Instruction in Second Language Vocabulary Learning' (Chapter 2), Batia Laufer argues that input cannot be relied on as the main source of L2 vocabulary learning. Instead, Laufer suggests that word-focused instruction is more effective for L2 vocabulary learning than incidental word acquisition from input. Word-focused instruction can be divided into three different types: incidental focus on form (FonF), incidental focus on forms (FonFs) and intentional focus on forms (FonFs). Incidental FonF refers to attending to lexical units within a communicative and authentic task environment when the lexical units are necessary for the completion of a communicative task. In the case of an incidental FonFs the student practices the target lexical units in non-communicative and non-authentic tasks without being forewarned of an upcoming test. In an intentional FonFs, the student performs a non-communicative and non-authentic task knowing that he will subsequently be tested on them. Finally, word-focused instruction is related to several hypotheses relevant to learning, second language learning in general, and vocabulary in particular. For future research, Laufer points out a crucial question in understanding vocabulary learning is whether retention in long-term memory depends on task type or on the number of encounters with the same lexical unit.

L2 learners need a large vocabulary to function appropriately in a non-native language. Norbert Schmitt's 'Key Issues in Teaching and Learning Vocabulary' (Chapter 3) asserts that this is likely to be one of the biggest challenges that learners will face during their learning process, and so encourages L2 teachers to focus on vocabulary. The chapter outlines key issues in teaching and learning vocabulary, starting with the amount of vocabulary necessary to perform various activities in English (e.g. read authentic texts). It then discusses the types of word knowledge necessary to use a word appropriately in different contexts. The chapter addresses the incremental nature of vocabulary learning, including the necessity for recycling, both for consolidation of partially known words, and for enhancement of what is known about those words. This recycling can most efficiently be achieved by using an expanding rehearsal revision schedule. A model of vocabulary acquisition based on a word knowledge framework is then presented. Finally, a number of factors related to the most effective vocabulary teaching strategies are highlighted.

Recent research has shown that the transfer of passive L2 vocabulary into production is far from linear, and that the interactions between levels of vocabulary knowledge depend on factors such as L2 learning context, length of study, word frequency and learners' proficiency levels. In Chapter 4, 'A Dynamic Perspective on L2 Lexical Development in Academic English', Tal Caspi and Wander Lowie emphasize the notion that the L2 lexicon is a dynamic system, similar to natural self-organizing systems, in which developing components interact in complex ways, and variation is inherent to development. The chapter focuses on a case study of an adult native speaker of Mandarin immersed in an English-speaking academic environment in which the development and interactions of four levels of academic ESL vocabulary knowledge are examined: word recognition versus word recall in the passive knowledge dimension, and controlled versus free production in the active knowledge dimension. The authors illustrate the explanatory power of dynamic systems theory (DST), and the information on the developmental processes that data variation can yield when vocabulary is investigated from a dynamic perspective.

In 'The Effect of Lexicalization in the Native Language on Second Language Lexical Inferencing: A Cross-linguistic Study' (Chapter 5), Sima Paribakht reports on an introspective study that compared lexical inferencing behaviors of Persian-(also referred to as Farsi) and French-speaking readers of English when they encountered unfamiliar lexicalized words as opposed to those which are not lexicalized in their native language. For this study the author selected two groups of subjects, 20 Persian-speaking and 20 French-speaking intermediate level learners of English in educational contexts. The results of this comparative study provided further insights into factors that may influence the complex process of L2 lexical inferencing, and indicated many similarities but also some differences in these learners' guessing patterns of the target English words. The findings of this study are interpreted in the light of the linguistic features of the participants' native languages, their first language processing habits, and the context of their target language learning.

Tests of vocabulary breadth are generally thought to be good predictors of overall foreign language ability but scores on these tests correlate much less well with measures of oral fluency than with other aspects of ability. In Chapter 6, 'Aural Word Recognition and Oral Competence in English as a Foreign Language', James Milton, Jo Wade and Nicola Hopkins investigate measures of both phonological and orthographic word recognition and attempt to calculate the degree to which both forms of vocabulary knowledge contribute to communicative skill in a foreign language. The authors compare vocabulary size scores with overall and subskills scores from a standard English test (IELTS). It appears that while orthographic vocabulary size predicts reading, writing and overall scores well; scores in speaking are best predicted by phonological vocabulary size. Listening scores are predicted by both, which is probably a by-product of the test format used. Regression analysis suggests that orthographic vocabulary size may explain more than 50% of variance in writing grades and IELTS overall grades. Phonological vocabulary size may explain more than 40% of variance in speaking grades. A combination of both vocabulary scores may explain more than 50% of listening scores.

Chapter 7, 'A Cascade Model of Lexical Access to Explain the Phonological Activation of Recently Practiced Lexical Items' by Teresa López-Soto, reports on two similar experiments that explore how phonological activation can operate in triggering lexical patterns at production and reception levels for L2 learners. Data collection took place in two second-year university courses for Spanish-speaking undergraduates majoring in English language and literature at the University of Seville, Spain. The first experiment presented the participants with a collection of recently practiced words. These words were represented in three different sets of pictures which participants had to name accordingly: the first set typically contained semantically related words (e.g. bed – mattress), the second typically included phonologically related words (e.g. widow – willow) and the third typically contained rhythmically related words (e.g. access – praxis). The second experiment was a replication of the first; however, in this case a recorded version (spoken form) of the coupled words was played along with the target picture. The results show that naming latency is generally faster when the target word is presented with other words with a high neighborhood density.

In Chapter 8 'Concordances versus Dictionaries: Evaluating Approaches to World Learning in ESOL', Rachel Allan offers an explicit approach to vocabulary learning through the use of concordances and monolingual English learner dictionaries at different levels. The author recruited students of mixed nationalities from different levels of proficiency and used a cloze test and a word associates test to measure vocabulary gains in different aspects of word knowledge such as word form, synonyms, collocations and contextual use. The results indicated that the use of concordance tasks leads to deeper knowledge of the target words at higher levels whereas dictionary tasks had a more positive effect amongst lower level learners, at least in productive terms. The author concludes that there may be a threshold for use of concordances and that an initial induction into what concordances are and how to use them will benefit learners. Finally, learner responses to concordance tasks are analyzed. Questionnaire results from the students indicate that reactions to concordances very much depend on individual learning styles and preferences. In general, higher level learners appreciate the value of concordances more than lower levels.

In Chapter 9, 'Evidence of Incremental Vocabulary Learning in Advanced L2 Spanish Learners', Diana Frantzen provides additional evidence that supports the claim that some L2 vocabulary learning takes place on an incremental basis, explaining the incidental acquisition hypothesis (Coady, 1993). The data examined were gathered in a classroom experiment on vocabulary acquisition reported in Frantzen (1998), centered on vocabulary learning and in Frantzen (2003), centered on the students' inferencing ability when the tested words were supplied in context. In the present chapter, using data obtained from advanced Spanish learners' performance on two sets of pre- and post-tests (each set employing both no-context and with-context formats), the author focuses on evidence of incremental learning that was revealed incidentally in the other two studies. The participants' performance was tracked over time through comparisons of their answers on each of the four tests. The examination revealed several patterns among the learners as they approached (but did not always attain) understanding of the target words. They made incremental gains which manifested themselves: (1) by their use of approximations (showing partial knowledge of a word's meaning); and (2) by the fact that many answers indicate an awareness that certain previous guesses were no longer viable.

In Chapter 10, 'Conspicuous by Their Absence: The Infrequency of Very Frequent Words in some English as a Foreign Language Textbooks', Jim Lawley suggests that some EFL materials often deliberately avoid high-frequency words because of the assumption that this vocabulary is somehow difficult for learners. The author discusses some problems which teachers and students may encounter if they use a major textbook which does give special emphasis to these words, and speculates that a lexical syllabus, which focuses on the most frequent words in their most common patterns of usage, may not fit easily into conventional EFL coursebooks. In view of this, Lawley suggests that one possible solution would be to provide bilingual word lists in which high-frequency words are presented in groups for easy learning. The author concludes that bilingual word lists might not only help students save time as they do not have to struggle to understand the mechanics of new exercise types but also help them learn independently of the teacher and other students.

Although L2 teachers acknowledge the central importance of vocabulary, their concerns currently center on what and how to teach vocabulary. In Chapter 11, 'The Treatment of Lexical Aspects in Commercial Textbooks for L2 Teaching and Learning', María Dolores López-Jiménez addresses the selection, presentation and practice of lexical units (*one*-word and *multi*-word units), vocabulary recycling, learning strategies and the presence/absence of glossaries with L1 translation equivalents in current textbooks for the teaching and learning of English (EngTBs) and Spanish (SpaTBs) as non-native languages at different proficiency levels. The results reveal that in the EngTBs and SpaTBs assessed, vocabulary selection criteria are seldom identified; vocabulary practice is mainly comprised of closed exercises, and vocabulary learning strategies are hardly included. In the EngTBs, the students' L1 is nonexistent as a presentation technique and bilingual glossaries are absent in most. In the SpaTBs, lexical collocations are not explicitly practiced and vocabulary is scarcely recycled. It is concluded that textbook writers tend to provide a rather traditional treatment of vocabulary, and economic interests are given preference over pedagogical ones, especially in the case of the EngTBs.

Vocabulary has always been a very popular topic among software packages. Unfortunately, the so-called first-generation vocabulary applications were restricted to the operation of mechanical activities, which provided learners with instant feedback – the 'correct solution'. These lexical learning experiences, however, have been strongly criticized because they are not informed by psycholinguistic and pedagogic principles of vocabulary acquisition. In Chapter 12, Carmen Pérez Basanta presents 'A Second-generation CALL Vocabulary-learning Program *ADELEX*: In Search of a Psychopedagogic Model'. The ADELEX acronym means Assessing and Developing Lexical Competence. This second-generation CALL program was designed at the University of Granada, Spain, to enhance the lexical competence based on current psycholinguistic thinking on the mental lexicon and vocabulary acquisition. Its instructional design is delivered through online learning within a constructivist framework via the digital platform WebCT (Web Course Tools). The author describes it as a fully virtual program whose syllabus is drawn from a variety of linguistic sources, including lexicology, lexicography, semantics, psycholinguistics, discourse analysis and corpus linguistics to develop vocabulary acquisition. The chapter focuses on two key issues concerning this learning experience: (1) main psycholinguistic hypotheses ('context availability', 'imaginability hypothesis' and 'depth of processing') and its implications in web-based vocabulary processing; and (2) the search for a pedagogic model in order to optimize CALL efficacy.

In Chapter 13, 'Word Associations as a Vocabulary Teaching Strategy in an Advanced L2 Reading Class', Zorana Vasiljevic examines the effectiveness of different approaches to vocabulary instruction in an advanced reading class. The author presents an experiment focused on adult learners who have limited contact with the target language. Three types of instructions were compared; on the one hand, instruction through word associations, on the other hand, vocabulary teaching through explicit definitions and finally, inferring word meaning from context. These three approaches were then evaluated based on their contribution to the growth of both receptive and productive word knowledge. The results suggest that when learners have limited exposure to L2 input, explicit instruction seems to be a more effective way of approaching L2 vocabulary. The data collected also suggest that instruction through word associations offers potential advantages to high-level learners, which are reflected primarily in the quality of L2 vocabulary knowledge. The chapter concludes with some pedagogical implications in which the author gives some advice to instructors in similar instructional settings and urges them to evaluate their practices and experiment with new approaches to vocabulary teaching.

We hope this volume contributes to a better understanding of the issues central to vocabulary acquisition, teaching and learning. These issues are complex but of great importance in today's world. While much remains to be discovered, the chapters of this volume clearly point to the importance of the role of formal instruction, explicit teaching and intentional learning.

Part 1
Development of a Model for Vocabulary Teaching and Learning

Chapter 2
Form-focused Instruction in Second Language Vocabulary Learning

BATIA LAUFER

Introduction

How do we acquire second language vocabulary? Believers in the pervasive importance of input claim that we acquire most words through exposure to language input, particularly to reading input, rather than by decontextualized learning of words. This position is usually referred to as the 'default hypothesis' since it is justified in negative terms: the number of words that is learnt is too vast to be accounted for by instruction (Nagy et al., 1985; Sternberg, 1987). This reasoning seems to be supported by first language vocabulary data. According to modest estimates, the number of words English-speaking high school graduates know in English is about 20,000 word families (Nation, 1990), while other estimates suggest a larger number of about 50,000. Yet these figures are very different from the vocabulary size of foreign learners. For example, Japanese college learners of English as a Foreign Language (EFL) were found to know 2000–2300 word families after receiving 800–1200 h of instruction (Barrow et al., 1999; Shillaw, 1995). Indonesian EFL university learners knew 1220 word families after 900 h of instruction (Nurweni & Read, 1999), Israeli high school learners knew 3500 word families after 1500 h of instruction (Laufer, 1998). In Spain, University students majoring in Audiovisual Communication knew 3950 lexical items (2470 word families) after 900 h of instruction and students of English Philology knew 5954 lexical items (3720 word families) after 1100 h of instruction (Miralpeix, 2007). Spanish 4th graders who studied 419 h reached the vocabulary size of 600 word families (Jiménez-Catalán & Terrazas-Gallego, 2005–2008).

The above figures show that an average number of words learnt per hour of instruction amounts to 2–3. As it is not impossible to learn an average of 2–3 words per hour of instruction, L2 learners might have been instructed most of their vocabulary rather than picked it up from input. Whether L2 vocabulary in the above examples was the results of exposure to input, explicit instruction, or both, the vocabulary size of high school graduates and many university students as suggested by the figures above may be adequate for carrying out simple language tasks, like an every day conversation, but it may not be sufficient for more sophisticated activities. To understand a radio interview with minimal support, that is without the necessity to use a dictionary too often, the listener would need to know 6000–7000 word families, to comprehend newspapers and novels, the reader needs 8000–9000 word families (Nation, 2006).

The gap between what learners know and what they should ideally know means that we (educators and language-learning researchers) should be looking for more effective methods of vocabulary learning. If one believes in the default hypothesis in L2 vocabulary learning, that is, the notion that most vocabulary in L2 is acquired from input, mainly the reading input, then the answer is clear. Learners should read a lot, and vocabulary learning will take care of itself. I have argued that there is a fundamental fault in the default hypothesis (Laufer, 2003, 2005a, 2005b), and showed that we cannot take for granted any of the assumptions that underlie this position: the assumption that learners notice unfamiliar words in the text, that they can infer their meaning, that successful guessing leads to word memorization, and that there is enough input for recurrent exposures to the new words. There is empirical evidence (for surveys of research, see Laufer, 2003, 2005a, 2005b) that learners do not necessarily notice unfamiliar words in the input. When they do, guessing is not always possible. If it is possible, it does not necessarily lead to the retention of the guessed word, and, finally, a necessary condition for 'picking up' words is massive exposure to the foreign language, which can hardly be expected to occur in classroom learning context. Moreover, studies that examined the amount of word acquisition from context showed that only a small number of L2 words can be 'picked up' from exposure to texts without any subsequent vocabulary practice.

Experiments which used relatively short texts (up to 7000 words) and measured short-term retention report very small gains: 1–5 words per text (Day *et al.*, 1991; Horst *et al.*, 1998; Hulstijn, 1992; Knight, 1994; Paribakht & Wesche, 1997; Pitts *et al.*, 1989; Waring, 2003; Zahar *et al.*, 2001). Slightly higher gains (six words per text) are reported by Dupuy and Krashen (1993), but this study included the use of video in addition to reading. Furthermore, learners knew that they would be tested, which may have led to some intentional memorization of words. In Cho and Krashen (1994), the subject who engaged in pleasure reading without using a dictionary learnt seven words from a booklet of 7000 words. Learning is usually measured in such experiments by checking whether the learner can recall the meaning of the target word, or recognize its meaning among several given options.

In view of the flaws in the default hypothesis and the empirical evidence presented above, it is questionable whether most L2 vocabulary is acquired incidentally from input. Instead I suggest an alternative hypothesis, according to which *word-focused instruction may be more effective for vocabulary learning than incidental word acquisition from input.*

Word-focused Instruction

Word-focused instruction is related to the construct of form-focused instruction (FFI) which has been proposed in the area of grammar, but can easily be adapted to vocabulary as well. Two major types of FFI have been discussed in the literature: Focus on Form (FonF) and Focus on Forms (FonFs). FonF refers to attending to linguistic elements during a communicative activity (DeKeyser, 1998; Ellis, 2001; Long, 1991). The term 'form' includes the function that a particular structure performs. For example, attention to the 'form' *-ed* subsumes the realization that *-ed* signals an action performed in the past. Originally, Long (1991) defined FonF as incidental, that is, employed only when a learner's need arises, and implicit so as not to interfere with interaction. Later, however, these requirements were modified to include: (1) planned FonF designed to elicit specific linguistic forms during a communicative activity (Ellis *et al.*, 2002); and (2) a range of techniques, from implicit, for example recasts, input enhancement, to more explicit, for example indication that an error has been made, or stating a rule (Doughty & Varela, 1998). According to the proponents of FonF, all the various FonF tasks are expected to occur within a communicative task environment. In terms of vocabulary instruction, FonF refers to attending to lexical items (single words and multiword units) within a communicative task environment when these lexical items are necessary for the completion of a communicative, or an authentic language task.

FonF has been contrasted with FonFs, that is, the teaching of discrete linguistic structures in separate lessons in a sequence determined by syllabus writers. In vocabulary, FonFs refer to teaching and practicing discrete lexical items in non-communicative, non-authentic language tasks. The distinction between FonF and FonFs, according to Ellis (2001), has also to do with how students view themselves and the language: in a FonFs approach, students view themselves as learners of a language and the language as the object of study; in FonF, on the other hand, learners view themselves as language users and language is viewed as a tool for communication.

To illustrate FonF and FonFs in vocabulary, we will consider 10 new words that are taught to a group of learners. These words have to be understood in a text in which they appear before a group discussion can take place. Therefore, learners decide to look them up in a dictionary. Looking them up constitutes FonF, since these words are attended to in order to complete a communicative/authentic language task. However, the same 10 words may be presented with their L1 translations in a decontextualized list and supplemented by two vocabulary exercises: (1) match each word in column A to its definition in column B and (2) fill in the words in 10 sentences, one word in each sentence. In these two tasks, attending to the words constitutes FonFs as the tasks are not connected with a communicative or authentic language activity, but the words are the objects of study.

FFI can occur in incidental and in intentional learning conditions. In incidental vocabulary learning, learners are typically required to perform a task involving the processing of some information without being told in advance that they will be tested afterwards on their recall of that information. Hence, contrary to what is sometimes assumed, in an incidental learning situation, learners do not work without attention to the learned words. They attend to them without the intention to remember them later on. The example above of looking up unknown words in a dictionary while reading a text is a case in point. Dictionary search requires the learner to attend to the words. But if they do not try to memorize the looked up words, any subsequent learning that will occur will be intentional. As mentioned earlier, the activity of looking up unfamiliar words which are necessary for text comprehension is a FonF task leading to incidental learning. Another example presented above, matching new words with their definitions, which is a FonFs activity may also lead to remembering some of these words without trying to do so, that is, to incidental learning. Even though the words are decontextualized, we cannot claim that the learning is intentional if no effort is made to commit them to memory. Hence, incidental vocabulary learning can be induced by FonF and FonFs tasks.

In an intentional learning situation, participants are most often told in advance that their recall will be tested afterwards (see Hulstijn, 2001, for an extensive treatment of incidental and intentional learning). However, learners can also impose an intentional condition on themselves by making a decision to commit words to memory even if no test will take place. Since an attempt to memorize words requires attention to decontextualized words and is not essential for performing an authentic language task, intentional learning is associated with FonFs only. Table 2.1 illustrates the above argument schematically.

I hypothesize that all three types of word-focused instruction in Table 2.1 are more effective for vocabulary learning than encountering new words in the input.

Table 2.1 Types of word-focused instruction

	FonF	*FonFs*
Incidental	+	+
Intentional	−	+

First, I will support this hypothesis by some empirical evidence from vocabulary research. Then I will support the hypothesis by several theories from the field of second language acquisition.

The Effectiveness of Word-focused Instruction: Empirical Evidence

Incidental FonF

Most FonF studies I found in L2 literature adopted an incidental design, that is, learners performed a task involving the target words without knowing that they would subsequently be tested on them. Some studies examined vocabulary learning from written language and some – from spoken language. The evidence regarding FonF is indirect since these studies were not designed to specifically contrast FonF and non-FonF conditions, but examined other issues in vocabulary learning. However, in each study, there was a comprehension-based condition compared with a condition that required some kind of Focus of Form, for example, dictionary work, negotiation of word meaning in the input, or output, attention to marginal glosses. Therefore, I chose these studies to support my argument in favor of FonF.

Luppescu and Day (1993) and Knight (1994) found that students who read a text and looked up unknown words in the dictionary remembered them better than students who read the text without a dictionary. Hulstijn *et al.* (1996) and Laufer (2000) found that looking up new words in a dictionary during a reading task was more effective than reading with the same words glossed in the text margin by the researcher. While the former two studies used paper dictionaries, the latter used electronic dictionaries and all the look ups of the learners were registered in log files. This way it was possible to verify that the acquired words had indeed been looked up by the students.

Similar to studies on reading, studies of word acquisition from oral language invariably concluded that whenever learners focused on unfamiliar vocabulary by asking for clarifications during interaction, they had a better chance of retaining these words than when they did not attend to words in this way (De la Fuente, 2002; Ellis & He, 1999; Ellis *et al.*, 1994; Newton, 1993).

What is it in a FonF task that makes learners pay attention to a word? Some studies investigated whether the relevance of words to task completion had an effect on the amount of attention. Hulstijn *et al.* (1996), Laufer and Levitzky-Aviad (2003) and Peters (2007) designed tasks in such a way that some words in the texts that learners read were relevant to task completion and some were not. The studies were carried out with electronic dictionaries. The log files showed that learners clicked more often on relevant words and consequently remembered them better.

Another factor that may affect the amount of attention learners pay to vocabulary is how demanding the task is in terms of how many language details have to be attended to. In the studies above, some learners had to answer specific questions while others were asked to summarize the text. The 'question groups' looked up more unfamiliar words, except in Hulstijn *et al.* (1996), but even in his study, when the question group was asked to describe the appearance of a specific character, the participants looked up more words from the relevant paragraph that did the summary group. In sum, there is ample evidence that FonF is beneficial to learning new words from written and oral language and can be manipulated through task relevance and task type.

Incidental FonFs

Here, I refer to studies where learners are asked to perform some activities with target words in non-communicative, non-authentic language tasks, and are subsequently tested on some aspects of knowledge of these words. Since they are not forewarned of an upcoming test, any learning that has occurred is considered incidental. Though the studies did not specifically investigate FonFs, they had at least one condition where learning was focused on the words as isolated items, without any related communicative activity. In most cases, this condition was compared with acquiring words from a reading activity.

Paribakht and Wesche (1997) compared learners in a 'reading only' condition with learners in a 'reading plus' condition. In the latter, the task consisted of reading a text and doing a range of vocabulary exercises including recognition of meaning and form, producing morphologically related words, supplying the words in various contexts and so forth. The 'reading only' group, however, read additional texts. Vocabulary gain tests showed that the 'reading plus' acquired significantly more words than the 'reading only' group.

Laufer (2003) compared learning of 10 unfamiliar low-frequency target words from reading with marginal glosses with learning from a sentence writing activity. The 'reading' group encountered the words in a text. The 'writing' group was given a list of the 10 target words with explanation and translation of meaning, and was asked to write a sentence with each word. In the test, the participants had to provide the meaning (in L1 or L2) for the 10 target words. Two weeks later, the same test was repeated. The 'sentence writing' group received significantly higher scores both on the immediate and on the delayed tests.

Hill and Laufer (2003) compared vocabulary gain from reading aided by an electronic dictionary with word gain from a FonFs condition that included two multiple choice word selection tasks: selecting the meaning of the target word and supplying the target words for their synonyms or paraphrases. The FonFs yielded significantly higher word retention scores on an unexpected test of meaning recall of the target words.

Some additional studies which showed the superiority of FonFs over a meaning-based condition are Rosszell (2003), where the learners prepared word sheets that contained information on the target words and wrote original sentences with them, and Kitajima (2001), where learners who were told to structure their conversations around new words, could use, two months later, almost twice as many words as learners who were exposed to the same words in the input and did not perform the FonFs activity.

Horst *et al.* (2005) investigated vocabulary learning through the use of word banks, online dictionaries, concordances, cloze exercises, hypertexts and self-quizzes. This kind of practice and learning in a computer-assisted environment can be considered a particular case of FonFs. They calculated how many words were learnt when learners entered them into the program in comparison to words that were encountered in texts, but not entered into the program. While the gain of the un-entered words was about 16%, the gain of the entered words was around 37%.

Clearly, FonFs activities, which are not communicative and not authentic, are, nevertheless, effective for vocabulary learning. Particularly so are activities that require retrieving the word itself and using it, that is, productive activities. Rosszell's (2003) learners remembered over 50% of the target words on a delayed test of active knowledge, Kitajima's (2001) – over 80%. Moreover, there is some evidence from Horst *et al.* (2005) that learners show interest in productive activities. When given a choice of various computer exercises, they took the trouble to generate novel cloze passages where they had to replace the target words in gaps in texts of their own choosing.

Intentional FonFs

In my survey of studies which adopt an intentional design, I came across two major types of studies. Some studies introduced an intentional stage after some kind of an incidental stage including either a communicative task, or a FonF task such as reading, or looking up unfamiliar words in a dictionary (Laufer, 2006; Mondria, 2003; Peters, 2007). Other studies investigated learning words in bilingual lists (Mondria & Wiersma, 2004; Prince, 1996; Qian, 1996), or in minimal context in the computer environment (Groot, 2000).

In the first type of studies, it is interesting to find out the contribution of each stage to learning. This can be done by comparing the acquisition of the same words in incidental and intentional conditions.

Laufer's (2006) study attempted to do this. In the incidental stage, learners read a text and used a dictionary to look up unknown words that were relevant to comprehension questions. At the end of the task, they were unexpectedly tested on the comprehension of 12 target words. Following a short break, in the intentional stage, the same learners received a list of the same 12 target words with definitions of meaning, examples and translations and were asked to spend 15 min on memorizing the words and their meanings for an upcoming test. On the completion of the memorization task, the lists were collected and the participants received the same test as after the incidental stage. The test was repeated two weeks later. After the incidental stage, learners remembered on average about 47% of the target words. After the intentional stage, the score increased to 88%. Two weeks later it was 62%, which was lower than on the immediate test following intentional learning, but higher than on the immediate test after incidental learning. Also Mondria (2003) found that the memorization contributed most to the retention of words, more than inferring their meaning from context and subsequently verifying the meaning in the dictionary. In his experiment, learners remembered 6% of the target words after inferring their meaning from context, another 9% after verifying the meaning in the dictionary, and an additional 32% after memorizing the list for a test. In other words, learners remembered 47% of the target words after they focused on the words for comprehension purposes and memorized them for a test.

Contrary to these results, Peters (2007) found no significant difference between incidental and intentional learning on word retention. In her study, learners read a text, looked up unfamiliar words in an electronic dictionary and answered comprehension questions. One group was forewarned of an upcoming vocabulary test, another one was not. On a series of subsequent vocabulary tests (recall, recognition, in isolation, in context) the two groups were not significantly different in the number of words they remembered. Hulstijn (2001) claims that what affects learning is not whether learning is incidental or intentional, but what learners do with the word, how they attend to it, or how elaborately they process it. Similarly, Laufer and Hulstijn (2001) suggested that retention depends on the amount of learners' involvement in the task and not in the forthcoming test or absence of it. Apparently, Peter's learners invested most of their effort during the task completion stage and not during the memorization stage. Laufer's and Mondria's learners must have worked more seriously with the words during the memorization stage. However, Peter's learners in both groups remembered about 28% of the target words when recall of meaning was tested in isolation (a test similar to Laufer and Mondria's studies). In view of this relatively low figure, compared to Laufer and Mondria above, one could postulate, albeit cautiously, that the participants in Peter's study did not invest much effort in memorizing the vocabulary. For most average learners, however, tests provide an instrumental motivation to attend to the material which is not attended to without the test. Hence, intentional FonFs will, in all likelihood, be conducive to learning.

The second type of FonFs studies is often unpopular among language educators who adhere to communicative teaching, and object to learning from lists, arguing that this method is old-fashioned, unnatural, shallow and possibly effective only for short-term retention. However, empirical evidence shows that this position is unjustified.

On the immediate posttests of the studies by Groot (2000), Mondria and Wiersma (2004), Prince (1996), Qian (1996), all of which used vocabulary lists, the percentage of correctly remembered target words was 67–99% on tests of passive knowledge, that is, recognition, or recall of meaning, and 32–79% on tests of active knowledge, that is, recognition or recall of the word form. On the delayed tests, the scores (in studies that provided such results) were 36–76% and 13–61%, respectively. Each study reported the results differently, either by means of raw scores, or percentages. When raw scores were presented, I calculated the percentage of the acquired words out of the total number of target words, in order to present a uniform picture of the results. A possible explanation of the effectiveness of list learning is that it is not necessarily shallow. When facing a memorization task for an upcoming test, learners may try their best and employ a variety of mnemonic techniques to reinforce word in memory. These were shown to play a positive role in retention (for a review, see Hulstijn, 1997).

Comparing FonF and FonFs

I am not familiar with any studies that set out to compare the two instructional conditions. I have recently conducted three experiments involving such a comparison.

In one study (Laufer, 2006), 158 high school learners of English as L2 studied 12 unfamiliar words. Half of the learners who were assigned to the FonF group, read a text containing the target words, looked them up in a dictionary, discussed the text in small groups and answered comprehension questions for which it was necessary to understand the target words. The other half of the participants, FonFs group, received the target words in a list with their meanings (translations and definitions in English), and with examples of usage. They performed two word-focused activities: choosing the correct meaning of the target word from four options, and completing gapped sentences with a word from the list of the target words. On a subsequent test which required the learners to provide the meaning for the 12 target words in English, or in their L1, the FonFs group significantly outperformed FonF group.

In a recent experiment (Laufer & Girsai, 2008), 48 high school learners of English as L2 were exposed to 17 target lexical items, eight unfamiliar words and nine collocations, in a text. Half of the learners were assigned to FonFs condition and practiced the target lexical items by means of translations from English into Hebrew and later from Hebrew into English. During the exercise, the differences between the two languages were pointed out by the teacher. Another half of the learners were assigned to FonF condition. They encountered the target vocabulary in the text, and performed a meaning-oriented activity with various FonF activities in which the new words and collocations figured as well. On subsequent tests of passive and active knowledge, learners in the 'translation group' (FonFs) outperformed the FonF group. The difference was particularly noticeable in the active test of collocations, in which the FonFs group knew six times as many collocations as the FonF group. Since collocations are known to be particularly difficult even for advanced learners (Alternberg & Granger, 2001; Granger, 1998; Howarth, 1996; Kaszubski, 2000), it is plausible that FonFs is particularly beneficial for words with a high learning burden.

Empirical Evidence: Concluding Remarks

All the studies surveyed so far show the effectiveness of word-focused instruction, whether in its own right, or compared to exposure to words in the input. Similar results were obtained in different sociolinguistic contexts. The participants of some of the studies surveyed here were learners who studied L2 in classroom context, or Foreign Language context. Others studied L2 in the L2-speaking environment, or in second language context. It is often argued that the richer input which is characteristic of second as opposed to foreign language context will provide enough repeated exposure to vocabulary for incidental learning. However, I do not know of empirical studies which showed that a particular number of exposures to a word in communication was more effective than a word-focused activity. Until such studies appear, we cannot dismiss the conclusion that doing something with a word is more effective than simply coming across it a number of times.

Word-focused instruction: Theoretical justification

Theoretically, word-focused instruction can be related to several hypotheses in second language acquisition in general: the 'noticing' hypothesis (Schmidt, 1990, 1994, 2001), the limited processing capacity hypothesis (Van Patten, 1990), and the 'pushed output' (Swain, 1985; Swain & Lapkin, 1995). It can also be related to the 'involvement load' hypothesis, which was proposed in connection with vocabulary learning in particular (Laufer & Hulstijn, 2001). The FonFs aspect of FFI can be justified in terms of skill acquisition theory (Anderson, 1982; Bley-Vroman, 1988; DeKeyser, 1998).

Except for the 'involvement load' hypothesis, all other hypotheses were formulated in connection with grammar learning. However, they can readily be adapted to vocabulary. According to Schmidt (2001), many features of L2 input are likely to be infrequent, non-salient, and communicatively redundant. Therefore, they may go unnoticed unless attention is drawn to them. This is certainly true for many words. Some words are not necessary for the understanding of the overall meaning. Some are easily guessed. However, when they are easily guessed, they are also easily forgotten (Mondria & Wit de Boer, 1991).

Van Patten (1990) claims that learners have a limited capacity for simultaneously processing L2 meaning and form. They will naturally attend to meaning rather than to form while communicating, and it is up to the teacher to draw their attention to form. In the area of vocabulary, this is true in the case of not noticing words in the input, but it is particularly true when vocabulary is used in writing. Learners with good passive vocabulary knowledge often prefer to use simple and frequent words to convey their message, even in an argumentative essay (Laufer, 1998).

According to the 'pushed output' hypothesis, when learners are 'pushed' to stretch their linguistic resources, they are forced into using a more syntactic processing mode than they would in comprehension; they notice elements in the L2 and modify their output. In vocabulary, learners can be forced to reformulate their messages by correcting the use of the words they chose, or selecting different, more suitable words.

The involvement hypothesis (Laufer & Hulstijn, 2001) was proposed as an attempt to operationalize the concepts that have been used in connection with good retention of information in general: depth of processing, degree of elaboration, quality of attention, richness of encoding (see e.g. Craik & Lockhart, 1972), but the hypothesis was developed in the context of vocabulary instruction in particular. It postulates that the most effective tasks are tasks with a high involvement load, that is, tasks which combine three elements with regard to the words being practiced: 'need', 'search' and 'evaluation'. 'Need' is present in the task when the word is deemed necessary for task completion. 'Search' is the attempt to find the meaning of an unknown L2 word or, conversely, to find the L2 word form expressing a given concept, as, for example, in the case of looking up a word in a dictionary or inferring its meaning from context. 'Evaluation' implies some kind of selective decision about the word's meaning, or form in which the word's context is taken into account. It entails a comparison of a given word with other words, a specific meaning of a word with its other meanings, or comparing the word with other words in order to assess whether a word does or does not fit its context, as, for example, in the case of sentence writing. 'Search' and 'evaluation' are form-focused activities performed with a word. As for higher effectiveness of tasks with higher involvement load, empirical evidence was found to support the involvement load hypothesis fully, or partially (Hulstijn & Laufer, 2001; Laufer, 2003; Webb, 2005).

The FonFs aspect of FFI can be justified theoretically in terms of skill acquisition with its three stages. The first stage is achieving the declarative, or factual, knowledge through explanation of rules. The second stage entails proceduralized knowledge, which is responsible for knowing what is to be done with language data. The third stage is automatization of procedural knowledge, that is, using language according to rules without thinking about them (Anderson, 1982; Bley-Vroman, 1988; DeKeyser, 1998). Achieving declarative and procedural knowledge in vocabulary involves mastering the various components of word knowledge: form (spoken and written, morphology, grammatical behavior, meaning, relations with other words). Achieving the automatization stage involves quick access to the information that is stored in the memory about the word. This is particularly difficult in classroom instruction. Words do not appear in the input as often as grammatical structures, since textbook materials may be thematically, and therefore lexically, unrelated. Moreover, memory research suggests that rehearsal of information, vocabulary in our case, should take the form of expanded rehearsals (Baddeley, 1997; Bjork, 1988; Pimsleur, 1967). Therefore, repeated encounters with words have to be planned and introduced artificially through word-focused activities in class. Snellings *et al.* (2002) provide empirical evidence that it is possible to increase learners' word retrieval speed through various form-focused exercises in four weeks.

Summary and Suggestions for Further Research

I argued that word-focused instruction may be more effective for L2 vocabulary learning, particularly in classroom context, than incidental word acquisition from input, and based the argument on the flaws in the default hypothesis and the empirical evidence from various 'vocabulary-through-input' studies. This does not mean that input is not useful for providing initial information about words, or for helping to consolidate already existing knowledge, or to reinforce a word's memory trace. I believe, however, that it cannot be relied on as the main, and certainly not the only, source of L2 vocabulary learning. I suggested that word-focused instruction can be of three types: incidental FonF, incidental FonFs and intentional FonFs. In research studies and in teaching practice, the latter can follow an incidental learning stage, or exist on its own. I provided empirical evidence from studies conducted in different language learning contexts and with learners of different ages, which demonstrated the effectiveness of word-focused instruction. Of particular interest were the FonFs tasks, including activities that cannot be considered authentic or communicative by the proponents of the communicative language teaching. Finally,

I related word-focused instruction to several hypotheses which are relevant to learning, second language learning in general and vocabulary in particular. These are the skill acquisition theory, the 'noticing' hypothesis, the 'pushed output' hypothesis, the 'limited processability' hypothesis and the 'involvement load' hypothesis.

For further exploration of word-focused instruction, several lines of research could be considered. Comparisons could be made between FonF and FonFs tasks, in order to find out whether focus on the task (as in FonF condition) matters more than focus on the target item (as in FonFs condition). Second, tasks with different involvement loads could be compared with regard to their effect on vocabulary learning, or tasks with the same involvement load, but different distribution of the involvement components, in order to further explore the task features that are responsible for learning. A crucial question in understanding vocabulary learning is whether retention depends on what one does with the word rather than how often one meets it. Put differently, the question is whether task type is just as important, more so, or less so than the number of tasks in which a new word appears, or the number of times a new word is seen by the learner. Research could compare vocabulary learning along two dimensions: varying task type and the number of exposures to the investigated words. Studies addressing these questions have started to appear (Folse, 2006; Webb, 2005), but more investigations along these lines will constitute a welcome addition to the growing research on vocabulary instruction in a second language.

Chapter 3
Key Issues in Teaching and Learning Vocabulary

NORBERT SCHMITT

Introduction

Vocabulary has always been an essential component of language teaching, and after a long period of relative neglect, it is now widely recognized as such. This has partly been due to a period of sustained attention and research which picked up momentum in the early 1990s. From this time, a number of influential books focusing on vocabulary were published (Bogaards & Laufer, 2004; Coady & Huckin, 1997; Folse, 2004; Nation, 1990, 2001; Schmitt, 2000; Schmitt & McCarthy, 1997). At the same time, research articles focusing on vocabulary issues appeared with regularity. One result of this research is that there is much more information concerning how to set up a principled approach to teaching vocabulary than before this vocabulary goldrush.

Key Issues

This resurgent research has raised many issues, which can inform vocabulary teaching, and this chapter will concentrate on six in particular:

- A large vocabulary is needed to function in an L2.
- Various kinds of word knowledge are needed to use a word well.
- Vocabulary learning is incremental.
- Vocabulary learning requires consolidation.
- Vocabulary learning requires enhancement of partial knowledge.
- Teaching vocabulary.

This chapter discusses each of these issues in turn, and attempts to demonstrate how they can inform a more coherent and principled approach to the teaching of second language vocabulary. The majority of vocabulary research has been on English as a second language (ESL), and thus the chapter normally uses English as the target language in the discussions.

However, many or most of the points made will also be pertinent to the teaching of other modern languages.

A Large Vocabulary is Needed to Function in a Language

In order to understand the best way to help learners acquire vocabulary, one must first know the extent of the vocabulary learning task. This involves knowing how many words need to be learned. There are a number of ways of looking at the amount of vocabulary which learners need to acquire. One way is to consider the vocabulary size of native speakers, who presumably have an adequate vocabulary size to use a language. In English, educated speakers (e.g. university students) appear to have a vocabulary size in the range of 15,000–20,000 word families (Goulden *et al.*, 1990). Of course, learners are unlikely to master this many words, but the good news is that they can operate efficiently in English with a much smaller vocabulary size.

Perhaps a better way of establishing vocabulary learning goals is to ask how much vocabulary is necessary to achieve the types of language activities which learners want to do. The first obvious step is communicating in daily conversation. This has traditionally been set at 2000 word families based on an older study of Australian worker oral communication (Schonell *et al.*, 1956). However, newer research has pushed this target upwards. In 2003, Adolphs and Schmitt found that that 3000 word families might be a better target, as this figure covered nearly 96% of the Cambridge and Nottingham Corpus of Discourse English (CANCODE), a modern 5 million word corpus of unscripted spoken discourse. Nation (2006) subsequently calculated that 6000–7000 word families are required, based on a higher 98% coverage figure. As it is still not clear exactly what percentage of lexical coverage is necessary, the best conclusion possible at the moment is that the vocabulary requirement is between 2000–3000 and 6000–7000 word families (Schmitt, 2008).

Another common goal is to read authentic materials such as books and magazines. Research by Laufer in 1992 suggested that this requires at least 3000 word families. However, with this vocabulary size, many words will still be unknown, and learners will still need considerable support from a teacher or dictionary. Hu and Nation (2000) found that around 98–99% coverage is necessary for comprehension from written texts, and based on this Nation (2006) calculated that 8000–9000 word families are necessary to read a range of authentic texts.

Nation (personal communication) suggests that general vocabulary ends at about 5000 word families. If learners wish to operate in a technical field, then it makes sense to learn this general vocabulary plus the technical vocabulary for the field. Beyond this, if a learner wants to be able to use

English well in a variety of contexts, then 10,000 word families is a good target as a wide vocabulary (Hazenberg & Hulstijn, 1996).

The new vocabulary requirements may seem daunting, but even so, they may underestimate the real learning burden. Each word family[1] contains several members. In some cases, there may only be a couple of word family members (*matrix, matrixes*). In other cases, inflections and derivative forms may result in a few more forms (*pilfer, pilfered, pilfering, pilfers, pilferage, pilferer*). In still other cases, the word family may be made up of a large number of members (*possess, possessed, possessing, possesses, possession, possessor, possessive, repossess, repossession*). Overall, we can see that the number of individual word forms to use English is much greater than the word family figures would suggest.

Therefore, the bottom line is that a large number of word forms are needed to operate in a language. While grammar is a closed system with a limited set of rules, vocabulary is open-ended, with even older native speakers learning new words. As such, it is likely to be the biggest hurdle in learning a language. This is especially true in English where the vocabulary is particularly large and complex. English has the largest vocabulary of any known language (Schmitt & Marsden, 2006), having absorbed loanwords from a vast number of other languages. In addition, many of its semantically related words carry no formal similarities. For example, a person who *swims* is a *swimmer*, and in this case the formal similarities make it easier for a learner to make the connection. But many other related words have totally different forms: a person who *steals* is a *thief* or *robber*, unless he robs a house, in which case he is a *burglar*. Likewise, the synonyms *intelligent, smart, bright* and *clever* have no formal similarities to show they mean much the same thing. This lack of a transparent clue to meaning from the word form means that learners must essentially memorize the different word forms individually. Between the large vocabulary size of English and the often unhelpful nature of its word forms, Nation and Meara (2002) suggest that there is often a 'Lexical Bar' to learning English.

Various Kinds of Word Knowledge are Needed to Use a Word Well

If you asked the average educated person on the street (or even many language teachers) what it means to know a word, they would probably say something like knowing what the word *means*, and knowing how to *spell* it. In fact, this is not a bad answer for *initial* knowledge of a word. If one thinks about it, a form-meaning linkage is the most basic vocabulary knowledge possible. If a word's form is known, but not its meaning, it cannot be used. The converse is also true. Thus, a form-meaning link is the minimal specification for knowing a word, and being able to use it in any practical way. It therefore makes sense to encourage learning form-meaning links as the initial step of vocabulary learning.

However, this form-meaning link should be seen as only the first step. It may be possible to use a word with this level of knowledge in a basic way, but it is unlikely that the word can be used appropriately, confidently and idiomatically in a range of different contexts. For this to happen, a wider specification of knowledge is necessary. The idea of a range of *word knowledge* types was first expressed by Jack Richards in 1976, and has been refined by Paul Nation. The listing in his 2001 book (Nation, 2001: 27) is the most comprehensive, but his 1990 listing provides a concise account of the most important types:

- meaning;
- written form;
- spoken form;
- grammatical characteristics;
- collocation;
- register constraints;
- frequency;
- associations. (Nation, 1990: 31)

The first three of these word knowledge types relate to the meaning and form, which have already been discussed. However, in English, many words are polysemous, and so learning the full meaning content of a word also entails learning a number of different meaning senses, some of which may be semantically unrelated. Grammatical characteristics entail information about word class (e.g. noun, verb, etc.) and morphology (e.g. grammatical inflections (*walk – walked*) and derivative affixation (*fool – foolish*).

The other four types of word knowledge are quite different in that they are almost completely dictated by context. Collocation is the relationship between words that occur together, register concerns the stylistic and connotative appropriateness of a word for a particular context, frequency is how often a word occurs in discourse and associations are other words related to the target word by semantic or formal links. All of the word knowledge types are necessary to use a word in a target-like fashion in a variety of contexts, and so need to be acquired by learners.

However, as opposed to meaning, form and grammatical characteristics, which can (largely) be learned about a word in isolation, the 'contextual' word knowledge types are much more difficult to teach explicitly. Their contextual nature necessitates numerous exposures with the word in diverse contexts in order to master it. For example, while it may be possible to explicitly teach a few collocations for a word, good intuitions about all of the words which do and do not collocate with that word would be impossible to teach. Such intuitions could only be acquired by large amounts of exposure. This suggests that some word knowledge aspects are relatively amenable to explicit teaching, while the contextual aspects will require an approach based on promoting extensive exposure. (See more on this in the section 'Teaching Vocabulary'.)

Therefore, it takes knowledge of various word knowledge types to master a word, but let us go back to the initial stage of learning, that is, forming the first form-meaning link. Which of the two is the more difficult to learn? As with other aspects of language learning, it depends on the situation. If a person is learning a completely new concept (e.g. the physics concepts behind the term *spin* as described by Stephen Hawking in *A Brief History of Time*), then the meaning may well be more difficult. But cases like this may actually be the exception. Most second language learners already know a vast number of concepts from their previous L1 and general knowledge of the world, for example, what *tables, love, swimming, beautiful* and *slowly* are. In these cases, the meanings are already known, and it is only a matter of learning the new L2 labels (written and/or spoken word forms) for those meanings. In other words, learning the word form may require more effort than the meaning.

Furthermore, L2 learners are often confused by a word's form, particularly if two or more forms are similar to each other. Batia Laufer and her colleagues have explored this issue in depth and found that their students often made errors caused by similarity in word form. Bensoussan and Laufer (1984) found that compound words were sometimes misinterpreted:

outline interpreted as 'out of line'
discourse interpreted as 'without direction'.

In fact, these guesses show good strategy use, and in many cases an analysis of word part like these would lead to correct interpretations. But word part analysis in English does not always yield the correct meaning, and in these cases the students were misled. Laufer (1988) made an extensive study of the different ways that word forms can be similar to each other (which she calls *synformy*) and found that some types of synformy are more problematic than others. She found that the categories of synformy that caused the greatest confusion were where words were similar except for suffixes (*comprehensive/comprehensible*), and were similar except for vowels (*adopt/adapt*). In contrast, words which were similar except for consonants (*price/prize*) were less prone to confusion.

Another way in which word form can be problematic is in knowledge of the various members of a word family. Bauer and Nation (1993) suggest that 'if learners know one member of a word family (*suspicious*), they can recognize the other members (*suspect, suspiciously*)'. While probably true in receptive terms, it is not true productively. Schmitt and Zimmerman (2002) gave advanced L2 learners one word form in a family, and found that they typically knew some, but not all, of the other derivative forms. They typically knew noun and verb forms better than adjective and adverb forms. Thus it is not possible to assume that learners will know all of the word forms for the members of a word family, just because one of the members is known. Taken together with the synformy results, it seems important not to assume that learning the form of a word will be easy. In fact, in many cases learning the word form may be more difficult than learning the meaning.

Vocabulary Learning is Incremental

It is widely known that people cannot learn a word from a single meeting; rather learners need multiple contacts with words to acquire them. The real question is *how many* exposures are necessary to learn a word. Nation (1990) surveys the research and finds results ranging from 5 to 16 or more exposures. This variation is a result of the different types of exposure in the various studies. Evidently, the number of exposures required to learn a word depends on a number of factors, including type of exposure, level of engagement and congruity between L2 and L1 form.

One way of learning words which has been studied extensively is incidental learning from reading. In L1 reading studies (mainly of school children), the research designs have tended to explore the chances of learning a novel word from a single exposure. The range found extends from about 5% to 14% at best (Nagy, 1997). Thus, the chances of learning a word from a single exposure are small, but young readers in school typically read a relatively large amount of text, and so the amount of learning overall can be substantial.

In L2 reading studies, the research designs typically expose learners to texts in which novel words occur with varying frequencies, and then test which words are learned. There is a great amount of variation in the results, and all that is safe to conclude is that learning does occur, but is generally not robust (Horst & Meara, 1999; Paribakht & Wesche, 1993; Pigada & Schmitt, 2006). Given the low rate of uptake, any meaningful incidental learning requires a program being in place which maximizes the amount of reading which is done, such as an extensive reading program (e.g. Day & Bamford, 1998).

The other way of learning vocabulary is through intentional techniques where words are explicitly taught and/or intentionally focused upon by the learner through learning strategies. Not surprisingly, research has shown that when learners' attention is explicitly focused on learning vocabulary, the uptake is stronger than in incidental learning. However, the efficiency depends on the level of engagement with the vocabulary learning task. With high-engagement techniques like the Keyword Method (Hulstijn, 1997), relatively few meetings (perhaps even only one) may be enough to make the form-meaning link. Other techniques, which involve less mental effort and engagement with the word (such as rote written repetition of a word), may require many more meetings.

The implications of the fact that it takes mastery of several types of word knowledge to employ a word properly, and that learning a word is incremental in nature, means that vocabulary programs need to build recycling into the curriculum. This can be done by choosing textbooks where vocabulary recycling is a design principle. Unfortunately, many teachers have to use a prescribed textbook, many of which do not recycle vocabulary in any principled way. In these cases, the teachers will have to insert supplementary activities into their classes. These could include vocabulary games, explicit review sessions, or something as simple as using previously taught vocabulary in the example sentences which the teacher uses to illustrate the highlighted language points of the day.

Vocabulary Learning Requires Consolidation

We have seen the recycling of vocabulary is essential to learning. However, consolidating previously met vocabulary entails more than just recycling. It is also important *how* the students revise their vocabulary. The way human memory works plays a part in this, particularly how the mind forgets information. It seems that when learning new information, most forgetting occurs soon after the end of the learning session. After that major loss, the rate of forgetting decreases (Figure 3.1).

By understanding the nature of forgetting, it is possible to organize a recycling program which will be more efficient. The forgetting curve in Figure 3.1 indicates that it is critical to have a review session soon after the learning session, but less essential as time goes on. The principle of *expanding rehearsal* was derived from this insight, which suggests that learners review new material soon after the initial meeting and then at gradually increasing intervals (Baddeley, 1990; Pimsleur, 1967). One explicit memory schedule proposes reviews 5–10 min after the end of the study period, 24 h later, one week later, one month later and finally six months later

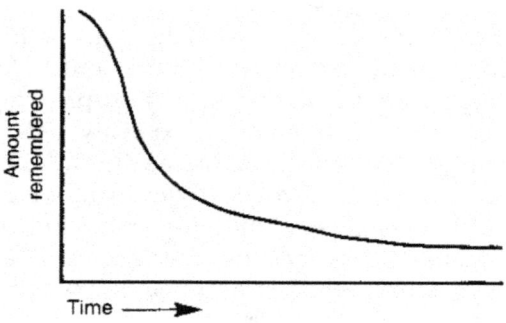

Figure 3.1 Typical pattern of forgetting (Schmitt, 2000: 131)

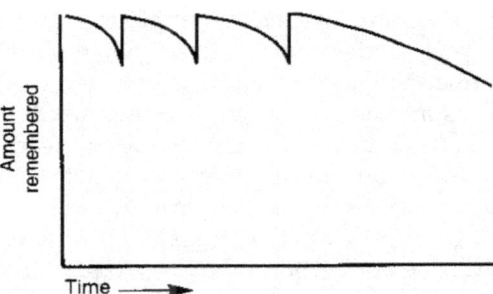

Figure 3.2 Pattern of forgetting with expanding rehearsal (Schmitt, 2000: 131)

(Russell, 1979). In this way, the forgetting is minimized (Figure 3.2). Students can use the principle of expanding rehearsal to individualize their learning. They should test themselves on new words they have studied. If they can remember them, they should increase the interval before the next review, but if they cannot, they should shorten the interval.

Landauer and Bjork (1978) combined the principle of expanding practice with research results demonstrating that the greater the interval between presentations of a target item, the greater the chances it would be subsequently recalled. From this, they suggest that the ideal practice interval is the longest period that a learner can go without forgetting a word. Research by Schouten-van Parreren (1991) shows that some easier words may be overlearned (in the sense that more time is devoted to them than necessary), while more difficult abstract words are often underlearned. A practice schedule based on the expanding rehearsal principle may help in avoiding this problem.

Another memory-based technique is attaching 'new' knowledge to established knowledge. The main way of doing this is by finding some preexisting information in the long-term memory to 'attach' the new information to. In the case of vocabulary, it means finding some element already in the mental lexicon to relate the new lexical information to. This can be done in various ways. One is through imaging techniques like the Keyword Approach. Another is through grouping a new word with already-known words which are similar in some respect. The new word can be placed with words with a similar meaning (*prank: trick, joke, jest*), a similar sound structure (*prank, tank, sank, rank*), the same beginning letters (*prank: pray, pretty, prod*), the same word class (*prank: cow, greed, distance*), or other grouping parameter, although by far the most common must be meaning similarity. Since the 'old' words are already fixed in the mind, relating the new words to them provides a 'hook' to remember them by so they will not be forgotten. New words which do not have this connection are much more prone to forgetting.

Although grouping can work well when attaching new information to established knowledge, it does not work well when simultaneously introducing new information which is similar in some way. In fact, if two or more similar words are initially taught together, it might actually make them more difficult to learn. This is because students learn the word forms and learn the meanings, but confuse which goes with which (*crossassociation*). As a beginning teacher I often confused my students in this way by teaching *left* and *right* together in the same class. After extensive drilling, I would ask the students at the end of the class to raise their left hands. To my consternation, a large number always raised their right. The problem was that the words were too similar, with all the semantic features being the same except for 'direction'. Research shows that crossassociation is a genuine problem for learners (Higa, 1963; Tinkham, 1993; Waring, 1997), with Nation (1990) suggesting that about 25% of similar words taught together are typically crossassociated. Antonyms are particularly prone to crossassociation, because they tend to come in pairs like *deep/shallow* or *rich/poor*, but synonyms and other words from closely related semantic groupings (e.g. days of the week, numbers, foods, clothing) are also at risk. Nation (1990) suggests the way to avoid crossassociation is to teach the most frequent or useful word of a pair first (e.g. *deep*), and only after it is well established introducing its partner(s) (e.g. *shallow*).

Vocabulary Learning Requires Enhancement of Partial Knowledge

So far, the chapter has discussed the necessity of consolidating knowledge of partially learned words. However, recycling is as much about enhancing knowledge as well as it is about consolidation. This is because the initial learning of a word is likely to establish only its form-meaning connection, and perhaps a bit of knowledge of its grammatical characteristics, including morphology. But this is not enough to demonstrate target-like use, and so additional exposures are necessary to start promoting acquisition of the contextual facets of word knowledge.

Each of the word knowledge types is mastered to greater or lesser degree at any point in time. Henriksen (1999) suggests that for any lexical aspect, learners can have knowledge ranging from zero to partial to precise. This would mean that all word knowledge ranges on a continuum, rather than being known versus unknown. Even knowledge as seemingly basic as spelling can behave in this manner, ranging on a cline something like this:

| cannot spell word at all | knows some letters | phonologically correct | fully correct spelling |

◄---►

(Schmitt, 2000:118)

Key Issues in Teaching and Learning Vocabulary 37

Moreover, all of the word knowledge aspects probably range along a cline like this. However, some word knowledge aspects are likely to become acquired sooner than others, with the contextual aspects lagging behind. Although I do not yet have direct empirical evidence to support this, my intuition is that vocabulary learning typically progresses something like the following account.

In the initial stages (first few exposures), a learner knows a limited amount about a new word. The knowledge is limited both in terms of *which* word knowledge types are known, and the *degree* to which they are known. It is likely that not much more than some knowledge of form and of a single meaning sense is known, plus perhaps some initial knowledge about the grammatical characteristics of a word. Based on a word knowledge framework, Figure 3.3 illustrates what early knowledge of a word may be like.

After a number of further exposures, the lexical specification starts filling out. As long as there are no synformy or crossassociation issues, it is likely that the word form (written or spoken, or perhaps both) will soon become relatively well mastered, as well as knowledge of the initial meaning sense. However, the meaning and grammatical characteristics are not fully mastered, because the learner is unlikely to know the various meaning senses a polysemous word has, and is unlikely to know all of the word forms for the members of the word family. The contextual word knowledge types will start filling in, but because these must be acquired over time, the knowledge state is only partial at this stage (Figure 3.4).

By the time a learner (or native speaker) has engaged with a word over time, it can become mastered to the extent that it can be considered known. But what does this mean? The word form should be well known by this time, and most of the possible meaning senses. However, even native speakers are often unaware of some unusual meaning senses, and so most learners may never reach the full mastery of all meaning senses. Eventually, the learner should learn how to use most of the members of a word's family, but even natives are unsure about some derivative forms, and so less-than-complete mastery may be the norm. As for the contextual word

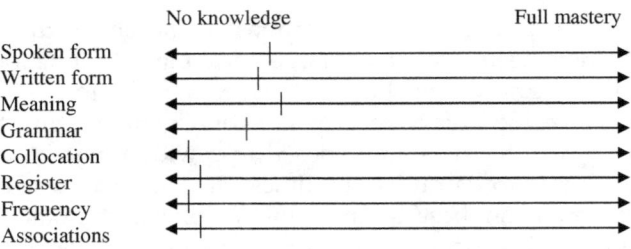

Figure 3.3 Early knowledge of a word

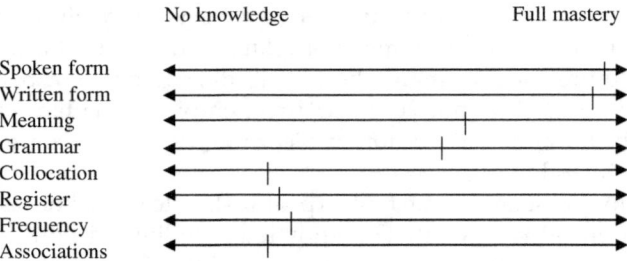

Figure 3.4 Developing knowledge of word

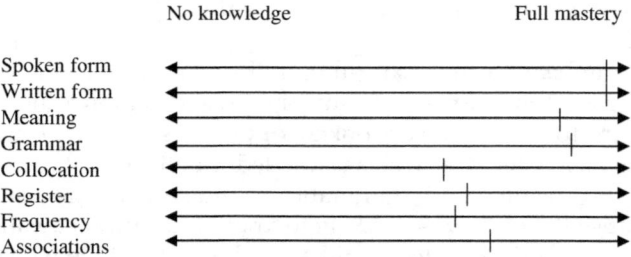

Figure 3.5 Advanced knowledge of word

knowledge types, only the most advanced learners are likely to get the amount of exposure in the L2 to build intuitions, which would rival natives in terms of automaticity, confidence and idiomaticity (Figure 3.5).

If vocabulary acquisition occurs something like the above account, then recycling is doubly critical. Learners need numerous encounters with words not only to consolidate already-accrued knowledge, but also to master the various types of word knowledge. In the end, recycling is as much about enhancement as consolidation.

Teaching Vocabulary

What are the pedagogical implications of the above discussion? In essence, learners need a relatively large vocabulary to function in a language, and must know a lot about each word in order to use it well. This kind of extensive vocabulary knowledge is only going to come from long-term study, where learners are exposed to a wide range of words, and exposed to those words numerous times. But how can teachers ensure this? First, there is no 'best' teaching methodology. As in all things concerning language instruction, the best teaching method depends on many factors which vary from situation to situation.

One important factor is the words themselves: different words/phrases might need different teaching strategies. There are a number of ways of conveying the meaning of a new word:

- definition or explanation;
- demonstration or gesture;
- synonym or antonym;
- giving examples;
- define in situational context.

Now let us consider a number of words to teach. Although you could conceivably use any of the above techniques to explain the meaning of any of these words, certain approaches seem more suitable for certain words:

butcher – this word may be best described with a definition: a person who sells meat
bite – very visual, and easy to clearly define with a simple gesture
filthy – a synonym can describe this state easily: 'very dirty'
awake – an antonym would work well here: 'not asleep'
vehicle – perhaps giving examples is the clearest technique here: 'car, truck, bus'
jealous – this concept is more difficult to define; perhaps a better approach is describing a situation where a person could become jealous

Just as different words may be more amenable to certain techniques of illustrating meaning, different words may be best taught and learned with different methodology. One example of this is using the Keyword Approach (Hulstijn, 1997). It works well with words that are easy to make an image of (*table*), but may be less effective for words expressing abstract concepts (*distance*).

A second factor is the learners themselves. Each learner is an individual, and different learners may favor different approaches. This is particularly noticeable with vocabulary learning strategies. Learners typically use a variety of vocabulary learning strategies (Schmitt, 1997). However, more strategy use is not always better. What is more important is *how well* the strategies are used. That is, what seems to make the difference is using strategies appropriate to the learning goal. While most specialists seem to promote 'deeper' strategies that require more extensive engagement with vocabulary, even relatively 'shallow' strategies, like rote memorization, can be effective if learners know how to apply them well, are diligent in their use, and are mainly interested in the initial form-meaning connection.

A third variable is the general teaching approach, that is intentional versus incidental learning. These approaches are complementary and yield different benefits.

- Intentional learning:
  - generally leads to more robust and faster learning;
  - generally involves deeper engagement leading to better retention;
  - can focus on important vocabulary selected by the teacher (e.g. high frequency, technical, targeted).

On the other hand,
- Incidental learning:
  - can address words which cannot be explicitly taught for time reasons;
  - fills out the kinds of contextual word knowledge which cannot easily be explicitly taught;
  - provides recycling for words already taught explicitly;
  - vocabulary learning occurs while improving other language skill areas (e.g. reading).

In short, intentional learning is focused and effective, but limited in terms of the number of words (and word knowledge types) it can address. Incidental learning is slow and untargeted, but can fill in the 'contextual' types of word knowledge, and provide recycling for words already partially learned. From this, we can see that both approaches are necessary, as they compensate for the gaps left by the other approach.

Conclusion

Learning a sufficient amount of vocabulary is one of the biggest challenges facing language learners. Teachers should face this challenge squarely, and provide their students with plenty of vocabulary to learn and use right from the beginning. Although some may say this is too difficult, I believe most students expect to have to learn a lot of vocabulary in their language studies. Keith Folse made this point forcefully in his 2007 presentation at the American Association for Applied Linguists (AAAL) conference, remarking that if he was a student and was told that he would only be learning 50 or 60 words over a several-week-long course, he would be insulted. It is important for L2 teachers to challenge their students by emphasizing vocabulary, and by doing so giving them a fighting chance to learn the vocabulary they need to function in their second language.

Note
1. A word family is a base word with its inflections and derivatives (*stimulate + stimulated, stimulates, stimulating, stimulation, stimulant,* and *stimulative*). (Schmitt & McCarthy, 1997: 331).

Chapter 4

A Dynamic Perspective on L2 Lexical Development in Academic English

TAL CASPI and WANDER LOWIE

Introduction

Vocabulary development has been studied in a wide variety of contexts, focusing on several knowledge dimensions that range from passive to active, from incidental to explicit and from learning to acquisition. In this chapter, we will focus on how these different kinds of word knowledge change and affect each other over time, by applying a Dynamic Systems Theory (DST) perspective. DST has been extensively used to analyze a range of natural, social and behavioral phenomena and has recently been applied to L2 development (de Bot *et al.*, 2007; Larsen-Freeman, 1997). DST is essentially a theory of change, and its most important merit for L2 development is its emphasis on the developmental process itself, rather than on products of this process at a single moment in time. In addition, DST allows for the combination of several factors affecting development into a single model. This chapter will concentrate on the varied developmental rates of lexical knowledge levels and the influence of word frequency, learner proficiency and learning context and duration on their interactions, which result in non-linear transfer of passive L2 vocabulary knowledge into production (Laufer, 1998; Laufer & Paribakht, 1998; Schmitt & Meara, 1997). We will trace the development and interactions of four L2 lexical knowledge levels: word recall and recognition in the passive knowledge dimension, and controlled and free production in the active knowledge dimension. We will demonstrate that the two dimensions are strongly interrelated and that patterns of variation in their development and interaction are compatible with characteristics of dynamic systems.

The chapter begins with an overview of DST, its relevance to language and the value of data variation in research from a DST perspective. After reviewing dynamic models of vocabulary knowledge and relating them to empirical findings, we conclude with a case study which illustrates how academic English (L2) vocabulary development can be investigated from a dynamic perspective.

Language as a Dynamic System

DST began in the fields of ecology, meteorology and physics and has since expanded to embrace diverse areas, among them human cognition and learning. Dynamic systems have been identified in virtually any field that involves growth and interaction. A classic example of a dynamic system is a flock of birds, in which dynamic interactions between individual birds generate a continually changing and self-organizing formation (Figure 4.1).

Generally speaking, a dynamic system is a set of changing components that influence one another. These components (individual birds in our example above) can be described as dynamic subsystems nested in the greater system, and which in turn comprise interacting, developing subcomponents. Not only do the components of a complex system change over time, but their interaction itself is also dynamic and changes with time. Because change over time always follows from a previous state of the system, systemic 'growth' cannot be fully predicted in the long run. This is perhaps best illustrated by another famous example of a dynamic

Figure 4.1 Simulation of bird-flocking behavior as the cumulative, unplanned result of complex and iterative interaction between members of the flock. (Image copyright of flight404.com)

system, the weather. Based on today's pressure areas, temperature, humidity, and so forth, tomorrow's weather can be predicted fairly accurately. The forecast for next week is much more uncertain and we can say virtually nothing about next month's weather.

The iterative growth of a dynamic system is inherently non-linear, as small changes at one stage may lead to drastic qualitative changes in its developmental pattern. The relevance of the initial conditions and iterative chance is illustrated by one of the best know applications of DST, the 'Butterfly Effect'. Put forth by Lorenz (1963 in Hilborn, 2004, 1972), this paradigm shows how the componentiality and interconnectedness of a dynamic weather system can result in far-fetched changes through iterations over time. It illustrates the effect that even seemingly minute factors can have on the overall development of a dynamic system, due to its nested and complex nature. The phenomena at hand, or the product, of a dynamic process can therefore not be studied in isolation from the process itself, as it is inherently inseparable from it.

The consequence of the iterative development and the ever-changing interactions of a dynamic system's components is that the system is 'self-organizing'. The self-organization of a dynamic system is limited by availability of systemic resources. These resources can consist of factors internal to the system ('internal resources', such as stamina in our bird example) or can come from the outside ('external resources', such as the weather and food conditions in the bird example). As a result of the limitations of the resources, the developmental pattern of the system alternates between 'attractor' and 'repellor' states. Attractor states are configurations that the system is inclined to remain in unless perturbed by a sufficient amount of resources; while repellors are states in which the system is seldom or never found.

It has been repeatedly argued (for instance by de Bot *et al.*, 2007; Larsen-Freeman, 1997; Van Geert, 1991, 2008) that language, both for the individual learner and for a language community, can be regarded as a dynamic system. Like other dynamic systems, language develops non-linearly and is affected not only by input, but also by interactions between its componential subsystems, such as specific languages known. Within these languages, another level of subsystems such as grammar, vocabulary and phonology can be considered as nested, interacting subsystems. The dynamic nature of language development is further emphasized by the initial state and varied resources. Some of the resources, such as working memory capacity and language learning aptitude, are inherently limited for a particular learner, while other resources, such as motivation, are more easily affected by the sociolinguistic setting in which the language is learned. Like all dynamic systems, language growth is restricted by the limitations on its resources, and shows patterns of repellors and attractors, characterized in L2 as 'fossilization'. The main merit of DST with respect to language is its ability to describe and explain its development, both within communities and in individual learners, with general principles that characterize other natural phenomena. This aim is achieved by identifying dynamic processes of interaction between components of linguistic knowledge that result in non-linear development across various areas of language.

Applying the dynamic perspective to language development implies that if, for instance, we want to know why a specific learner has acquired only a limited number of linguistic structures after a period of exposure to target language input, the answer may lie not only in the direct, or linear effect of this input on the specific area of the linguistic knowledge, but also or even predominantly in the interactions of this area with other areas of the learner's knowledge. To illustrate this principle, we use an example from a paper by Verspoor *et al.* (2004), which applied dynamic principles to the analysis of aspects of the development of beginner level EFL writing by a Dutch native speaker. One of their findings was that instances where the participant used Dutch words instead of English words (presumably because she did not know or remember the English words at the time of writing) coincide with a decrease in the number of incorrect English words in her writing. The findings implied that a decrease in writing complexity was accompanied by an increase in overall accuracy. Plotted against time, this concurrence was seen to be robust in the first half of the study period, after which changes in the ratios of Dutch words and incorrectly used English words started to run parallel (see Figure 4.2). The parallel development was seen to reflect a possible settling of the system. This example illustrates how a dynamic approach accounts for the change of language components in dynamic relation to each other rather than in isolation. This example also shows how a DST approach views process and product as inseparable, and how variability in the data can be meaningfully used rather than being discarded as 'noise'.

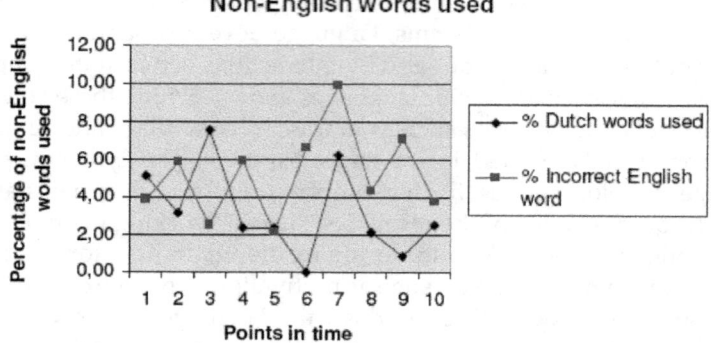

Figure 4.2 The ratio of Dutch words versus the ratio of incorrect English words, as used in the ESL writing of a Dutch native speaker. (Derived from Verspoor *et al.*, 2004)

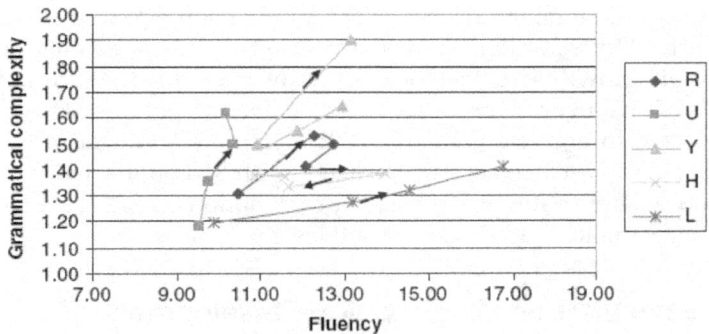

Figure 4.3 Change and direction of the growth rate of fluency as a function of the growth rate of grammatical complexity in the written essays of five participants data. (Larsen-Freeman, 2006, with permission of Oxford University Press.)

Similarly, Larsen Freeman (2006) has investigated the development of aspects of written L2 in relation to each other (Figure 4.3). She plotted the changes, or growth rate, of fluency, as manifested in the average words per *t*-unit, in relation to grammatical complexity, as manifested in average number of clauses per *t*-unit. The growth of one component of linguistic knowledge is this system presented as a function of the growth of another yielded a concentric pattern reminiscent of attractor state plots.

In contrast with the study mentioned above, the bulk of language studies concentrate on attempts to link growth effects and external factors linearly, thereby disregarding the data of variation both between and within individual learners as noise or measurement error. However, this variation can be 'substantial, stable, and have [its] own developmental course' (Bates *et al.*, 1995: 1). Recent dynamic approaches to L1 (Ruhland, 1998; van Dijk, 2003) and L2 development (*cf.* de Bot *et al.*, 2007; Larsen-Freeman, 1997) emphasize that its trajectory is far from a straightforward linear transition from a complete lack of knowledge to full command. They focus instead on patterns of variation that accompany developmental trends.

From this perspective, variation is inherent to, and in fact enables, language change and evolution by altering the languages of individuals and their communities (Larsen-Freeman, 1997). Increased variation coincides with periods of accelerated development known as 'developmental jumps' (Thelen & Smith, 1994). Acquisition has been shown to be a series of changes in relative frequencies of strategies, leading to a decrease in less mature strategies, rather than an abrupt replacement of older strategies with new ones (van Geert & van Dijk, 2002). Moreover, variation not only reflects change, but can also be regarded as the condition that enables it (Bertenthal, 1999).

All levels of language development and use, on every time scale, are characterized by variation. At the macro level of a learner's lifespan, periods of rapid growth, like the 'vocabulary spurt' during the second year of a child's life (Ganger & Brent, 2004), alternate with periods of vocabulary attrition due to non-use (Hansen, 2001). At the microlevel of the millisecond, rapid word retrieval alternates with strenuous word finding. Here, too, a detailed longitudinal study of variation in lexical use can yield valuable information about the mental lexicon.

A Dynamic View on L2 Vocabulary Development

Vocabulary, the largest area of linguistic knowledge, is also the area most affected by attrition, both in individual learners and in language communities (Gross, 2004). Traditional accounts of the mental lexicon describe it as a static dictionary-like structure that exists independently of its use; more recent accounts address its complexity, componentiality and interconnectivity and the dynamic nature of lexical processing (Elman, 1995, 2004; Meara, 2005; Singleton, 1999). However, as in most L2 studies, lexical studies typically focus on pre- and post-treatment group effects rather than on developmental processes in individuals, and eliminate variation by applying regression analysis to data.

The dynamic approach perceives the mental lexicon as comprised of word representations which are 'highly context-sensitive, continuously-varied, and probabilistic' (Elman, 1995: 199). These representations are 'trajectories through mental space' (Elman, 1995: 199) rather than fixed constructions. In this episodic view, word recognition, recall and production are graded processes affected by interactions that determine the speed of word retrieval in a given context. In other words, a word does not have a fixed meaning that is stored in the lexicon, but a particular set of meanings in a particular context at particular moment in time (for a detailed account of the episodic lexicon, see Goldinger, 1998). The state of the dynamic lexicon, at any given moment, is a function reflecting its prior state (Elman, 1995: 203). Although so far DST has not been applied to empirical L2 vocabulary data, current lexical models using the activation metaphor are largely compatible with dynamic views (Jacquet & French, 2002).

A simulation of a strongly simplified model of the bilingual lexicon as an on–off network of a small number of items has shown that it exhibits interactive relations and iterative development characteristic of dynamic systems (Meara, 2005). The interacting L1 and L2 lexicons typically settle in a steady attractor state, in which L1 vocabulary is dominant and L2 is dormant (Meara, 2005). The dominant L1 lexicon remains relatively stable, while the L2 lexicon was unstable and sensitive to perturbation. Thus, activating L1 lexical items did not produce large or lasting effects, whereas activating even a small number of L2 items sometimes generated extensive iterative activation patterns. These patterns were comparable with the 'butterfly effect' (Lorenz, 1963 in Hilborn, 2004), a phenomena characterizing unstable dynamic system in which, through a series of iterations, slight changes in parameters have profound effects on the entire system. In Meara's model, this manifested in large vocabulary gains, rendering the L2 lexicon temporarily dominant within the bilingual system. When activation of the L2 items stopped, the system returned to the L1 dominance–L2 dormancy equilibrium. Meara concluded that his simulation mirrored the Boulogne Ferry Effect, in which dormant French vocabulary of British passengers on the cross-channel ferry is activated by a sudden exposure to a small number of vocabulary items (2005).

While Meara's simulation successfully models the dynamic nature of the lexicon, it does not incorporate the ever-changing, interactive and hierarchical nature of word knowledge, which can be described as a continuum ranging from 'barely knowing [a word] receptively to being able to use it productively with stylistic and collocational appropriateness' (Schmitt & Meara, 1997). Similarly, most vocabulary studies focus on single words rather than on the overall state of the mental lexicon (Read, 2000). In addition, it has been recommended that cross-sectional, group-trend findings be supplemented with case studies of vocabulary development (Schmitt & Meara, 1997; Singleton, 1999).

The current study, therefore, is a longitudinal study of the development and interactions of two levels of lexical knowledge in two dimensions within an individual learner: free versus controlled production in the active knowledge dimension; and recall versus recognition in the passive knowledge dimension. Free production is spontaneous usage of target words in writing (Laufer & Nation, 1999). Using the initial letters of target words as cues, controlled production is elicited by a context from which the target word is missing (a gap fill task) (Laufer & Nation, 1995), recall by supplying the word's meaning through a dictionary definition (Laufer et al., 2004), and recognition by supplying the meaning as one option out of four (Laufer et al., 2004) (see also section 'Hypotheses').

Empirical findings: The L2 lexicon as a dynamic system

So far, DST had not been explicitly applied to empirical lexical data, and vocabulary studies generally refer to the lexicon as a collection of stored lexical items, sometimes in connection with activation models. Yet the results of several studies suggest that L2 lexical development is compatible with the characteristics of a dynamic system.

While in L1 there is no large difference between passive and active vocabulary knowledge dimensions, in L2 they develop in markedly different rates. These rates are manifested in the number of vocabulary items that can be retrieved or used in each knowledge dimension, and vary across learner proficiencies, learning contexts and durations and word frequencies. For instance, it was shown that at least two years' immersion in an L2 environment was necessary for passive knowledge to transfer into production, and even then, an increase in passive vocabulary knowledge does not necessarily manifest in free production, and depends on the learning context (EFL or ESL), learner proficiency (manifested in passive vocabulary size), and word frequency (Laufer, 1998; Laufer & Paribakht, 1998).

In other words, although relationships between passive vocabulary knowledge and controlled or free production[1] were predictable, correlations between these knowledge levels were neither uniform nor stable, and differed as a function of word frequency and learner proficiency (which affects passive vocabulary size) (Laufer & Paribakht, 1998). Laufer and Paribakht (1998) show that while more frequent words were found to be likelier to transfer into production in general, controlled production did not develop at the same rate as passive vocabulary in any learning context or duration. Consequently, they suggested that some passive vocabulary items might never transfer into production. When passive vocabulary knowledge was categorized in accordance with learners' proficiency levels, free production was shown to progress only when a threshold between intermediate and advanced proficiency was crossed.[2] In an ESL context, there was a significant correlation between passive vocabulary knowledge and free production across learners, regardless of proficiency. However, this correlation was not found within each proficiency level separately. This indicated that passive vocabulary knowledge, controlled production and free production develop at different rates in different proficiency levels, or stages of learning. Free production, in particular, was found to develop more slowly and unpredictably than passive vocabulary knowledge.[3]

Laufer and Paribakht also found that word frequency influenced the correlation between passive knowledge and controlled production. However, the strongest influence was attributed to the length of stay in an ESL learning environment. At least two years were needed before the correlation between controlled active and passive vocabulary was affected, but no significant effect was found on free active vocabulary. They explained the latter finding by a plateau reached by free active vocabulary. Yet they could not specify the cause and nature of this plateau, nor could they determine whether 'the different developmental rates (of the types of vocabulary knowledge) reflect the nature of lexical learning or rather are "a consequence of the learning context"' (Laufer & Paribakht, 1998: 387).

Similarly, in a study of vocabulary gains over a year of L2 immersion, Schmitt and Meara (1997) found that there was an overall increase in vocabulary size, which did not manifest in certain word frequencies.

Moreover, in certain learners, rather than the group as a whole, a decrease over time in certain word frequencies was even noted.

As mentioned earlier, dynamic systems are characterized by changing interactions between their components over time. These changes in turn affect the degree to which input from the environment influences the system. The findings of the aforementioned empirical studies, such as the changing interactions between passive and productive lexical knowledge levels over time and across learning contexts, can be seen as compatible with DST.

Following these findings, the current study investigates the L2 lexicon from a dynamic perspective, by focusing on the development and interactions of passive and productive lexical knowledge levels. This study is described in the following section.

The Case Study

To test the applicability of DST to lexical development, we investigated development and interactions of four vocabulary knowledge levels: word recognition versus word recall in the passive knowledge dimension; and controlled versus free production in the active knowledge dimension. We targeted academic ESL vocabulary, as included in the University Word List (UWL) (Xue & Nation, 1984) and the Academic Word List (AWL) (Coxhead, 2000). The limited scope of this vocabulary enabled us to assess a percentage of known vocabulary at each knowledge level, while the fact that it is distributed across frequency levels allowed us to control for the frequency effects found by the empirical studies mentioned in the previous section (Laufer, 1998; Laufer & Paribakht, 1998; Schmitt & Meara, 1997). The decision to test words from both lists was derived from the need to create a large item database that would enable repeated test administration while avoiding practice effects. Both lists contained words shown to be indispensable for successful completion of academic studies in English. The UWL was shown to successfully discriminate between proficiency levels (Laufer & Nation, 1999), while familiarity with the AWL, in combination with the most-frequent 2000 English words that constitute 79.9% of written English, was found to be essential for academic success (Beglar & Hunt, 1999).

The UWL contains 808 words common in academic texts, divided into 11 frequency levels, and excludes the most frequent 2000 words listed in the General service List (West, 1953). The AWL includes 570 word families in 10 frequency bands, which are characterized by high degrees of frequency and coverage in texts across academic topics and disciplines. Like the UWL, it excludes the most frequent 2000 words of the General Service List (West, 1953).

Participants, materials and procedures

Since this was a longitudinal study of development, we focused on one case study. The study participant was a 28-year-old female native speaker of Mandarin enrolled in an English-speaking Master's program. Prior to her academic studies, the participant successfully completed a standardized English examination (TOEFL or IELTS), and was employed as trainer for English teachers at a university in China.

Data were collected during the first semester of the participant's studies, when it was expected that her academic English vocabulary would undergo change due to language contact in the academic environment.

During 3.5 months, the participant completed 12 different versions of a test assessing passive knowledge and controlled production of academic English vocabulary knowledge (see section 'The Longitudinal Academic Vocabulary Test'), and wrote 23 assignments which were used to assess her free production of academic English vocabulary. The participant completed a test every 7–10 days, and wrote two assignments a week. These assignments were home compositions on assigned topics that constituted a part of her coursework, and were therefore not restricted in time, amount of their revision, or accessibility to resources such as dictionaries.

Samples of approximately 350 words were extracted at random from different parts of these assignments, in accordance with the view that 300-word essays are needed in order to obtain stable vocabulary size estimates (Laufer & Nation, 1995) and the fact that lexical ratio and density measures are highly dependent on text size.

The participant's free production of academic English vocabulary was operationalized as the ratio of academic word types to the total number of word types, to correct for multiple uses and overgeneralization of academic vocabulary items. Controlled production, word recall and recognition were tested by a test designed for longitudinal assessment of academic word knowledge on the basis of words sampled from the UWL and AWL. This test is presented in the following section.

The longitudinal academic vocabulary test

To assess the development of controlled production, recall and active recognition of academic English vocabulary, we devised a testing method which henceforth is referred to as the Longitudinal Academic Vocabulary Test (LAVT) (see Appendix I). The LAVT design incorporates adaptations of two testing methods: the productive version of the Levels Test (PVLT) (Laufer & Nation, 1995) and two parts of the monolingual version of the Computer Adaptive Test of Size and Strength (CATSS) (Laufer et al., 2004): active recognition and active recall.

The LAVT consists of controlled production, paired in the study with free production of academic English vocabulary manifested in written assignments, active recall and active recognition. The term 'active' refers here not to production, but to the fact that the target word itself is elicited rather than its meaning, in accordance with the knowledge continuum specified by Laufer *et al.* (2004). This continuum consists of four consecutive levels of word knowledge. The lowest level of knowledge in this continuum is passive word recognition. 'Passive' in this case refers to knowledge of word meaning, and 'active' to knowledge of the word itself. Passive recognition was operationalized by Laufer *et al.* as the ability to identify the target word's definition out of four possible options (2004). The second word knowledge level is active recognition, which is operationalized as the ability to recognize the target word out of four options when presented with the word definition (Laufer *et al.*, 2004). The third level is passive recall, which was operationalized as the ability to recall the meaning of the word when presented with the word itself. Finally, the highest level of word knowledge, according to this continuum, is active recall, which is the ability to recall a word when presented with its meaning and the initial letter of the word serving as a cue that prevents the recall of a synonym (Laufer *et al.*, 2004).

Within this continuum, we focus on active word recall and recognition, in which the word itself rather than its meaning is elicited. We excluded passive word recall and recognition from our study, because we found that the elicited definitions were often elicited partial, ambiguous or context-dependent meanings, and that the learner population that we focus on, namely non-native users of academic English of intermediate to high proficiency, showed a near-complete acquisition of the target vocabulary at this level, leaving little room for development.

A key consideration in designing the LAVT was preventing practice effects between different test versions as well as test parts. Since it is a test aimed at repeated administration, obviously if the same words were tested, any development seen would reflect the effect of the test itself rather than represent academic vocabulary knowledge. We therefore compiled a database of test items based on words that are randomly extracted from all UWL and AWL sublists by spaced sampling, a procedure in which items at preset intervals, starting from randomly determined points, are picked. No distinction was made between based and derived forms. From this database, we randomly generated each test version. This procedure in turn generates a need to ensure equivalent forms reliability. A significant correlation ($p < 0.01$) between two LAVT versions completed by Dutch-speaking first year English students ($n = 32$) at the same time proved that the method of randomly generating LAVT versions from an item database indeed results in equivalent test versions (see Table 4.1).

Table 4.1 Results from a cross-sectional study of LAVT equivalent forms reliability

Test part	Pearson's r coefficient	Number of participants
Controlled production	0.775	27
Active recall	0.844	32
Active recognition	0.733	31

Hypotheses

We expected to see an increase in recognition, recall and controlled production of academic vocabulary and a relative stability in the amount of academic vocabulary produced in free production, in accordance with previous findings (Laufer, 1998; Laufer & Paribakht, 1998). The dynamic approach to learning in general and language development in particular anticipates variation in interactions between knowledge levels and a consequent variation in development, due to the limited resources of the developing system. Therefore, we expected that levels within each dimension of knowledge, passive and productive, would exhibit a competitive relationship in which increase in one level would entail a decrease in the other. Also in accordance with the characteristics of dynamic system development, we anticipated that these levels of knowledge that showed an increase would also show a higher degree of developmental variation, in comparison with levels which decreased or remained in a stable degree of consolidation. This variation will be manifested in fluctuation above and below the linear trend.

Analysis and results

Two-tailed Pearson's r correlations were calculated between all four vocabulary knowledge levels. It was found that neither active recall and active recognition, nor controlled and free production, correlated significantly with each other. However, controlled production correlated significantly with active recall (0.644; $p < 0.05$), and active recognition and free production showed a near-significant negative correlation (−0.588; $p < 0.05$).

Following this step, the development of the paired knowledge levels within the passive and productive dimensions was plotted separately. Linear regressions added to the data showed that while one level increased, the other decreased. This was more apparent in the productive dimension, where free production decreased as the amount of known academic vocabulary in controlled production increased, than in the passive knowledge dimension, where active recognition decreased only slightly as active recall increased (see Figures 4.4 and 4.5). When we inspected the variation

L2 Lexical Development in Academic English 53

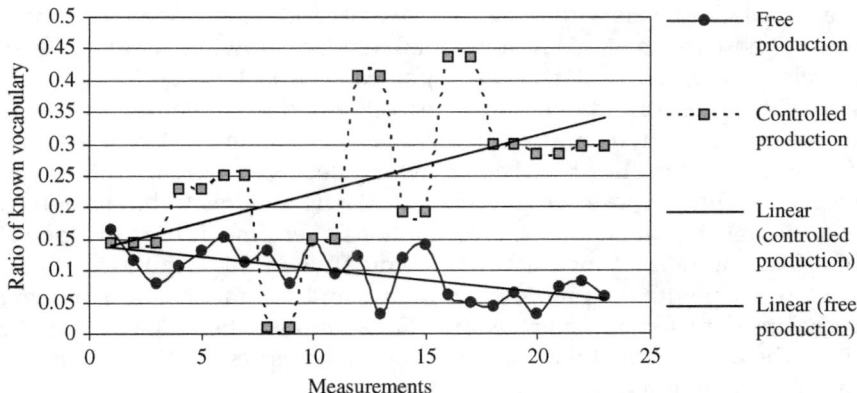

Figure 4.4 Raw data and developmental trends of free and controlled production of academic English vocabulary. Due to the smaller number of controlled production results (since 12 tests and 23 written assignments were completed by the participant during the study period), the CP results were connected by a moving average of two data points)

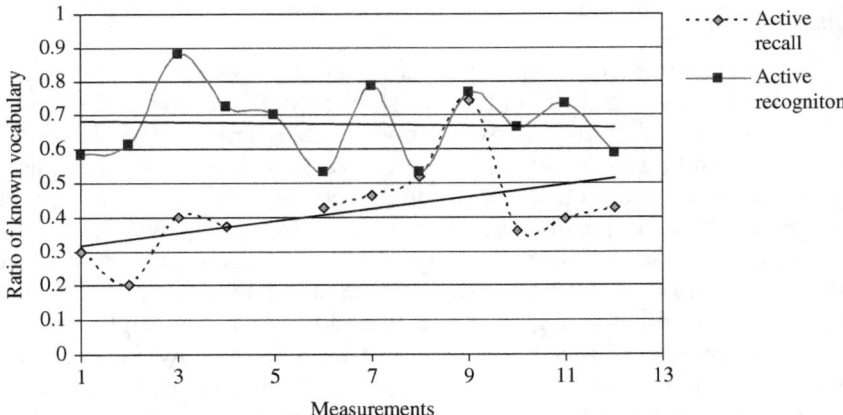

Figure 4.5 Raw data and developmental trends of active recall and recognition of academic English vocabulary

around the trend, it became evident that it was larger in the knowledge levels which increased – controlled production and active recall – rather than in the levels which decreased – free production and active recognition.

A correlation was calculated between the data residuals, the values from which the growth over time, manifested in the trend, has been subtracted. This correlation yielded a representation of interactions between the knowledge levels within the passive and productive dimension which was not obscured by the developmental trend, or growth over time. These correlations were not statistically significant, probably due to the small size of the data set and due to the variability of the correlation over time. However, from a dynamic perspective, we were still interested in seeing if and how the interaction between knowledge levels within each dimension varies. For this purpose, we employed a moving window technique which enables tracking fluctuations in correlations over time. It uses 'windows' of a fixed number of measurement points (five in this case), which partially overlap with the preceding windows and include the measurement occasions depicted in the preceding window minus the first and plus the next. The movement of the window enables the representation of changes in correlations as a developmental trajectory.

Applying this technique showed fluctuations between positive and negative correlations in both pairs of vocabulary knowledge. These fluctuations were more pronounced in the interaction between the productive knowledge levels, as can be seen in the number of transitions from positive to negative correlations and in the 'heights' and 'depths' of the developmental trajectories' 'peaks' and 'valleys' (see Figures 4.6 and 4.7).

Discussion

The development of lexical knowledge levels was shown to be consistent with the key principles of DST. First, in both the passive and productive knowledge dimensions, while one level of knowledge showed a developmental increase, the other decreased. This discrepancy was more apparent in the productive knowledge dimension, while in the passive vocabulary knowledge, the regression or linear trend of active recognition was characterized by a very small slope angle. Considering that passive vocabulary knowledge has been shown to consolidate earlier and to higher degree than production (e.g. Laufer & Paribakht, 1998), this might indicate that it is a more stabilized subsystem of L2 lexical knowledge. Such a system would exhibit less competition and more stable interaction between its components. In contrast, the interaction between the productive knowledge levels is more competitive and varied, a finding which may be explained by the fact that productive knowledge is a less stable subsystem of the L2 lexical knowledge system, since it is acquired later and at a slower pace, and therefore exhibits a more obvious competitive interaction (Figures 4.4, 4.6 and 4.7).

Although in both the passive and the active knowledge dimensions, the knowledge levels that increased also showed more variation in cross-sectional studies (*cf.* Laufer & Paribakht, 1998) controlled and free production did not develop simultaneously, and controlled production showed a large degree of fluctuation. The increase in controlled production, which

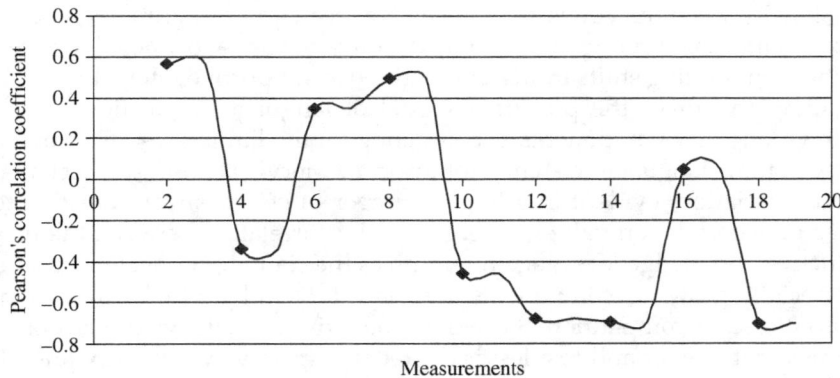

Figure 4.6 Moving window (five measurement points) of correlation between controlled and free production of academic English vocabulary

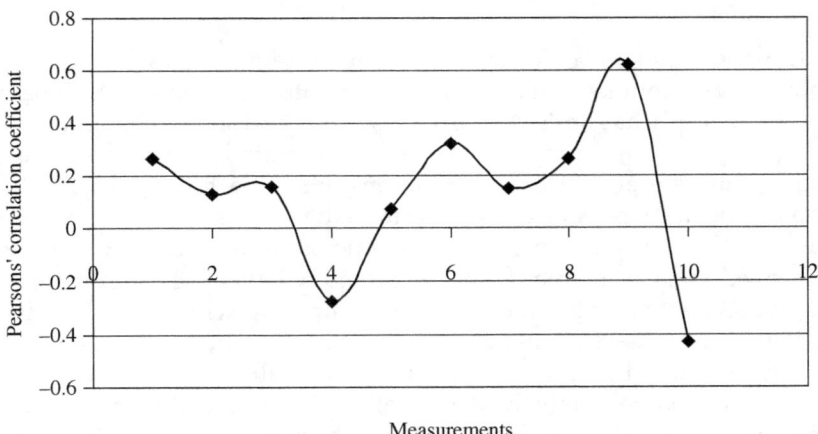

Figure 4.7 Moving window (five measurement points) of correlation between active recall and active recognition of academic English vocabulary

was larger than the increase in active recall (again evident in the slope of the linear trend), was accompanied by a higher degree of variation around the linear trend. This is in line with the 'growth-accompanying variation' characteristic of dynamic systems, again suggesting that each knowledge level within the two knowledge dimensions of passive and productive knowledge acts as a componential subsystem of a dynamic system. This finding resonates with studies of first and second language from a dynamic perspective, which found that acquisition data showed a generally increasing bandwidth in addition to a general increase in its level (van Geert & van Dijk, 2002; Verspoor et al., 2008).

Finally, the interactions between active recall and recognition and controlled and free production fluctuated from a negative to a positive correlation, suggesting shifts from a competitive to supportive interaction. This finding reinforces the precursor model of language acquisition, which views language components as competing for the limited resources of the developing language system (Robinson & Mervis, 1998). The fact that more variation, evident in a larger number of changes from positive to negative correlation values, emerged in the correlation between the productive knowledge levels again reinforces the claim that developing, and especially growing, components are characterized by a higher degree of variation and competition. Since the productive knowledge dimension is consolidated later and to a lesser degree than passive vocabulary knowledge, we suggest that it can be viewed as a less stable system, which is more sensitive to perturbation.

Conclusion

Dynamic systems are characterized by non-linear, unpredictable and iterative development that tends toward attractor states. A dynamic system typically has limited internal resources and shows changing interactions between its components, which alternate between competition and mutual support. These interactions are impacted by, and in turn impact, the influence of external input on the system. In our study of the development of academic English lexicon in a non-native speaker immersed in an academic setting, we asked whether the development of passive and active lexical knowledge is compatible with DST. We focused on longitudinal assessment of two pairs of passive and active knowledge dimensions: word recognition versus word recall; and controlled versus free production, respectively. We hypothesized that while certain knowledge levels would increase, namely the passive levels and controlled production, free production would remain at a plateau or decrease. We based our hypothesis both on previous empirical findings (Laufer, 1998; Laufer & Paribakht, 1998; Schmitt & Meara, 1997) and on DST, which considers limited systemic resources as a determining factor affecting interactions between system components. More stable systems, such as passive knowledge, exhibit more supportive componential interactions or a milder competition, than those found in less stable systems – such as active vocabulary knowledge. Less stable systems also show more fluctuation in interactions between their components of less stable systems. We also expected to see more variation in knowledge levels that increased, in accordance with the view that variation is inherent to, and in fact enables, growth in a dynamic system (Thelen & Smith, 1994; Van Geert & van Dijk, 2002).

The findings of this study were compatible with our hypotheses. Passive academic vocabulary knowledge of the participant increased or declined only slightly, while there was a decline in free production. Increasing levels of vocabulary knowledge showed greater fluctuation and variability. The interactions between levels of lexical knowledge, expressed in a moving window of correlation between data residuals, also showed a pattern of increased fluctuation and variability. These findings suggest that the L2 lexicon is a dynamic system, comprised of interacting, developing subsystems, and can have theoretical and pedagogical implications. Bearing in mind that the case study presented in this chapter was fairly short and that replication in other learners over longer durations is necessary, we would nevertheless like to suggest that the dynamic perspective can explain and supplement cross-sectional findings on the non-linear nature of lexical knowledge level development and interaction. It also highlights the discrepancy between learners' passive and productive lexical knowledge levels and the need to take the non-linear and stochastic nature of L2 vocabulary learning into account. Often the expectation is that learners' passive vocabulary knowledge, manifested prior to their academic studies in testing, would be immediately transferred into production. However, as the current study hopefully showed, when language in general and lexicon in particular are viewed and investigated from a dynamic perspective, the unpredictable, non-linear nature of their development can be anticipated and to a certain degree explained. Obviously, this is a short case study, which can only serve to illuminate certain characteristics of L2 lexicon. If we want to determine the compatibility of DST to the mental lexicon, this study should be expanded, while still focusing on individual learners and variation as complementary to group effects and general trends. We therefore would like to suggest the explanatory power of DST with regard to language development in general and L2 lexicon in particular and its potential contribution to research. We hope that this study will be followed by further investigations of the mental lexicon from a dynamic perspective, in learners of varied proficiency and language backgrounds, in varied durations and learning contexts, and with a focus on additional aspects of L2 lexical knowledge.

Notes

1. As generated by Lexical Frequency Profiles (Laufer & Nation, 1995) of the participants' written assignments, and the controlled and passive versions of the Levels Test (Laufer & Nation, 1995, 1999).
2. For example, a 0.7 ratio means that when 400 words are known passively, 2800 are known actively, resulting in a 1200 word difference. When the passive vocabulary reaches the level of 5000, the active becomes 3500, yielding a 1500 word difference, and when it reaches 6000, the active arrives at 4200, which is a 1800 difference (Laufer & Paribakht, 1998).

3. A large amount of vocabulary might need to be learned passively before transferring into free active level (Laufer & Paribakht, 1998).

Appendix I: Examples of LAVT Items

(1) Controlled production:
This debate is becoming too a_____ – let's have some hard facts!;
Truth and beauty are a_____ concepts.
(2) Active recall:
To act or work together for a particular purpose, or help someone willingly when help is requested c_____
(3) Active recognition
To communicate with or react to
(a) interfere; (b) interlock; (c) interact; (d) intervene

To take part in or become involved in an activity
(a) sustain; (b) capture; (c) participate; (d) emphasize

Part 2
Empirical Studies on Lexical Processing in English and Spanish

Chapter 5
The Effect of Lexicalization in the Native Language on Second Language Lexical Inferencing: A Cross-Linguistic Study

T. SIMA PARIBAKHT

Introduction

Research indicates that lexical inferencing, or how one makes an informed guess about the contextual meaning of an unfamiliar word, is the main strategy that learners use when they encounter unfamiliar words when reading (Fraser, 1999; Paribakht & Wesche, 1999). It can also be the first step in learning a new word. Thus, given its crucial role in both second language (L2) reading comprehension and lexical development, a precise understanding of the process of inferencing and factors that contribute to its success is important for both theory and instruction.

Previous studies have demonstrated that L2 readers use textual cues from all levels of language, interacting with their world knowledge in lexical inferencing (e.g. Ames, 1966; Bengeleil & Paribakht, 2004; Carton, 1971; Haastrup, 1991; Paribakht, 2005; Paribakht & Wesche, 1999). Research on the topic has also identified a number of learner, text and contextual factors that influence the success of L2 lexical inferencing. These include the importance of the word to text comprehension (Brown, 1993), the degree of textual information available in the surrounding text (Dubin & Olshtain, 1993), the learner ability to make effective use of extra-textual cues (de Bot *et al.*, 1997; Haastrup, 1991), the learners' preconceptions about the possible meaning of the word and their attention to the details in the text (Frantzen, 2003), reading proficiency (Bengeleil & Paribakht, 2004; Haastrup, 1991), vocabulary recognition knowledge (Coady *et al.*, 1993; Laufer, 1997), and depth of vocabulary knowledge (Nassaji, 2004).

Despite a large body of research on L2 lexical inferencing, little is known about the influence of the readers' native language on the inferencing process. It is not yet clear how the readers' first language (L1) knowledge may affect their use of various knowledge sources (KSs) in L2 lexical inferencing and their success in comprehending the target word meaning. Cross-lingual studies of L2 lexical processing have addressed the impact of differing orthographies (e.g. Chikamatsu, 1996; Ghahremani-Ghajar & Masny, 1999; Gholamain & Geva, 1999; Koda, 1989; Koda *et al.*, 1998). Other research has looked at the effect of cognate recognition (Ard & Holmburg, 1983; Hancin-Bhatt & Nagy, 1994; Tréville, 1996), as well as L1 syntactic effects on L2 lexical inferencing (e.g. Nagy *et al.*, 1997).

An earlier related study by Paribakht (2005) examined the effect of the learners' L1 (i.e. Farsi/Persian) lexicalization patterns (i.e. whether or not there are lexical equivalents – single or compound lexical items, including lexical phrases – in the learner's L1 for the L2 target words) on their L2 (English) lexical inferencing behavior while reading. Her study showed that lexicalization patterns in L1 did not affect the types and relative frequencies of KS use in the participants' L2 lexical inferencing, but it had a clear effect on their success rate in inferring accurate meanings for the unfamiliar L2 target words. The participants were by far more successful in guessing the meanings of lexicalized (L) than non-lexicalized (NL) target words. She concluded that NL words may constitute a notable challenge in L2 readers' successful comprehension and interpretation of L2 texts, and may, partially account for certain L1-related problems that L2 readers from different linguistic backgrounds encounter in decoding L2 text meanings and subsequent vocabulary development. Do such results hold across L2 learners from other linguistic backgrounds? Do lexicalization patterns of L1 have a similar effect on learners of English from other linguistic backgrounds? An examination of this issue may help to better understand the nature and extent of L1 influence on L2 lexical inferencing, and may also bring to light L1 specific features that may have an impact on the readers' L2 text comprehension and vocabulary learning. The results may also offer implications for L2 reading and vocabulary instruction.

Research Questions

The following research questions directed the study[1]:

(1) Are there similarities and differences in the kinds, patterns and frequencies of contextual cues and other KSs that Persian and French-speaking readers of English draw upon in inferring the meanings of L2 words which are lexicalized versus those which are not lexicalized in their L1s?
(2) How do the two linguistic groups compare with respect to their success in inferring the meanings of unfamiliar target words which are/are not lexicalized in their L1s when reading English texts?

Methodology

Participants

Two groups of 20 students at an intermediate level of English reading proficiency from colleges and universities in Iran and Canada were selected for the study, based on a Reading Comprehension Test developed at the University of Ottawa[2].

Instruments

Target words and texts

The target words for the study consisted of two sets of 50 English words each, 25 of which are lexicalized and 25 not lexicalized[3] in the respective language (see Appendix A for the lists of target words). Fifteen of these words were the same in the two sets (nine are lexicalized both in Persian and French and six which are neither lexicalized in Persian nor in French). The common words are indicated with an '*' in the French target word list in Appendix A.

To select the NL words, native speakers of each language group, bilingual in English, prepared lists of words which to their knowledge had no equivalents in their respective languages. The final lists were prepared after consulting several dictionaries and other native speakers. The lists consisted of words which represented concepts generally familiar to educated speakers of the two language groups but for which no single or compound lexical equivalents exist in their respective languages (e.g. *to elope, to indulge, proactive, prognosis* and *to stalk* for Persian speakers; and *to backfire, to crave, gaze, spree* and *sleet* for French speakers). In the selection process a representation of four word classes was sought (10 nouns, 8 verbs, 4 adjectives and 3 adverbs in each set).

The list of lexicalized target words consisted of words that in a previous research had been shown to be relatively difficult for high intermediate university ESL learners (Paribakht & Wesche, 1997). The L word list included 25 words representing the same four word classes (10 nouns, 8 verbs, 4 adjectives and 3 adverbs).

The selected target words were grouped thematically in mixed (L/NL) sets and were used to compose six general interest paragraphs, using seven to nine words per text for each group. The themes of the texts used for Persian speakers were *'Marriage'*, *'Preserving the Environment'*, *'The Ice Age'*, *'The World's Forgotten Poor'*, *'Big City Dreams'* and *'Genetic Engineering'*, and for French speakers they were: *'Human Clones'*, *'Human Rights'*, *'Global Warming'*, *'An Author's Life'*, *'Knowing the Future'* and *'Weddings and Marriage'*. The paragraphs were formatted for use in data collection with the target words bolded, in large print, one paragraph to a page (see Appendix B for a sample text).

Procedures

Introspective methods of data collection were used, involving individual research sessions for each participant with a researcher. Several days before the individual research sessions, the participants met in groups and were trained in think-aloud procedures.

In the individual research sessions, the English texts were presented to the participants, one at a time and in the same order. The participants were asked to first read the text quickly for general comprehension and then to read it again and try to guess the meanings of the unfamiliar target words indicated in bold font. They were also instructed to verbalize what they were thinking and doing while carrying out the task, using their L1, English or both languages, according to their preference. The same bilingual research assistant conducted all the interviews for each group and prompted the participants as needed.

Results

Research question 1: Are there similarities and differences in the kinds, patterns and frequencies of contextual cues and other KSs that Persian and French-speaking readers of English draw upon in inferring the meanings of L2 words which are lexicalized versus those which are not lexicalized in their L1s?

Qualitative analysis

Paribakht's (2005) taxonomy was used as a basis for identifying the contextual cues and KSs used by the French-speaking participants in inferring the L2 target word meanings. The analysis showed that the two groups basically used the same types of KSs in inferring the meanings of the target words. The exceptions are that *L1 Word Collocation* was used only by the Persian speakers in inferring the meanings of both L and NL target words, and *Word Collocation* was not used at all by the French speakers in inferring the NL words. The analyses have also brought forth an additional KS, *L1 Word Form* that was used only by the French participants in inferring both L and NL words. See Figure 5.1 for the modified taxonomy including all the KSs identified in the Persian and French speakers' data, together with the definition of each KS. This is followed by examples for each KS from transcripts of participant think-aloud protocols.

*Examples of use of different KSs taken from the participants'
interview transcripts[4]*

Word Association
P: [**bleak**], ça serait (terne) parce que je vois le mot *depressing*.
   ([**bleak**], It would be (dull) because I see the word *depressing*.)

The Effect of Lexicalization in the Native Language 65

> **I. Linguistic Sources**
>   **A. L2-Based Sources**
>   **1. Word Level**
>   **a. Word Association**
>   Association of the target word with another familiar word or a network of words
>   **b. Word Collocation**
>   Knowledge of words that frequently occur with the target word
>   **c. Word Morphology**
>   Morphological analysis of the target word based on knowledge of grammatical inflections, stem and affixes
>   **d. Word Form**
>   Knowledge of form (orthographic or phonetic) similarity between the target word, or a part of it, and another word, and mistaking the target word for another word resembling it.
>   **2. Sentence Level**
>   **a. Sentence Meaning**
>   The meaning of part or all of the sentence containing the target word
>   **b. Sentence Grammar**
>   Knowledge of the syntactic properties of the target word, its speech part and word order constraints
>   **c. Punctuation**
>   Knowledge of rules of punctuation and their significance
>   **3. Discourse Level**
>   **a. Discourse Meaning**
>   The perceived general meaning of the text and sentences surrounding the target word (i.e. beyond the immediate sentence that contains the target word)
>   **b. Formal Schemata**
>   Knowledge of the macro structure of the text, text types and discourse patterns and organization
>   **B. L1-Based Sources**
>   **L1 Word Collocation**
>   Knowledge of words in L1 that have collocational relationship with the L1 equivalent of the target word, assuming that the same relationship exists in the target language
>   **L1 Word Form**
>   Knowledge of form (orthographic or phonetic) similarity between the target word or a part of it and a L1 word
> **II. Non-linguistic Sources**
>   **World Knowledge**
>   Non-linguistic knowledge, including knowledge of the topic of the text and other related background knowledge

Figure 5.1 Taxonomy of knowledge sources used in L2 lexical inferencing by Persian and French speakers

Word Collocation
P: [**musters**], c'est un membre du couple *musters the courage*, ça va avec "courage"; ça doit être une expression.
([**musters**], It's a member of the pair 'musters the courage'. It goes with "courage"; it must be an expression.)

Word Morphology
P: [**genocide**], I think means... if we parsed it, it'd mean 'to kill someone'... *geno* means 'gene' and its derivative *generation* means generation, and *çide* means 'to kill'. So, [**genocide**] should mean (to kill a generation).

Word Form
P: [**keenly**], ça ressemble à [kindly], oui, ça pourrait faire du sens ... ça va dans les environs de (kindly).
([**keenly**], It looks like "kindly". Yes, that could make sense ... it's close to (kindly).)

Sentence Meaning
P: [**trickle**] means (to drip, to come down).
I: How did you guess? What helped you?
P: *Down the mountain,* and *water tricles down the mountain* must mean (it's dripping, falling down).

Sentence Grammar
P: [**devastated**] should be describing *landscape* which means 'land or view' ... It must be an adjective describing *landscape*.

Punctuation
P: [**lounges**] ... because a comma separates this word from the other words coming after it, we can say it's a noun, intending the names of things ... intending to separate the things that they have in mind.

Discourse Meaning
P: Given the whole meaning of the text, I think [**snoop**] means (to control).
I: How did the overall meaning of the text help?
P: It cautions that if medical facilities aren't carefully controlled ... It gives the example that if criminals aren't controlled in the sphere of medical profession...Given the first sentence and this example, I think it means controlling crimes. Given that the whole paragraph is about the science of genetics and the control of crimes by doctors ... Doctors can have a role in controlling crimes only when they've made progress in genes. That's to say, controlling people's genes can control crimes.

Formal Schemata
P: *likewise brutal* **retaliation** ... the sentence before it *such a terrible outcome* ... I think *brutal* is a member of it as well. That is, a general thing that this is a subset of it. It wants to give us an example.

L1 Word Form
P: [**untimely**], ça ressemble au mot français 'intimement'.
([**untimely**], It looks like the French word 'intimement').

L1 Word Collocation
P: I think [**intrusion**] here means (to interfere) because it's talking about people and here *into their lives* means direct movement into their lives which I think considering our Persian words can be interpreted as (to interfere in one's life).

The Effect of Lexicalization in the Native Language 67

World Knowledge

P: [**retaliation**], j'ai déjà vu le mot ailleurs parce que je joue à des jeux vidéo puis j'ai un vidéo qui porte ce nom-là.
([**retaliation**], I've seen the word elsewhere, because I play video games and I have a video which has this name.)

Quantitative analyses

In the quantitative analysis of the data, the frequency of use of each KS, patterns and sequences of KSs used in inferencing, and the level of success in identifying an appropriate target word meaning were calculated for the two language groups and word sets.

KSs used in L2 lexical inferencing

In calculating the frequency of use of different KSs by the participants, the number of times each KS was used in inferring L and NL target words was calculated. These were then converted into percentages for different word categories and language groups. See Appendix C (Tables 5.1 and 5.2) for the frequency of use of each KS for each word set and each language group. Figures 5.2 and 5.3 show the frequencies of use of the main categories of KSs and their graphic presentation, by the two groups for L and NL target words.

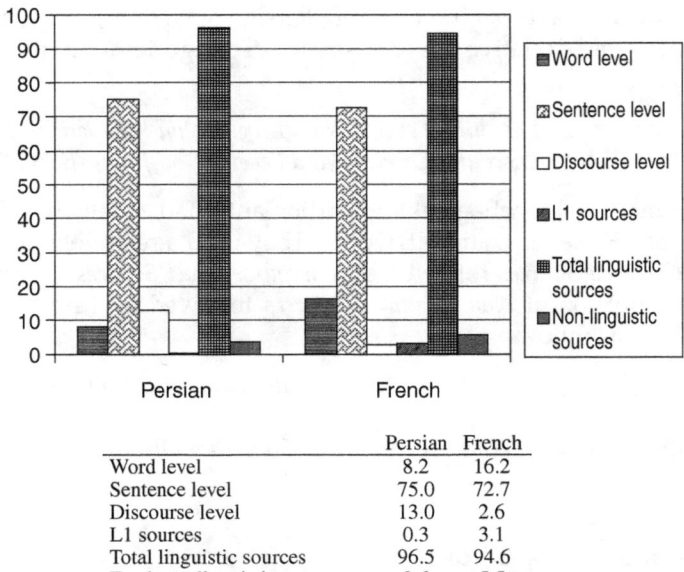

	Persian	French
Word level	8.2	16.2
Sentence level	75.0	72.7
Discourse level	13.0	2.6
L1 sources	0.3	3.1
Total linguistic sources	96.5	94.6
Total non-linguistic sources	3.6	5.5

Figure 5.2 Main knowledge sources used – L words

68   Part 2: Empirical Studies on Lexical Processing in English and Spanish

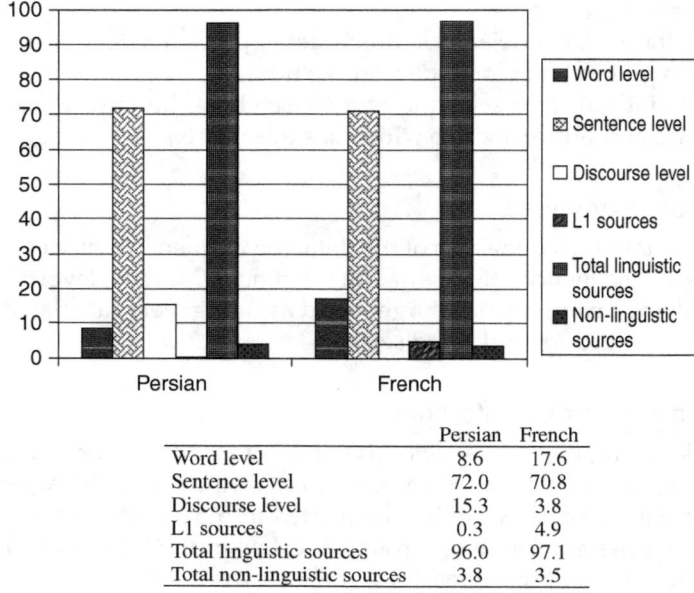

	Persian	French
Word level	8.6	17.6
Sentence level	72.0	70.8
Discourse level	15.3	3.8
L1 sources	0.3	4.9
Total linguistic sources	96.0	97.1
Total non-linguistic sources	3.8	3.5

Figure 5.3 Main knowledge sources used – NL words

Within-group comparisons

As Figures 5.2 and 5.3 indicate, the Persian-speaking participants had similar patterns of relative use of the main KS categories for both L and NL words:

L   *Sentence Level > Discourse Level > Word Level > Non-linguistic > L1 Sources*
NL *Sentence Level > Discourse Level > Word Level > Non-linguistic > L1 Sources*

However, the French-speaking participants had somewhat different patterns of KS use for L and NL words. They used a relatively higher percent of *L1-based Sources* followed by *Discourse Level Sources* for NL, but a higher proportion of *Non-linguistic Sources* followed by *L1-based Sources* for L words, as follows:

L   *Sentence Level > Word Level > Non-linguistic > L1 Sources > Discourse Level*
NL *Sentence Level > Word Level > L1 Sources > Discourse Level > Non-linguistic*

Across-group comparisons

Sentence level cues were the main source for both Persian and French speakers and they were used almost with the same frequency by both

The Effect of Lexicalization in the Native Language 69

groups in inferring the two sets of target words. However, word level cues were used almost twice as often by French speakers than by Persian speakers in inferring both L, and NL words, but discourse level cues were used by far more often by Persian speakers than French speakers in inferring both target word sets.

It is also noteworthy that French speakers used by far a higher percent of L1-based KSs than Persian speakers. The use of *Non-linguistic* source was similar across the two language groups for the NL words (3.5 vs. 3.8), but higher for French speakers in inferring L words (5.5 vs. 3.6).

The patterns of use of the main categories of KSs by the two language groups for L and NL words are thus as follows:

L Words
Persian group: *Sentence Level > Discourse Level > Word Level > Non-linguistic > L1 Sources*
French group: *Sentence Level > Word Level > Non-linguistic > L1 Sources > Discourse Level*

NL Words
Persian group: *Sentence Level > Discourse Level > Word Level > Non-linguistic > L1 Sources*
French group: *Sentence Level > Word Level > L1 Sources > Discourse Level > Non-linguistic*

The patterns for the total words (L and NL), as shown in Figure 5.4, are:

Persian group: *Sentence Level > Discourse Level > Word Level > Non-linguistic > L1 Sources*
French group: *Sentence Level > Word Level > Non-linguistic > L1 Sources > Discourse Level*

Use of individual KSs

A detailed analysis of frequencies of use of specific KSs within each language level for each group and word set revealed the following patterns:

Persian group

Word sets	Word level	Sentence level	Discourse level
L	WM > WF > WC > WA	SM > SG > P	DM > FS
NL	WM > WF > WC = WA	SM > SG > P	DM > FS
Total	WM > WF > WC > WA	SM > SG > P	DM > FS

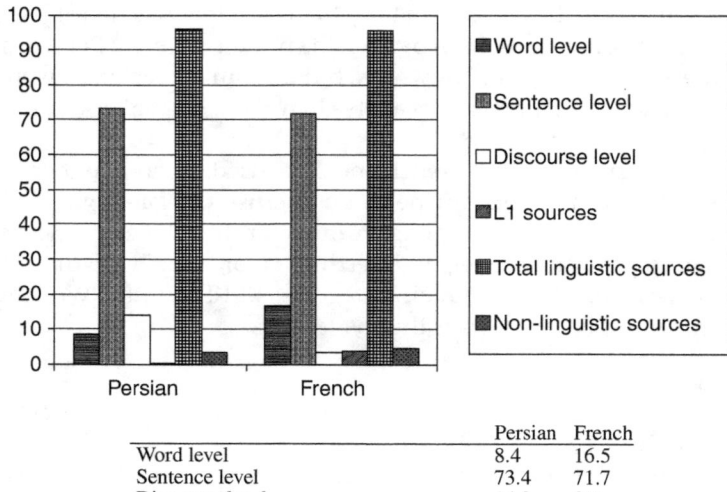

	Persian	French
Word level	8.4	16.5
Sentence level	73.4	71.7
Discourse level	14.2	3.7
L1 sources	0.3	4.0
Total linguistic sources	96.2	95.5
Total non-linguistic sources	3.7	4.5

Figure 5.4 Frequency of use of the main knowledge sources in inferring total L2 target words (L and NL) by the two groups

French group

Word sets	Word level	Sentence level	Discourse level
L	WM > WF > WA > WC	SM > SG > P	DM > FS
NL	WM > WF > WA	SM > SG > P	DM > FS
Total	WM > WF > WA > WC	SM > SG > P	DM > FS

Key for abbreviations:

Word level	Sentence level	Discourse level	Non-linguistic
WA = word association	SM = sentence meaning	DM = discourse meaning	WK = world knowledge
WC = word collocation	SG = sentence grammar	FS = formal schemata	
WM = word morphology WF = word form L1WF = L1 word form	P = punctuation	S = text style/register	

Within-group comparisons indicate that both groups have almost identical rankings of KS use for L and NL words, except that French speakers did not use *Word Collocation* at all for NL words. Across group comparisons also indicate that the two groups had similar relative frequency patterns of individual KSs use within *Sentence Level* and *Discourse Level*, but a slightly different frequency distribution within the *Word Level* cues. While both groups used *Word Morphology*, followed by *Word Form* most frequently, Persian speakers relied more on *Word Collocation* as a third source, whereas French speakers drew more upon *Word Association* for both L and NL words and did not use *Word Collocation* at all for NL words.

Since Persian- and French-speaking participants exhibited some apparent differences in their use of word level KSs, a more detailed analysis was carried out at this level and the results (out of 100%) are presented in Figures 5.5–5.7.

Overall, across levels of language, the relative frequency of specific KS types used with L and NL and total words for the two groups are as follows:

	Persian-speaking group	*French-speaking group*
L:	SM > SG > DM > WM > WK	SM > SG > WM > WF > WK
NL:	SM > DM > SG > WM > WK	SM > WM > SG > L1WF > WF
Total:	SM > DM > SG > WM > WK	SM > SG > WM > WF > WK

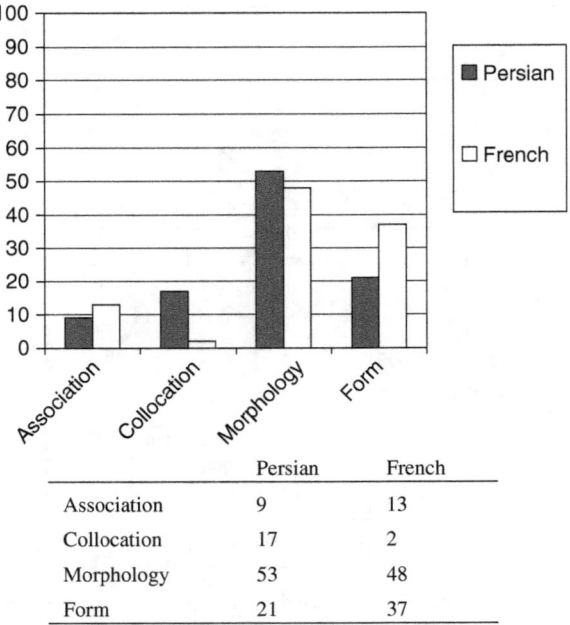

	Persian	French
Association	9	13
Collocation	17	2
Morphology	53	48
Form	21	37

Figure 5.5 Frequency of use of word-level knowledge sources – L target words

72   Part 2: Empirical Studies on Lexical Processing in English and Spanish

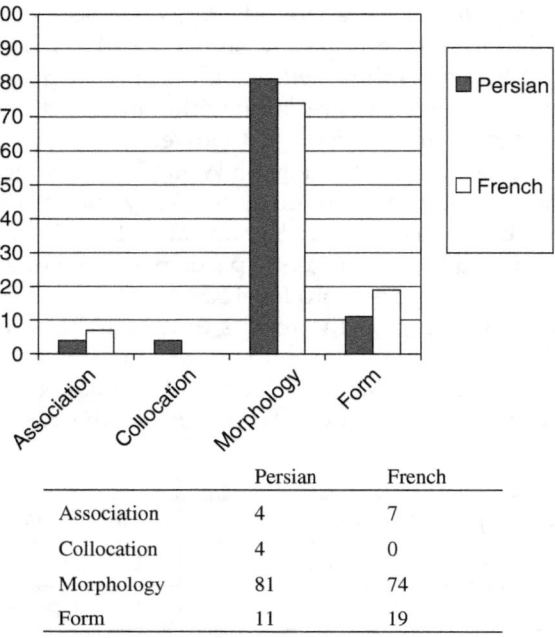

Figure 5.6 Frequency of use of word-level knowledge sources – NL target words

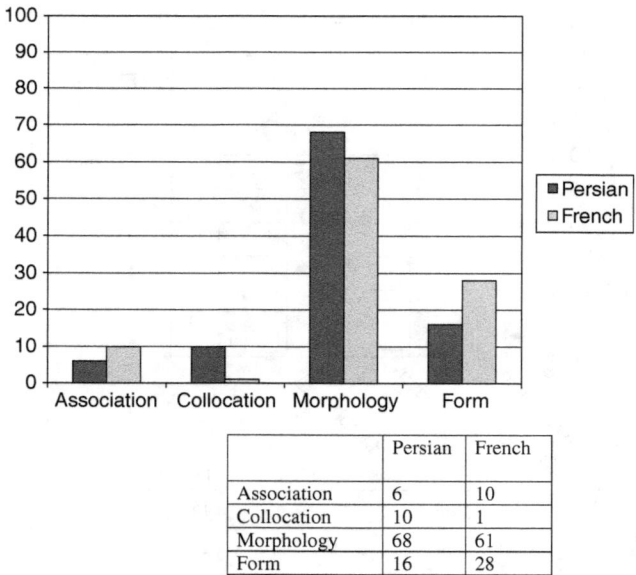

Figure 5.7 Frequency of use of word-level knowledge sources by the two groups for total words

These analyses indicate that *Sentence Meaning* was by far the most important single KS used by both groups in inferring the meanings of both L and NL target words.

The comparisons indicate that while Persian speakers relied on similar proportions of the main individual KSs in inferring the two word sets, with the exception of *Sentence Grammar*, which was used more often for L words, French speakers used similar frequencies of KSs for L and total words but have a somewhat different frequency pattern of KS use for the NL words. Whereas they used *Sentence Grammar* more often for L words, they relied on *Word Morphology* more frequently for NL words. It is also shown that for both groups, *Sentence Grammar* is the second most important KS in inferring the L words, but for NL words Persian speakers rely more often on *Discourse Meaning*, whereas French speakers draw more on *Word Morphology* for inferring the meanings of NL words. It is also noteworthy that while for French speakers *Word Form* and *L1 Word Form* were important KSs in inferring both L and NL words, Persian speakers only rarely used *Word Form* and never used *L1 Word Form* in their inferencing.

Success in L2 lexical inferencing

Research question 2: How do the two linguistic groups compare with respect to their success in inferring the meanings of unfamiliar target words which are/are not lexicalized in their L1s when reading English texts?

The participants' inferred meanings for the unfamiliar target words were evaluated as 'successful' if an appropriate inferred meaning or a synonym was provided, 'partially successful' if an approximate meaning was given, or a 'failure' if an inaccurate meaning or no meaning was inferred[5]. Figures 5.8 and 5.9 present the relative degrees of success for the two participant groups in inferring unfamiliar L and NL target words. The analyses show a strong effect for lexicalization. They indicate that both groups were more successful in inferring the meanings of L than NL words. Persian speakers were three times more fully successful in inferring the L than the NL words (17% vs. 6%), and the French speakers also had a higher level of full success for the L words (34% vs. 28%). Across-group comparisons show that French speakers were by far more successful in inferring both L and NL target words, especially NL words, than the Persian-speaking participants.

Discussion and Conclusions

KS use

This study compared how Persian and French-speaking readers of English inferred the meanings of unfamiliar English words, which are lexicalized in their L1s versus those which are not.

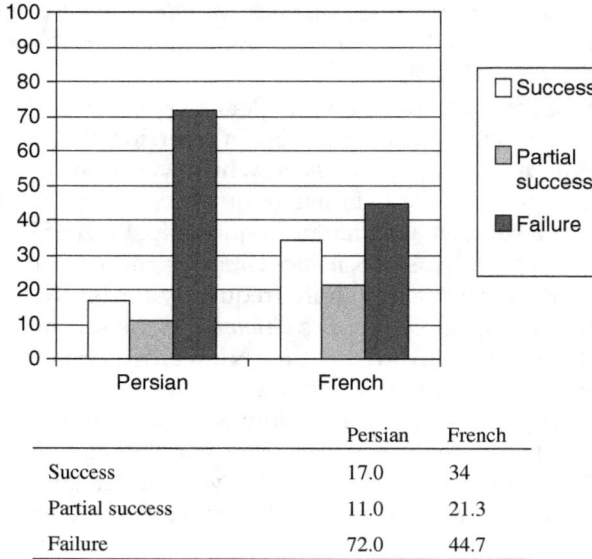

	Persian	French
Success	17.0	34
Partial success	11.0	21.3
Failure	72.0	44.7

Figure 5.8 Degree of success in inferencing by the two groups – L words

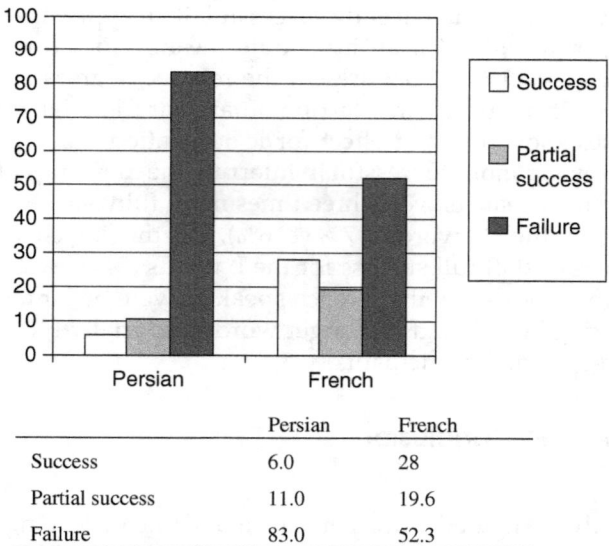

	Persian	French
Success	6.0	28
Partial success	11.0	19.6
Failure	83.0	52.3

Figure 5.9 Degree of success in inferencing by the two groups – NL words

The results indicated that the two linguistic groups drew upon the same types of KSs from different levels of the language system (i.e. word, sentence and discourse), as well as non-linguistic (world) knowledge in inferring the meanings of the unfamiliar target words, indicating that when dealing with lexical gaps in reading, learners appear to draw upon similar KSs to construct the words' meanings.

The specific KS types drew upon in the process were also basically the same, indicating that lexicalization did not affect the types of KSs these two linguistic groups relied on in L2 lexical inferencing. These results further support Paribakht's (1985, 2005) position regarding the existence of a common underlying strategic competence among speakers and readers in solving lexical problems.

The exceptions are as follows:

- *L1 Word Collocation* was used only by the Persian speakers, but only minimally (0.3% for both L and NL words), indicating that this is not a major contributing KS when inferring L2 word meanings.
- *Word Collocation* was used more often by Persian speakers than French speakers in inferring the L words and it was not used at all by French speakers in inferring the NL words. This difference is probably indicative of French speakers' limited exposure to the use of these words in their English readings and their limited familiarity with the contexts of use of these NL words in written English. Persian-speaking EFL learners appear to largely depend, however, on reading for the development of their English language knowledge, which may in turn have contributed to the development of their collocational knowledge of the target English words, especially the lexicalized ones.
- *L1 Word Form* was used only by the French participants in inferring both L and NL words.

This is not surprising considering that English and French share the same orthography, which may encourage French-speaking ESL learners to occasionally draw on the shared form features of L1 and L2 lexicon in their lexical inferencing. That is, sharing the same writing system may serve as a cue source for readers in L2 lexical inferencing.

The quantitative analysis of the data indicated that while Persian speakers had similar frequency patterns of KS use for both L and NL words (*Sentence Level > Discourse Level > Word Level > Non-linguistic > L1 Source*), French speakers' patterns of KS use were somewhat different for the two word sets. They used a higher percent of *Non-linguistic* sources (*World Knowledge*) for L than NL words, indicating that they had more relevant world knowledge concerning the L words.

Furthermore, French speakers' greater reliance on discourse level cues in inferring NL words than L words may indicate that these participants needed a larger meaning context for guessing the meanings of NL words. They also relied more often on their L1 for NL words than L words, possibly indicating that readers may draw more often on their L1 sources when dealing with more difficult tasks. In sum, within-group comparisons indicate only a minor lexicalization effect on the French speakers' frequency of use of KSs in L2 lexical inferencing.

Across-group comparisons revealed that both groups relied primarily on sentence level cues, mainly *Sentence Meaning*, indicating that the target word's immediate context is the primary source for them in inferring both L and NL word meanings. It is striking, however, that while French speakers relied twice as often on word-level cues (primarily *Word Morphology*) for both L and NL words, Persian speakers drew by far more on discourse level cues (mainly *Discourse Meaning*) in inferring the meanings of the two word sets. These patterns may at least be partially explained by the differences in Persian and French orthography. Persian orthography does not represent all the vowels of the language, limiting the reliability of word level cues as a source of information for inferring word meanings while reading in Persian. Readers are instead accustomed to relying on the context (sentence and discourse) to identify the exact word they are reading and to pronounce it correctly when reading aloud. This L1 processing strategy appears to be carried over to L2 lexical processing in that even though more word level cues are available in English, Persian speakers appear to still rely more often on sentence and discourse level meaning in L2 lexical inferencing.

Furthermore, French speakers appeared to be more inclined to draw on L1-based KSs than Persian speakers in L2 lexical inferencing (for both L and NL). This is probably related to these readers' perception of the proximity of their L1s and English in that although Persian and French are both Indo-European languages, French is typologically closer to English than Persian (see Kellerman, 1977, 1978 for a discussion).

The fact that French speakers relied more on their world knowledge in inferring NL words than Persian speakers, may indicate that the former group has more relevant cultural and topical knowledge of texts originated in English. This is hardly surprising given the many shared social, historical and cultural elements in the two linguistic communities, particularly in the bilingual context of Canada, especially the Ottawa region.

The results also showed that *Sentence Grammar* was an important KS for both groups, indicating a possible training effect. Grammar instruction receives considerable instructional attention both in French and Iranian school systems. It may also be related to L1 processing effects as sentence grammar cues are abundant and important in both languages.

It is also apparent that French speakers relied more frequently on their knowledge of *Word Associations* than Persian speakers in L2 lexical inferencing. This is again understandable in light of our francophone participants' more exposure to the actual English language use in the bilingual context of Ottawa region, and their greater access to English culture and media in this ESL context, which may lead to greater development of associations with the target words. As noted earlier, Persian-speakers' more reliance on *Word Collocation* than *Word Association* may be related to their main source of English input being written texts. These participants may have gained some collocational knowledge about these words, but their lack of exposure to the English culture and context of the use of the language may have limited the possibility of forming associations with the target words in their EFL context.

In short, the findings of this study regarding types, frequencies and patterns of KS use by the two language groups reflect minimal lexicalization effects within each group but clear L1 influence on L2 lexical inferencing in cross-linguistic comparisons. The two language groups appear to share many patterns but also differ in significant ways in their KS use in L2 lexical inferencing.

Success

The success rates in inferring appropriate meanings for L and NL target words by the two participant groups show a strong effect for lexicalization. Both groups were more successful in inferring appropriate meanings for L words than NL words, indicating that the latter present a greater challenge to L2 readers. This extends the findings reported by Paribakht (2005) where she concluded that patterns of lexicalization in L1 may constitute a significant challenge to L2 readers in their lexical inferencing and subsequent reading comprehension and interpretation.

Across-group comparisons also showed that French speakers were by far more successful than Persian speakers in inferring the meanings of both L and NL target words. Several important factors may have contributed to the greater success rate of the French speakers. French and English share the same orthography and many cognates[6], which put the French speakers in an advantageous position to use that knowledge base in reading English texts and inferring the meanings of unfamiliar words. Furthermore, the proximity of the two cultures, as well as the ESL context of learning for the French-speaking participants, may have also played important roles. Collective contribution of all of these factors, among possibly other ones, presumably contributed to better text comprehension, which in turn facilitated French speakers' inferencing efforts, leading to more accurate guessing of the meanings of unfamiliar target words when reading English texts.

The findings of this comparative study provide further insights into factors that may influence the complex process of L2 lexical inferencing. They provide solid grounds to conclude that lexical inferencing in L2 reading is mediated by certain features of L1, including its lexicalization patterns, as well as factors such as the context of target language acquisition and use. They also shed light on L1-related challenges that learners from various linguistic backgrounds may encounter in L2 reading.

Notes

1. An earlier version of this paper was published in French, in collaboration with Marie-Cloude Tréville, in the *Canadian Modern Language Review*, March 2007, 63 (3), 399–428.
2. The *Reading Proficiency Test* has three subtests. Subtests 1 and 2 comprise two readings on 'Test Anxiety' and 'Sinister Statistics', and have six and nine comprehension questions, respectively. The third subtest is a multiple-choice cloze on 'Culture Shock' and has 30 items. The participants had 60 min to complete the test. Each comprehension question was worth 2 points and cloze items 1 point each, for a total possible score of 60. The participants who scored between 27 and 39 were selected for the study.
3. In recent years, equivalents for a few of these words have been coined in the media. However, these are not commonly known and used by most educated speakers of the respective languages.
4. Transcription conventions:
   'P' stands for participant and 'I' for interviewer.
   Normal font = translation of utterances from Persian or French to English
   Bold face = target words
   Italics = words/phrases read from the target text
   [ ] = words spoken in English
   ( ) = the inferred meaning(s)
   .... = pause
5. The scoring system for success was as follows: 2 points were awarded if the response was both semantically and syntactically appropriate, 1 point if an approximate meaning was inferred or if the inferred word was semantically accurate but not syntactically appropriate (e.g. a noun instead of a verb or adjective was given), and no point (i.e. zero) was given if the participant provided a wrong meaning or gave up.
6. The target words had been screened for cognates in this study, but cognates still existed in the texts surrounding the target words, which could have facilitated French speakers' reading comprehension.

Appendix A
Lists of target words

Target words for the Persian group		Target words for the French group	
English target words not lexicalized in Persian	English target words lexicalized in Persian	English target words not lexicalized in French	English target words lexicalized in French
1. glacier	1. to trickle	1. to clone*	1. keenly
2. breakthrough	2. intrusion	2. to implement	2. to thrive
3. presumptuous	3. deteriorating	3. mainstream	3. pawn
4. metropolitan	4. to tackle*	4. to backfire*	4. to withstand
5. lounge	5. to flee*	5. plight	5. retaliation*
6. catering business	6. devastated	6. clout	6. testimony*
7. genocide	7. desertification	7. grimly	7. to flee*
8. to snoop	8. to slam	8. overwhelmingly*	8. stowaway
9. sophisticated	9. testimony*	9. to glimpse	9. tattered
10. to tow	10. decay*	10. smouldering	10. strife
11. prognosis	11. layer*	11. to spark	11. layer*
12. overwhelmingly*	12. lethal	12. to draft*	12. decay*
13. intuitively	13. bleak*	13. slouches	13. to spawn
14. chronologically	14. ambivalence	14. bungling	14. to spray*
15. to trigger	15. to wipe out	15. afterthoughts	15. bleak*
16. to elope*	16. to blend	16. cut off	16. to tackle*
17. to stalk someone	17. to draft*	17. understatement*	17. dolefully
18. proactive	18. to spray*	18. to crave	18. warily
19. monogamy	19. masterpiece	19. gaze	19. omens
20. sleet*	20. retaliation*	20. poised	20. untimely
21. to indulge	21. innuendo*	21. blandness	21. craze
22. to clone*	22. inadvertently	22. arguably	22. to muster
23. to backfire*	23. retroactively	23. spree	23. giddy
24. understatement*	24. frivolously	24. sleet*	24. innuendo*
25. courtship	25. annoyance	25. to elope*	25. to strum

N.B. Common words in the two lists are indicated by an asterisk.

Appendix B

Sample text (used with the French group)

AN AUTHOR'S LIFE

The life of a successful author is one to which many people aspire. After all, wouldn't writing best-selling novels and winning prizes be a great way to make a living? An author's life may not be as ideal as it appears, however. Many writers spend years simply observing the world around them before a person or an event *sparks* their imagination, inspiring them to put pen to paper. Even then, the time it takes to *draft* a masterpiece may seem endless, causing some to give up before they have written more than a few pages. Others, not wanting to be considered *slouches*, may toil on, and, when inspiration leaves them, spend hours staring **dolefully** at a blank sheet of paper. In the end, a few of those who set out to write award-winning books will submit their work to publishers for evaluation. Editors will **warily** survey these latest offerings from new writers, knowing that much time and effort has been expended by each one, but also well aware that for every rejection sent out, another aspiring author will be only too willing to submit new work. Those who receive rejections will curse the *bungling* publisher who failed to recognize their talent. Some will continue trying, writing more and remaining hopeful; others will give up, their unpublished novels becoming mere *afterthoughts* when they later tell the stories of their lives. Ah, but those who do make the *cutoff*! For them, victory is sweet. Their talent has been recognized, and, after much rewriting, they will see their work in print. Who knows? A few of them may even win a prize!

N.B. The target words are in bold and the NL words are also italicized.

Appendix C

Table 5.1 Frequency of use of KS in inferring L, NL and total target word meanings by Persian speakers

Knowledge sources	L (25)		NL (25)		Total (50)	
	N	%	n	%	N	%
I. Linguistic sources						
A. L2-based sources						
1. Word level						
a. Word association	4	0.7	2	0.3	6	0.5
b. Word collocation	8	1.4	2	0.3	10	0.8
c. Word morphology	25	4.4	42	7	67	5.7
d. Word form	10	1.7	6	1	16	1.4
Total word level	47	8.2	52	8.6	99	8.4
2. Sentence level						
a. Sentence meaning	345	60.1	350	58.2	695	59
b. Sentence grammar	83	14.5	75	12.5	158	13.5
c. Punctuation	2	0.4	8	1.3	10	0.9
Total sentence level	430	75	433	72	863	73.4
3. Discourse level						
a. Discourse meaning	73	12.8	90	15	163	13.9
b. Formal schemata	1	0.2	2	0.3	3	0.3
Total discourse level	74	13	92	15.3	166	14.2
Total L2 sources	551	96.2	577	95.9	1128	96
B. L1-based source						
L1 Word collocation	2	0.3	2	0.3	4	0.3
Total L1 source	2	0.3	2	0.3	4	0.3
Total linguistic sources	553	96.5	579	96.2	1132	96.3
II. Non-linguistic sources						
World knowledge	21	3.6	23	3.8	44	3.7
Total non-linguistic sources	21	3.6	23	3.8	44	3.7
Total linguistic and non-linguistic sources	574	100	602	100	1176	100

Table 5.2 Frequency of use of KS in inferring L, NL and total target word meanings by French speakers

Knowledge sources	L (25)		NL (25)		Total (50)	
	n	%	n	%	N	%
I. Linguistic sources						
A. L2-based sources						
1. Word level						
a. Word association	15	2.1	9	1.3	24	1.7
b. Word collocation	2	0.3	0	0	2	0.1
c. Word morphology	56	7.8	87	12.5	143	10.1
d. Word form	43	6.0	22	3.8	65	4.6
Total word level	116	16.2	118	17.6	234	16.5
2. Sentence level						
a. Sentence meaning	420	58.7	403	58.0	823	58.3
b. Sentence grammar	98	13.7	84	12.1	182	12.9
c. Punctuation	2	0.3	5	0.7	7	0.5
Total sentence level	520	72.7	492	70.8	1012	71.7
3. Discourse level						
a. Discourse meaning	16	2.2	26	3.7	42	3.0
b. Formal schemata	3	0.4	1	0.1	4	0.3
Total discourse level	19	2.6	27	3.8	46	3.3
Total L2 sources	655	91.5	637	92.2	1292	91.5
B. L1-based sources						
1. L1 Word collocation	0	0	0	0	0	0
2. L1 Word form	22	3.1	34	4.9	56	4.0
Total L1 sources	22	3.1	34	4.9	56	4.0
Total linguistic sources	677	94.6	671	97.1	1348	95.5
II. Non-linguistic sources						
World knowledge	39	5.5	24	3.5	63	4.5
Total non-linguistic sources	39	5.5	24	3.5	63	4.5
Total linguistic and non-linguistic sources	716	100	695	100.6	1411	100

Chapter 6
Aural Word Recognition and Oral Competence in English as a Foreign Language

JAMES MILTON, JO WADE and NICOLA HOPKINS

Introduction

Vocabulary is recognized as a key area of language knowledge. As Wilkins succinctly notes (1972: 111), 'without grammar very little can be conveyed, [but] without vocabulary *nothing* can be conveyed'. In order to become proficient in a foreign language, therefore, a learner has to learn thousands of words and it has been argued that other aspects of language ability, such as knowledge of grammar in a foreign language, are dependent on the development of the foreign language lexicon (Ellis, 1997). Perhaps it is not surprising that, as a result, there is a general relationship between the number of words a learner knows and how proficient a learner is: the more vocabulary a learner knows the better he or she tends to be. As a consequence, a vocabulary size measure, or a measure of vocabulary breadth, can be used as a general indicator of language level and ability, as in Nation's (1990) *Vocabulary Levels Test*, Meara and Jones's (1990) *Eurocentres Vocabulary Size Test* (*EVST*) and Meara and Milton's (2003) *X_Lex*.

There are two things to be noted in these tests. One is that they assess vocabulary knowledge almost exclusively in terms of the orthographic form of the word. The *Vocabulary Levels Test*, *EVST* and *X_Lex* all use a presentation of the written form of a word only and, in the case of the *Levels Test*, written explanations. The second is that the measures they produce correlate well with reading, writing and grammatical knowledge in a foreign language but seem to be less useful in predicting the kind of oral fluency required for effective speech (Meara & Buxton, 1987).

One explanation of this derives from what we know about coverage in written and spoken corpora. Substantially more vocabulary is needed to achieve the kind of coverage associated with good comprehension in written text than in spoken text (Adolphs & Schmitt, 2003) and spoken communication has access to gesture and contextual information which written text usually lacks. It appears possible to be far more fluent with fewer vocabulary resources in speech than are needed in writing. It might be argued that vocabulary size and breadth tests concentrate on comparatively less frequent vocabulary which is much less useful in oral communication. Both the *Levels Test* and *EVST* have a 10,000 word range, for example. This concentration on infrequent vocabulary, however, might be much more useful in reading and writing where larger vocabulary resources are required. Perhaps these tests fail to assess in sufficient depth the frequent lexical levels which are important for speech. Their content validity may be at fault therefore if these tests are to represent oral language ability with any accuracy.

There is a second potential explanation, a construct validity problem, that current vocabulary levels tests tap into the orthographic recognition knowledge of learners only, and fail to assess phonological or aural word recognition which should be more relevant for speaking ability. Knowledge of the written forms of words ought to be an indispensable requirement of reading and writing but would be less important in speaking where knowledge of the phonological form ought to be more important. The reverse ought to be true as well, knowledge of phonological word form should be a requirement of speaking and listening in a foreign language but not so important in writing. It might be hypothesized that in order to anticipate the ability to handle oral language, a vocabulary levels test should attempt to measure knowledge of aural or phonological vocabulary rather than orthographic vocabulary.

There is a presumption here that the foreign language mental lexicon has two halves; an orthographic half, where written representations of words are stored, and a phonological half, where the aural representations are stored. There is an implication, too, that the two halves do not have to map on to each other exactly and that words can exist in one half without a corresponding entry in the other. The literature on the subjects sometimes appears to suggest this. Nation's (2001: 27) table of aspects of word knowledge, for example, clearly separates what a word sounds like from what a word looks like. Dual processing models (e.g. Coltheart & Rastle, 1994) suggest two separate routes to word recognition: a direct route based on visual recognition of a word's orthography and a more round-about route, which uses grapheme–phoneme conversion rules to convert the written form of a word into an aural form which can then be decoded. This suggests, at least to us, that existence in the lexicon may not require words to have both forms and that phonological word forms may exist without an orthographic equivalent. It certainly is not an absolute requirement of language learning to acquire both forms of a word. It is possible to learn a language entirely through speaking and listening and this is often done where orthographic forms, as in Chinese, are impenetrable to western learners, and in approaches such as total physical response.

Further evidence emerges from studies of language learning aptitude. One strand of this suggests that an important element in the ability to learn a foreign language is the ability to recognize foreign language sounds and link them to symbols. This quality is specifically tested for in Carroll and Sapon's (1958) *Modern Language Aptitude Test* and might be taken to imply that successful foreign language learning is heavily tied to the recognition and decoding of the written form. If foreign language use is to include the ability to read and write then the learner will need a transliteration process to handle words never seen before. Carroll and Sapon's conclusions may be colored by their use of school and college language scores as the basis for measuring foreign language success. These courses will inevitably have been academic in orientation and will have included a substantial requirement that the subjects handle the written form of the foreign language well. With language viewed in this light then it might be expected that the two halves of the lexicon would have to map closely and be equivalent in size.

Another strand considers this element of aptitude to be a more narrowly constructed phonological ability, the ability to recognize and distinguish foreign language sounds and not connected specifically to the written form (several studies in this area are reported in Sparks & Ganschow, 2001). Skehan (1993: 166) suggests this ability is particularly important at the outset of learning. It suggests that a requirement of foreign language ability is the presence of phonological forms of words in the foreign language. The two halves of the lexicon need not always map onto each other so closely and while an orthographic representation of a word might necessarily have a phonological equivalent, the reverse would not need to be true. Words could exist in the lexicon in phonological form without an orthographic representation. The need to have a phonological form of words in the lexicon does not imply that the representation has to be the correct foreign language one. Learners who read well in their foreign language may not recognize the correct aural version of a word when they hear it because their grapheme–phoneme conversion rules are faulty, but this need not inhibit comprehension in writing.

Notwithstanding these considerations, it seems possible that if orthographic word knowledge predicts ability to communicate through writing, then phonological word knowledge might predict oral/aural communication in the same way. There is very little evidence either to support or contradict this idea. Phonological tests of vocabulary breadth are a recent phenomenon. A dictation form of Nation's *Levels Test* (Fountain & Nation, 2000) can be found in Nation (2001: 429) but studies of how performance on this test ties in with overall ability or with performance in formal exams are lacking. *AuralLex* (Milton & Hopkins, 2005) is designed as a phonological test equivalent to the orthographic X_Lex (Meara & Milton, 2003) and we have some idea of how the two types of vocabulary recognition link to one another as learning progresses.

Milton and Hopkins (2006) tested 126 Greek- and Arabic-speaking learners of English and found that while both types of vocabulary increase in size with foreign language level, they do not increase proportionately. At the outset of learning, phonological vocabulary size generally exceeds orthographic vocabulary size but thereafter orthographic vocabulary increases at a faster rate. In intermediate and advanced learners orthographic vocabulary size exceeds phonological vocabulary size. A feature of advanced learners in this study was that their orthographic recognition of English words always considerably exceeded their aural recognition, often by a surprisingly large margin. It appeared that the Arabic- and Greek-speaking groups behaved rather differently with the Arabic-speaking learners being rather slower to develop the orthographic side of their vocabularies and much less likely to develop a very large vocabulary whichever way it was tested.

Milton and Riordan (2006) investigated Arabic and Farsee speakers using X_Lex and AuralLex and examined whether the relatively slow growth of orthographic vocabulary in Arabic speakers could be attributed to the effect of script decoding strategies since Farsee uses the same script. It appears this was not the case and they conclude that while Arabic speakers may be particularly tied to phonological decoding of written text, the cause of slow vocabulary growth lay elsewhere. Arabic speakers, taken as a group, tended to have vocabulary sizes of the same size in both orthographic and phonological form, while the Farsee speakers did not. It is suggested that the decoding strategies transferred from Arabic make reading comparatively inefficient and Arabic speakers in particular appear reluctant to lose these strategies. For these learners, the knock-on effect of reading less and less quickly is what contributes to the inability to take up new vocabulary. Less reading means that these learners would encounter and learn fewer infrequent words, which tend to proliferate in writing, and this would prevent orthographic vocabulary growing beyond phonological levels.

Neither study attempts to link vocabulary size to the assessment of overall ability, or the subskills of language, through formal exams such as the UCLES suite of exams or TOEFL although in both studies the authors point to the varying characteristics of learners from different national and language backgrounds. Native Arabic speakers, they report, tend to be good in oral communication despite having small assessed vocabularies and appear, in speech, to be far more able than their orthographic vocabulary scores suggest. Native-speaking Chinese learners generally display good vocabulary knowledge, measured orthographically, and while they can perform quite well in tests of reading comprehension, they struggle as a group to handle the spoken language to the same level of proficiency.

The case has been made here that vocabulary knowledge is an important element in the mix that makes up overall language skill but it is not, of course, the only element in such a mix. Foreign language skill will involve knowledge of other elements of language and an appreciation of non-linguistic factors. In writing, for example, the foreign language user will have to make a choice as to who the intended readership is, what the content should be, and make a choice of an appropriate register and style. In an exam, the learner will have to make a decision as to how real the task is and how much scope there is for displaying knowledge beyond the simple requirements of communication. All of these, in addition to the words which are chosen and whether they are grammatically put together, will influence the success of the communication and, in an examination, how it will be judged and graded. Usually it is difficult to assess what proportions of these elements are required for foreign language skill to develop, since skills and the elements which make them up are rarely quantifiable in the way that height or weight are. But vocabulary size, it can be argued, does provide interval data and it may be possible to estimate how much of the variation in language skill learners display can be attributed to the vocabulary knowledge they have and use.

A study which investigates both orthographic and aural vocabulary size may make these differences more comprehensible and enable us to explain the role of vocabulary knowledge in foreign language oral fluency much better than our current models of vocabulary learning permit. It should enable us to see the way the different types of vocabulary knowledge contribute to the separate subskills of language. It may even allow us to make some kind of calculation as to how great a contribution vocabulary knowledge makes to communication skills, which also require other knowledge.

Aim, Objectives and Method

The broad aims of this study are twofold. First, it is an attempt to link performance in overall language skill and the four subskills to measures of both phonological and orthographic vocabulary size. It is expected that, in line with previous studies, vocabulary size measures administered through writing will correlate with the subskills of reading and writing, which involve vocabulary in this form, and will not correlate well with scores in speaking, where knowledge of the written form superficially appears less useful. While fluency in speaking may require much less vocabulary knowledge, one might hope that a measure of phonological vocabulary size will correlate with speaking ability. It is less clear how this might link with the other skills and the answer to this may depend on how closely orthographic and phonological forms are connected in the learner's lexicon. However, it seems more than likely that the two systems may, from the point of view of estimating native-like forms of these words, function relatively independently and that phonological vocabulary size need not predict ability in reading and writing. In formal exams such as IELTS the listening subskill is tested using a methodology, which involves both reading and listening, and both forms of knowledge may play a role as a consequence.

Second, it is intended to try to calculate the proportion of variance in overall language skill and subskill scores which can be explained by the two types of vocabulary knowledge. We all agree that vocabulary knowledge is important for communication in a foreign language but this study will attempt to quantify how great the importance is.

There are a number of specific objectives, therefore, which involve collecting the following from a group of learners:

(1) Measures of orthographic vocabulary size.
(2) Measures of phonological vocabulary size.
(3) IELTS scores (as a measure of overall language skill and ability) and scores on the separate subskills: reading, writing, listening and speaking.
(4) Spearman correlation coefficients between the vocabulary size and IELTS test scores.
(5) The results of regression analysis using the vocabulary scores to try to explain variance in the various IELTS scores.

The subjects were 30 students of English language at Swansea University attending pre-sessional courses prior to undergraduate or postgraduate study. In all, 10 of the learners were native Arabic speakers, 10 were Chinese speaking and the remaining 10 from Japan and European countries. The learners ranged in ability between intermediate and relatively advanced.

The testing instruments were *X_Lex* (Meara & Milton, 2003), to estimate orthographic vocabulary size, and *AuralLex* (Milton & Hopkins, 2005), to estimate phonological vocabulary size. These tests are constructed in the same way and test knowledge of each of the first 5; 1000 lemmatised word frequency bands in English (where a word is taken to include a head word and its regularly formed inflections). The tests estimate overall knowledge of this vocabulary. The frequency bands are drawn from work by Hindmarsh (1980) and Nation (1984). They are Yes/No tests, which present learners with 120 words, one by one. In *X_Lex* the learners see the word on computer screen but the words are not heard. In *AuralLex* the learners hear but do not see the words. In *AuralLex* the screen gives the learner a button to press in order to hear the test word as often as is needed to form a judgment. In both tests learners have to indicate whether they know each word. There are 20 words from each 1000 word frequency band and a further 20 pseudowords, which are designed to look and sound like words in English but are not real words. The number of Yes responses to

Aural Word Recognition and Oral Competence in English 89

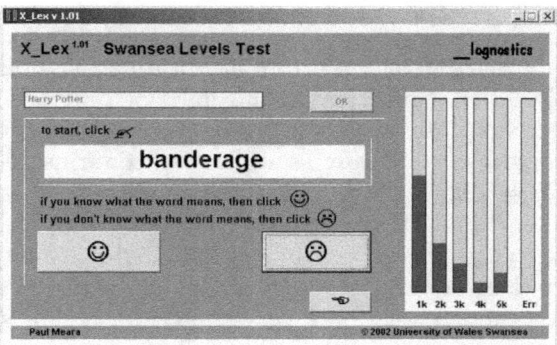

Figure 6.1 The presentation of test items in *X_Lex*

these pseudowords allows the score on the real words to be adjusted for guessing and overestimation of knowledge. The tests give an overall score of words known out of 5000. A screen image of the *X_Lex* test illustrates how the words are presented and how the profile is drawn for the learner as the test takes place. This is shown in Figure 6.1.

Statistical analysis is challenged by the fact that all the data may not be interval data. A good case can be made that the vocabulary scores are interval scores. Foreign language words are countable in a rather more meaningful sense than other aspects of foreign language knowledge and it can be argued that someone who knows 2000 words in a foreign language has twice the knowledge of someone who knows only 1000 words, for example. The IELTS scores, however, are grades and the numbers do not reflect knowledge or skill in the same way. While ascending scores represent ascending gradations of knowledge and skill, it is much harder to argue that somebody with an IELTS score of six has exactly twice the knowledge or skill or someone with an IELTS score of three. In calculating correlations, account can be taken of this difference by using Spearman's coefficient rather than Pearson's. This may be a better calculation in any case since Pearson assumes a linear correlation which may not be present in the data, a fact somewhat overlooked in many studies. In regression analysis the problems are rather greater since the dependent variable, in this case the IELTS scores, should be interval. Two approaches might be taken in handling these data therefore. One is to assume that the IELTS scores are interval and accept too that any conclusions reached, however insightful they appear, will be flawed. A second approach is to reduce the IELTS scores to a binomial variable, high and low, and carry out a logistic regression which accepts a binomial dependent. Both approaches will be taken. For the purpose of the logistic regression, all IELTS scores have been reduced to high, scores of five or above, and low, anything below five.

Results

Vocabulary size data collected from the group as a whole are summarized in Table 6.1. As expected in the light of previous observations concerning learners at this level, the mean orthographic score exceeds the mean phonological score. A paired sample t-test confirms this difference is significant $t(29) = 3.329$, $r < 0.01$. The three sub-groups, Arabic-speakers, Chinese-speakers and others, display differences in the relationship between these two aspects of vocabulary knowledge. Their separate sub-scores are shown in Table 6.2.

The mean vocabulary sizes are very similar for Arabic-speakers with the phonological score larger than the orthographic, but for the other speakers the orthographic scores exceed the phonological. The difference in the vocabulary scores is not significant for the Arabic-speaking learners, however, the differences between the two scores in the other groups is significant [$t(9) = 4.991$, $r < 0.01$ for Chinese-speaking subjects and $t(9) = 3.607$, $r < 0.001$ for other students]. The significance of these differences is discussed later. It should be noted that the standard deviations vary considerably both between tests and from group to group. This may be a product of the small sample sizes of the groups but may also reflect the considerable individual variation that test of this kind can produce.

Overall IELTS scores ranged between 3 and 7.5 and sub-scores similarly varied between three and seven. A summary of the scores on the sub-tests and the overall grade received is presented in Table 6.3. Table 6.4 presents the Spearman correlation coefficients which emerge when vocabulary size and the IELTS scores and sub-scores are analyzed.

Tables 6.5 and 6.6 report the results of regression analyses. Table 6.5 presents the model summaries which linear, step-wise regression produces when the IELTS scores and sub-scores are analyzed as dependent

Table 6.1 Mean scores on vocabulary size test

	Mean scores	SD	Max possible
X_Lex	2844.83	809.46	5000
A_Lex	2384.48	771.95	5000

Table 6.2 Mean vocabulary size scores broken down by language group

	Arabic n = 10		Chinese n = 10		Other n = 10	
	Mean	SD	Mean	SD	Mean	SD
X_Lex	2410	322.14	3272.22	625.55	2895	1091.49
A_Lex	2470	904.06	2394.44	658.80	2290	795.40

Table 6.3 Mean scores on IELTS test and subtests

	Mean IELTS scores	SD	Max possible
Reading	4.50	0.94	9
Writing	5.03	1.01	9
Listening	5.10	0.94	9
Speaking	4.88	1.09	9
Overall grade	4.90	0.88	9

Table 6.4 Correlations between vocabulary size scores and IELTS scores

	A_lex	Read	Listen	Write	Speak	Overall
X_lex	0.46*	0.70**	0.48**	0.76**	0.35	0.68**
A_lex		0.22	0.67**	0.44*	0.71***	0.55****

**Correlation is significant at the 0.01 level.
*Correlation is significant at the 0.05 level.

Table 6.5 Model summaries of linear regression

	Model predictor	R	R square	Adjusted R square	Standard error of the estimate
Read	1 xlex	0.70	0.50	0.48	0.68
Write	1 xlex	0.78	0.60	0.59	0.64
Listen	1 alex	0.68	0.46	044	0.70
	2 xlex	0.74	0.54	0.51	0.65
Speak	1 alex	0.65	0.42	0.40	0.84
Overall	1 xlex	0.77	0.59	0.58	0.56

Table 6.6 Model summaries of binary logistic regression

	Model predictor	2 log likelihood	Cox & Snell R Square	Nagelkerke R square
Read	1 xlex	27.53	0.30	0.41
Write	1 xlex	21.93	0.46	0.62
Listen	1. alex	25.18	0.32	0.45
Speak	1. alex	21.71	0.45	0.61
Overall	1. xlex	23.25	0.44	0.59

variables of the vocabulary scores. Only the predictor variables are included and the excluded variables are omitted. Table 6.6 presents the model summaries which binary logistic regressions produce where the IELTS scores recorded are either high, five or above or low, less than five. Again, only significant predictor variables are included.

Discussion

The results reported for the two vocabulary size measures are in line with those of previous research. In the group as a whole, learners appear to possess an orthographic recognition vocabulary larger than their phonological recognition vocabulary. Milton and Hopkins (2006) and Milton and Riordan (2006) report the same conclusion. Similar to these papers, the Arabic-speaking learners, as a group, appear different from the other groups in that for this subgroup, the two vocabulary scores are much closer in size with the mean phonological score actually slightly larger than the mean orthographic score. The significance of this information for how words are stored and processed is not clear especially as, as might be expected, there is variation within each group. It is not even clear whether the deficiency of words in the phonological form is the product of poor grapheme–phoneme decoding rules, implying that many words have a phonological representation but not one that matches native-like usage, or whether some words lack a phonological presence in the lexicon entirely. Nonetheless, it is clear that learners will bring different types of orthographic and phonological vocabulary knowledge to the task of foreign language communication. How does this knowledge influence the degree of success these learners have in written and oral communication?

As expected, orthographic vocabulary size proves to be quite a good predictor of overall academic language, communicative ability, at least as measured by IELTS. A significant correlation of 0.68 is rather impressive considering how many other elements of knowledge and ability must also impact on the IELTS scores. It must be remembered that the vocabulary size measures attempt to access only knowledge, while IELTS seeks to test skill in using that knowledge amongst other things. But the orthographic vocabulary size test does not appear to mesh equally well with all of the four components which comprise the overall IELTS grade. Significant correlations emerge between orthographic vocabulary size and reading, writing and listening. The correlation with writing scores, at 0.76, seems remarkably large given that the vocabulary measure tests a passive receptive knowledge of form only, while the IELTS writing component tests a productive skill. How do good learners manage to display in writing their knowledge and skill when they have only to produce a few hundred words, out of the thousands they know, and where most of the words they write will be highly frequent vocabulary which all learners will use? There is some evidence in speaking tests that assessors can be very heavily influenced by the occurrence of just a few, judiciously placed, infrequent words and expressions (Lorenzo-Dus & Meara, 2005) and maybe assessors in writing are influenced the same way. If this is so, then these words and expressions must be placed early in the text, since it also appears that writing assessors make their grade judgments within a few seconds of beginning to read Meara and Babi (2001). Correlations with the oral/aural skills of listening and speaking are much more modest, at below 0.5, although the correlation with listening is still significant. The orthographic vocabulary size test does not correlate significantly with scores on the IELTS speaking test.

In contrast, phonological vocabulary size measures fail to produce a significant correlation with the reading component, but do produce significant correlations with the writing, speaking and listening test scores. The correlations are quite strong at 0.67 with listening and 0.71 with speaking, but more modest with the writing scores at below 0.5. But they tell us that vocabulary knowledge and vocabulary size, are relevant to oral and aural competence, despite the observation that spoken language appears to involve the use of a much smaller lexis than written language. This observation confirms something which seems obvious, that learners appear to need knowledge of words in phonological form to speak well, rather than visual word recognition which explained so much in reading and writing. There is a convincing case to be made with these data that the subskills of language, as measured by the IELTS tests of those skills, access different lexical resources. The IELTS components which involve the written form of language will be governed to some extent by the learners' orthographic lexical resources. Components which involve the spoken form of language will be governed to some extent by the learners' phonological vocabulary resources. Components which involve both, and the listening test requires learners to interact with both a written test paper and an aural comprehension task, require both orthographic and phonological lexical resources. This makes sense and helps explain why vocabulary size measures in the past have failed to predict oral fluency satisfactorily.

This observation can help explain too the kind differences which learners from different language backgrounds display in communicative performance where learners who appear to have small vocabularies can also appear quite communicatively proficient especially in speech. Arabic-speaking learners tend to have *AuralLex* and *X_Lex* scores of very similar size. This might suggest, although it does not prove, one-to-one mapping of items in the mental lexicon, and their heavy dependence on phonological processing so recognition of written form would rely on recognition of phonological form. These learners can do well in oral communication with comparatively modest lexical resources because 2–3000 words (out of the most frequent 5000) will give good coverage even of fairly academic aural text, but this knowledge is not sufficient for handling written text, whether reading or writing, where far greater lexical knowledge is needed for fluency. They will tend, therefore, to do comparatively poorly in reading and writing tests. Other learners tend to have orthographic vocabularies larger than their phonological vocabularies. For these learners, 2–3000 words in the aural side of the lexicon will be matched with hundreds or, possibly, thousands more words in the orthographic side allowing for greater capability in handling written text. These learners are more likely to perform equally well in all components of the IELTS test.

The purpose of including regression analysis in this kind of study is to attempt to quantify the scale of impact which one component of knowledge, in this case vocabulary, can have on communicative skill and fluency. We know that vocabulary size is important for communicative fluency and correlates with general language ability measures, but how important is it? Is it the single most important factor which governs general ability or a factor of rather less impact which ranks alongside or behind other elements of language knowledge and skill?

The results of linear regression, remember, must be treated with some caution. The sample size is small and the IELTS scores analyzed here are not true intervals. Nonetheless, linear regression results suggest that the importance of vocabulary size may depend on which skill is required. Scores on the writing paper in IELTS appear quite heavily dependent on orthographic vocabulary size and the regression analysis suggests that nearly 60% of variance in the IELTS writing scores can be explained by differences in orthographic vocabulary size alone. Given that so many other factors are thought to be involved in producing a good and appropriate piece of writing, and some of these were listed earlier in this chapter, this result is a little surprising. The same analysis suggests that orthographic vocabulary size can explain 48% of variance in IELTS reading scores. These results are very much in line with a study by Stæhr (2008) which produces similar figures. Differences in phonological vocabulary size do not appear to contribute to variance in IELTS grades in subscores involving writing.

The opposite is true in the IELTS speaking test where phonological vocabulary size appears to explain 40% of variance while orthographic vocabulary does not appear to predict any at all. If the capacity for orthographic vocabulary scores to explain differences in writing is unexpectedly large, the explanatory power of phonological vocabulary in speaking is comparatively smaller. There are a variety of possible reasons why vocabulary size may not appear so important a determiner of success in speech as it appears to be in writing. It may be a problem with the vocabulary tests and their concentration on infrequent vocabulary items not relevant to fluent speech. But it may also be due to the nature of the relationship between vocabulary knowledge and oral fluency which may not be a simple linear one. Nation (2001: 147) points to the existence of a threshold, at around 80% coverage in writing and 2000 words, below which learners struggle to communicate at all and beyond which this skill is possible. This suggests an all-or-nothing threshold therefore, and the continuum of knowledge and skills necessary for good correlations will be missing. Beyond this threshold, speaking skill might be more dependent on other factors than simply the number of words a learner knows and can bring to bear on the communicative task. The binary regression analysis might be more insightful if this is the case.

Both types of vocabulary knowledge appear to contribute to variance in listening scores. The *AuralLex* scores alone explain 44% of variance which rises to 51% once the *X_Lex* scores are added to the model. Our initial interpretation of this is that success in the listening test may be dependent both on the learner's ability to successfully interpret the instructions and the questions, which are in writing, as well as their ability to aurally decode the content of the listening task itself. An interesting avenue of research would appear to lie in investigating the written element of this test and in testing the effect when the lexical content of the questions and rubric are very strictly controlled.

It might be expected that the overall IELTS grades, which combine written and aural subtests, would draw on both types of vocabulary knowledge. The regression analysis suggests, however, that it is orthographic vocabulary knowledge which is the more important factor. *X_Lex* scores appear to explain 58% of variance in overall IELTS scores while AuralLex scores are excluded from the model. IELTS is intended as a measure of English language performance for academic purposes and in one sense it would not be a concern to those of us who work in universities if IELTS has this bias for writing skills in particular. We can manage students who speak poorly but we struggle to cope with students who read and write poorly. We would want IELTS to identify these students particularly. But IELTS does claim to test all four skills and the dependence on orthographic vocabulary knowledge suggests that the oral and aural elements of the test may not be given the weighting many users expect.

Even if the precise figures are to be doubted, the relationship they suggest between vocabulary knowledge and overall language performance makes a crude kind of sense and repeats, as might be expected, what the correlations indicated. Orthographic vocabulary knowledge is important for skills which involve orthography such as reading, writing and the listening paper, which has a reading component in it. Phonological vocabulary knowledge is important for skills which involve speech such as listening and speaking. The only surprise has been just how important vocabulary knowledge appears to be in developing writing skills in particular and in overall language performance as measured by IELTS grades.

These scores might suggest that vocabulary size is the most important factor in determining success in the writing, reading listening and overall IELTS grades; more important than grammatical accuracy or the other factors we believe to be at work in the mix which makes up a productive skill in language. This echoes the feelings of learners themselves who report vocabulary as the most important factor in determining whether they can comprehend a foreign language text (Laufer & Sim, 1985).

It appears that the use of regression analysis is more of an art than a science and we expressed doubts as to whether linear regression was a completely satisfactory mode of analysis given the nature of the IELTS scoring system. For this reason, a binary logistic regression analysis was also carried out. The results produced by this method broadly confirm the previous analysis. Reading and writing subskill scores, above and below IELTS 5, continue to be explained to a considerable degree by the orthographic vocabulary size score, while the contribution of the phonological vocabulary size score is not significant. Variance in the overall IELTS grades again appear sensitive to orthographic but not to phonological vocabulary knowledge.

There are differences, however. The speaking subskill appears, again, to be sensitive to phonological vocabulary size but by this method of analysis, the relationship appears very strong. According to the method of analysis used, over 60% of variance in the ability to score IELTS 5 or more, might be explained by this single factor. We believe this lends support to the idea of lexical thresholds and that the relationship between knowledge and scores which measures oral performance may not be linear. The ability to perform well, or above five, in the IELTS test relies on having sufficient minimum phonological vocabulary. Additional vocabulary knowledge after this threshold may not produce higher grades. These results produce different results regarding the listening subskill scores. While linear regression suggested that phonological and orthographic knowledge combined to best explain performance on this test, binary logistic regression suggests a simpler relationship where phonological vocabulary size can explain much of the ability to gain five or more while the contribution of orthographic vocabulary knowledge is not significant. This challenges easy interpretation and this is probably because the listening test, alone among the subskill tests, appears to draw on both orthographic and phonological knowledge. If the relationship between phonological knowledge and oral/aural skill scores is not linear then binary regression analysis will be particularly sensitive to the effect of phonological vocabulary knowledge. It will be less suitable for detecting the effect of orthographic vocabulary knowledge, which may have an influence through the written questions, where the relationship between knowledge and performance is linear and the more you know the better you do. Notwithstanding these differences, however, this type of analysis confirms the manner in which the two different types of vocabulary knowledge impact on the ability to perform in and through English as a foreign language. Orthographic knowledge is important, and probably very important, for the ability to perform through reading and writing. Phonological vocabulary knowledge is important for the ability to perform through speaking and listening.

Conclusions

For practical purposes, phonological and orthographic vocabulary knowledge appear to be different, to interact only loosely with each other, and to interact differently with performance. The fact that a word is recognized in its written form, for example, does not mean it will also be recognized when heard. This conclusion seems very obvious given the emphasis modern teaching methods place on teaching all forms of vocabulary, both written and spoken. But it is clear that the take-up of this information varies from one individual to another and even between native-language groups, and the effect on language performance appears quite considerable. The ability to read and, especially, write in English is strongly tied to knowledge of the written form of words and, where learners fail to develop this knowledge, for whatever, reason, communication and performance suffers. The ability to speak and understand speech is tied to knowledge of the phonological form of words and, again, learners who do not develop this area will suffer in performance and communication. While there is a case for arguing that vocabulary size is possibly the most important factor in determining ability in these skills, it must be remembered that vocabulary knowledge appears closely tied to other aspects of language knowledge such as grammatical knowledge, so vocabulary size measures may reflect other types of knowledge as well which will also impact on performance.

While learners' knowledge of orthographic recognition of vocabulary is well researched, their phonological knowledge of word forms is much less well known. This reinforces recent opinion in vocabulary measurement (e.g. Nation, 2007; Richards & Malvern, 2007) that multiple measures are required to characterize learners' knowledge. The results of this study suggest that research in the area of phonological vocabulary knowledge is likely to be particularly fertile and as useful as other domains of lexical investigation such as lexical depth. They reinforce too the fact that we do not have a perfect picture of the structure of the mental lexicon and we do not really understand how these different types of knowledge mesh together and are stored and accessed. This study has not added to this knowledge except to say that the orthographic and phonological sides, insofar as they reflect native-like representations of words, can be very different. Results also suggest that while the simple linear relationship, suggested at the outset of this chapter, between vocabulary size and performance holds true for written performance, it may not be so true for all communicative skills. In reading and writing, the more you know the better you get by as a generality, at least up to the several thousands of words tested by the method used in this study. In speaking, the relationship is different and beyond a certain threshold more vocabulary knowledge does not appear to be so useful. It would be interesting to know, in the speaking subtest in particular, what is being tapped into to produce the higher IELTS speaking grades if it is not vocabulary knowledge.

One final conclusion which is suggested by this study is that overall IELTS scores are tremendously sensitive to vocabulary size and particularly orthographic vocabulary size. It is not clear if this is the intention of IELTS or the by-product of what it means to be proficient in a language from a written, educated and academic viewpoint. Rather than reflect the subskills which comprise the overall score equally, it appears to be heavily weighted to the learners' knowledge of written forms in one, admittedly key, area of language knowledge.

Chapter 7
A Cascade Model of Lexical Access to Explain the Phonological Activation of Recently Practiced Lexical Items

TERESA LÓPEZ-SOTO

Introduction

Many studies have claimed how vocabulary acquisition can be enhanced by reading, or by placing words in contexts. There are few studies which address the success of teaching the vocabulary of a foreign language by means of exposing students to the phonological representation of the words to be learned. Before any claim can be made regarding how much listening input can be of any benefit for the acquisition of vocabulary in learning a foreign or second language, some preliminary analyses must be done in order to demonstrate that learners do indeed activate phonological patterns prior to retrieving lexical items. This study aims at resolving this dilemma, which has otherwise been extensively demonstrated in psychological experiments (Caramazza, 1997; Navarrete & Costa, 2005).

The general theory assumes that speech production involves the retrieval of four different types of information: conceptual, lexical, phonological and articulatory. In naming a picture, for example, the speaker must first identify the conceptual reality, extract the phonological pattern, select the corresponding lexical representation and finally articulate the phonetic pattern that represents that lexical information. It is also generally assumed that the activation at the conceptual level is done following the so-called Cascade Model, in which, semantically related conceptual representations are activated together with the target item (Dell, 1986; Levelt, 1989).

These are the only propositions that seem to be accepted by scholars in the field, for at least three different theories or alternatives to the general theoretical framework have been offered to explain how information is passed in a feed-forward fashion from the conceptual level, to the lexical level and finally to the phonological level. Below there is a summary of these three proposals.

The Full-Cascade Model predicts that any activation at the conceptual level is followed by a linked activation at the lexical and phonological levels (Caramazza, 1997; Costa *et al.*, 2000, 2005; Dell, 1986; Dell *et al.*, 1997; Griffin & Bock, 1998; Harley, 1993; Rapp & Goldrick, 2000; Starreveld & La Heij, 1995). This model holds that phonological encoding can occur before lexical node selection, in which case, the phonological selection would come all the way along the layered structure. Figure 7.1 represents this framework. The activation of a semantically related network comes along with the activation of a phonologically related network.

The Discrete Model restricts the activation to the lexical level and predicts that the retrieval of the phonological pattern only takes place in the case of the target word (Levelt, 2001; Levelt *et al.*, 1999). This kind of serial model posits that phonological encoding begins only after lexical node selection has taken place, in which case, there would be no possibility of information-crossing across the lexical network. Figure 7.2 exemplifies this model.

In this final model, proposed by Bloem and La Heij (2003) (also, Bloem *et al.*, 2004), we find the theory that the activation at the lexical level is only done within the lexical network surrounding the target word and the subsequent triggering of the corresponding phonological patterns, as shown in Figure 7.3. This assumption would be mid-way between the Cascade Model and the Serial Model.

The three versions exemplified above coincide in that multiple lexical representations are activated in the process of accessing the lexical item.

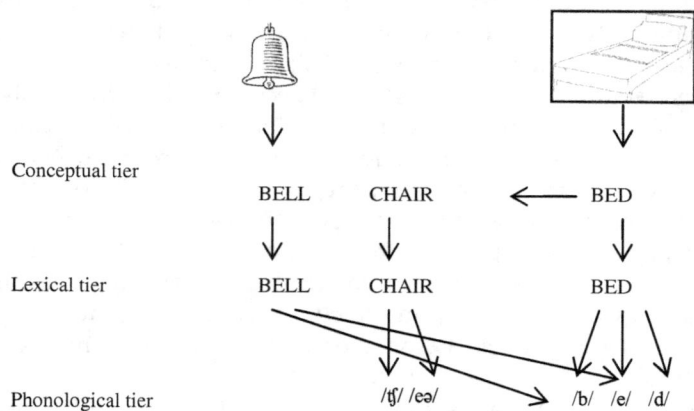

Figure 7.1 Outline of the Full-Cascade Model in which after the conceptual network activation, the activation of the semantically and phonologically related items follows (the framed picture contains the target word)

A Cascade Model of Lexical Access

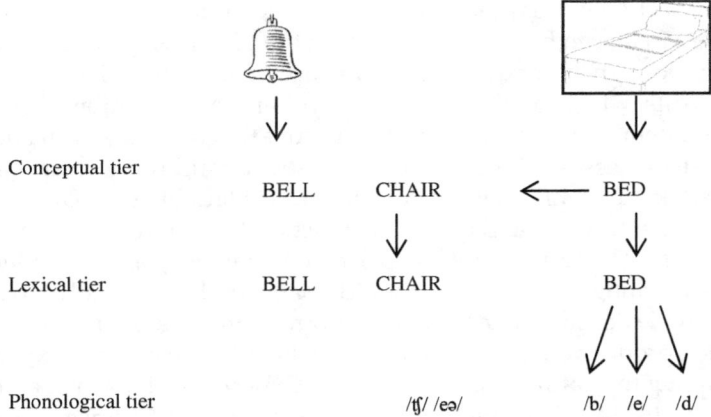

Figure 7.2 Outline of the Discrete Model that shows, after the conceptual network activation, how the information proceeds exclusively for the target word (the framed picture contains the target word)

The Discrete Model states that the phonological activation is exclusive of the target word information-passing line. Bloem and La Heij's Model is in favor of multiple activation of semantically related items while the Full-Cascade Model proposes the possibility of multiple activation of lexical and phonological representations.

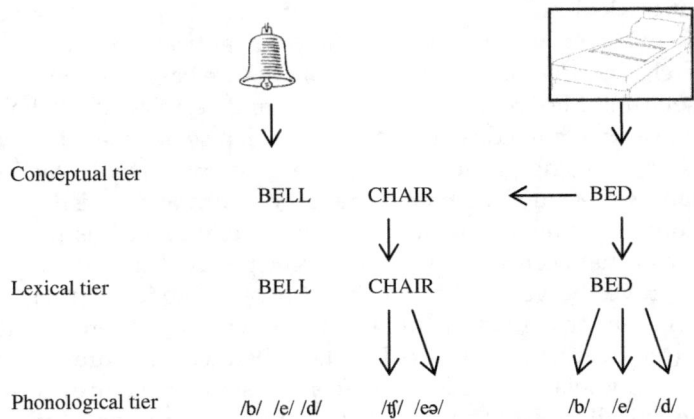

Figure 7.3 Outline of Bloem and La Heij's Model that shows, after the conceptual network activation, the subsequent activation of only the semantically related items within the conceptual network (the framed picture shows the target word)

The objective in this study is to find further evidence on how the Full-Cascade Model can be traced when the setting is the acquisition of vocabulary in a foreign (second) language. In particular, we describe two parallel experiments which analyze whether conceptual activation of recently practiced items is followed by a linked activation of both lexical and phonological processes. The context of the study is EFL, more specifically, intermediate-level EFL courses currently being taught at the University of Seville, Spain (Remedial English Phonetics and Listening Comprehension Techniques). The results of the experiments may be useful to understand how the teaching of vocabulary should be approached, as well as to understand how lexical and phonological information are stored and retrieved in speech production. For that reason, we have replicated one experiment by changing the nature of the stimulus: in Experiment 1, participants were instructed to find the target word by (1) looking at a series of pictures which were semantically related to the first target picture (the 'target picture' being the picture that had to be named and which referred to the recently practiced lexical item), and (2) looking at the first target picture which was followed by other 'distractor pictures' which corresponded to phonologically related words. In Experiment 2, distractor pictures were substituted by recordings of the distractor words.

When the model refers to the lexicalization phase, it really makes reference to the cognitive stage at which conceptual information is transformed into lexical representation. Bearing in mind that the networked activation is done at the conceptual level, the result of lexicalization is a construct formed by a semantically driven network. Thus, when lexically related items are mentioned, they should be considered as being semantically related at the lexicalization stage. For that reason, the item 'semantically related' will be used both for lexically and semantically related items.

Research objectives in the two experiments are based on the idea given by Morsella and Miozzo (2002) and Cutting and Ferreira (1999). Following these authors, we have designed a study which seeks to analyze naming latencies by exposing participants to a series of pictures. In each set, the participant is presented with both the target word and a distractor word (in the form of different pictures). The participant's task is to name the lexical word that corresponds to the target picture.[1] In our case, and in order to prove the validity of the Full-Cascade Model, participants are presented with the correct picture for the target word together with other pictures (the distractor pictures). The first distractor pictures correspond to semantically related words. The second distractor pictures correspond to phonologically related words. In our study, the notion of phonologically relatedness is two-fold: we have tested words which have a high neighbor density (they are minimal pairs or nearly minimal pairs) and, also, we have tested words which have the same rhythmical pattern (i.e. the number of syllables is the same and the stressed syllable is on the same position, but segmental density is low: 'suffer' versus 'pattern' would be rhythmically related in our study but not phonologically related).

The objective of the experiment is to investigate whether naming latency is faster when the distractor picture is phonologically related to the target word (whether it be segmentally or rhythmically related) or, whether naming latency is faster when the distractor picture is semantically related. With this study, we aim at proving whether there is multiple activation at the conceptual, lexical and phonological levels, in a cascade fashion, which spans its effects over semantically and phonologically related items. The innovative idea in this study is that the process has been applied to the field of second language learning. Thus, the objective is to analyze what kind of representation produces a faster latency in naming recently practiced lexical items: are semantically related networks more effective in retrieving lexicalization of new words? Or rather, is the explosion of phonologically related networks more efficient in retrieving lexicalization of these words? Traditionally, the design of activities for vocabulary learning has been extensively based on semantic networks and lexical families (Lewis, 1997b). The goal is, therefore, to understand how this process operates in the field of teaching, learning and acquiring new lexical items in an EFL setting.

Experiment 1

Method

Participants

In all, 31 native speakers of Spanish participated in the experiment. All were English language and literature majors at the University of Seville; all of them took part in the experiment in exchange for a course credit. Totally, 60% of the students were female and 40% male; the age range was 18–25. Eligibility was assessed through a proficiency pretest intended to select participants with a similar level in the target language (i.e. an intermediate level as defined by the University of Cambridge ESOL examination http://www.cambridgeesol.org/index.htm).

Materials

Participants were instructed to produce target words associated with six pictures which represented these target words. Each picture was shown together with seven other pictures which represented semantically related items. For example, a picture of a bed (the target word) would be shown in conjunction with seven other pictures representing a cushion, a blanket, a bedside table, some pajamas, slippers and so on. These latter pictures are described as being the 'distractor pictures'.

Participants would also have to produce target words associated with phonologically related words. Six target pictures would be associated with seven distractor pictures. In this second test, all target words and phonologically related words shared the same stress pattern and vocalic segments (e.g. distractor *hey!* vs. target-*pail*); consonantal segments were shared only 60% of the total (e.g. distractor-*knife packet* vs. target-*life jacket*). Target pictures and distractor pictures took the form of photographs in order to eliminate any possible color distinction.[2] Target pictures appeared first and were followed by distractor pictures, one at a time.

To further reduce the number of related trials, a second set of six filler target pictures (distractors) was presented twice along with seven distractor pictures (phonologically and semantically related) mirroring the same procedure described above. None of these filler target and distractor pictures were used in accounting for the final results. Finally, six filler target pictures were collected which were presented twice along with seven distractor pictures which, in this case, were completely unrelated to the target word. The objective in this case was to completely disguise the general organization of the experiment so that participants would find it difficult to infer the result by applying processes of logical reasoning.

In the overall experiment, each participant was presented with 42 experimental trials (six trials in the semantically related condition, in addition to six trials in the phonologically related condition (neighborhood density), plus six trials in the rhythmically related condition, plus 18 more filler trials, plus six trials in the unrelated condition). In total, 336 pictures were presented, 42 of them represented target words, while there were 294 distractors. The presentation of pictures followed a structure in blocks: first, a target picture followed by unrelated distractor pictures; second, a target picture followed by phonologically related distractor pictures; third, a target picture followed by rhythmically related distractor pictures; and, finally, a target picture followed by a semantically related set of distractor pictures. When the sets shown were rhythmically, phonologically or semantically related, a second round would follow containing the distractors. Special care was taken to choose completely unrelated target words, so that no kind of internal correlation could be established between the different target pictures.

Procedure

Participants were tested seated approximately 1 m away from each other and 10–15 m away from the screen in a classroom. Pictures were projected on a 3 × 4 m white screen. At the beginning of the experiments, participants were asked to write down the English word for the first picture they would see in each block, only after all the pictures in a set had finished being projected. They had to wear noise-isolating headphones and lights were dimmed. If they could not produce the word to name the target picture, they were instructed to leave it blank. The experimental phase involved the following events: (1) a fixation point (an asterisk) was shown in the center of the screen for 1.25 s. (that would stand for the opening of a new series of pictures); (2) a blank interval of 500 ms (white screen); (3) the picture stimulus was presented for 500 ms (the target word) in the center of the screen; (4) the picture stimulus was presented along with the distractor pictures for 1.25 s; and (5) a beeping sound together with a query signal (a question mark projected on screen) signifying the time to write down the target word for 1.25 s, without any additional time to wait for the subject's responses. The entire experimental session lasted 3 min (42 trials × 4.25 s = 3 min approximately).

Results

Only one type of answer was excluded from the final analyses: answers given in Spanish (0.15%). Answers that contained spelling mistakes were accepted after they passed a review by a native speaker to determine intelligibility. There were no instances of responses that would refer to the phonologically related distractor word. The results show that the number of correct answers was higher when a set of phonologically related distractor pictures was present. Table 7.1 shows the final percentage and error values.

The results of this experiment suggest that the phonological overlapping facilitates the naming response and may also indicate facilitation at the acquisition level.

Discussion

The results of the experiment replicate those of Morsella and Miozzo's (2002) study and suggest that phonological activation takes place before lexicalization. These results also corroborate the Full-Cascade Model in that the early phonologically networked construct has a direct effect on the naming of the target word. Discrete models, according to Levelt *et al.*'s (1999), state that one phonological activation takes place, that of the target word. Serial models, according to Bloem and La Heij's (2003) restrict the phonological activation to the target word and its semantically related items. Therefore, no phonological activation outside this network would take place.

Table 7.1 Percentage of correct naming responses and error rate (*E%*) for Experiment 1

Type of relationship	*Percent*	*E%*
Rhythmically related	30.01	0.06
Phonologically related	22.50	0.06
Semantically related	15	0.06

Experiment 2

Method

Participants

The same group of participants (31 total), EFL learners, students at the University of Seville, Spain, took part in a second experiment in exchange for a course credit. In total, 60% of the students were female and 40% male; the age range was 18–25.

Materials

The materials used in Experiment 2 are replicated from those used in Experiment 1, the only difference being at the procedure stage.

Procedure

Participants in Experiment 2 were presented with the same materials and in the same fashion, with one difference: after the target picture had been presented, a recorded transcription of distractor words would accompany the image representation. Thus, Experiment 1 included visual input only, while Experiment 2 combined visual and perceptual input. The naming procedure was the same: participants had to write down the name of the word which would represent the picture that appeared alone in the center of the screen.

Results

Following the same criteria as in Experiment 1, answers given in Spanish were excluded from the final analysis (0.0%). Semantically related distractor pictures elicited more errors than phonologically related ones. Table 7.2 shows the final percentage and error values.

In this case, a deviation of 3.7% must be mentioned. This figure refers to the number of times that participants wrote down the distractor word instead of the target word.

Discussion

The results of Experiment 2 corroborate the same conclusions reached after Experiment 1 in relation to the validity they give to the Full-Cascade

Table 7.2 Percentage of correct naming responses and error rate ($E\%$) for Experiment 2

Type of relationship	Percent	E%
Rhythmically related	34.95	0.05
Phonologically related	33.22	0.05
Semantically related	27.49	0.05

Model. It is worth mentioning how in 3.5% of the cases the phonological reproduction of the distractor word can override the naming of the correct target word. This may suggest the strength of the phonological patterns in producing the target word.

The fact that phonologically related words help activate lexical retrieval faster could also be related to experiments carried out by Damian and Bowers (2003). These authors demonstrated that, in naming a picture, participants do not necessarily have to activate the orthographic representation of the target. Following our results, similarity in spelling does not seem to interfere with a correct lexical retrieval. On the contrary, phonological similarity does help activate the correct lexical item, which could indicate that orthographic information comes after phonological information. A deviation of 3.7% indicating that the distractor word was chosen instead of the target word is not significant enough to state that spelling representation has a relevant influence on lexical activation.

General Discussion

We have reported two experiments assessing the effects of distractor objects during the naming of recently practiced EFL vocabulary by native speakers of Spanish. In choosing both the target and the distractor words, special care was taken so that they would belong to the set of recently practiced words by the participants. With this objective in mind, a series of preliminary tests and activities took place in different sessions in class. When a distractor word could not be easily found, nonsense words would take its place (e.g. distractor-*the Orr rotten's* vs. target-*the door opens*). Also, when new expressions were learned, moving pictures would substitute static ones in the experimental phases. Participants also took other tests on the use of English to demonstrate a similar level of English language proficiency (i.e. intermediate as defined by University of Cambridge ESOL examination (http://www.cambridgeesol.org/index.htm). Several rehearsal sessions (β testing) were organized with a different group so that final preparation of the layout and presentation of the experiments could take place with minimal margins of error produced by collateral variables.

Because results are very similar in the case of rhythmically related and phonologically related words, we will use the word 'phonological' to refer to these two different sets in discussing the results and giving a conclusion.

In Experiment 1, participants had to write down the English word for the target picture they would see on screen while ignoring the distractor pictures which would also be shown. The target picture was recognizable as it would be the only one to appear on the screen. Distractor pictures would always accompany the target picture. Naming correctness was higher when the name of the distractor picture was phonologically related to the name of the target picture. This experiment replicates previous observations by Morsella and Miozzo (2002) and Navarrete and Costa (2005), in which phonologically related items triggers the production of lexical items faster than lexically related items.

In Experiment 2, participants had to name the English word for the target picture they could see on screen while ignoring the distractor pictures which they could hear. The rate of accuracy was also higher when the distractor words were phonologically related to the target word.

Considering both experiments, results show that phonologically related words help retrieve recently practiced items faster than semantically related words. This is true for the two experiments, but it is even more noticeable in Experiment 2, where no distractor picture was shown but rather a recording was played. It seems that this materialization of the phonological structure of the related networks (pronunciation) enhances lexical retrieval (14 points in the case of phonologically related words and 12 points in the case of semantically related words).

Regarding the connection that could exist between a phonological stimulus and a productive retrieval ('productive' here meaning the spoken production of the word to be retrieved) further experimentation is needed. Further evidence is needed to understand how phonologically related terms have an impact on orally produced responses.

Going back to the data, a possible interpretation would be that lexicalization and, therefore, lexical retrieval operates at the same level as phonological activation. The results suggest that semantic networks do not have the impact that phonological networks have on retrieving recently practiced lexical items. These results also corroborate others which investigate lexicalization in the L1 (Navarrete & Costa, 2005) or in bilingual production (Costa *et al.*, 2005).

In the Introduction section, we presented three models to explain the cognitive stages in speech production. It is generally agreed that conceptualization takes place in a cascade fashion, meaning that one stimulus takes place and a network of concepts associated with the input is triggered. Theories are divergent in explaining what follows. Discrete models proposed by Levelt *et al.* (1999) restrict the flow of activation across levels of processing in that only the selected lexical representation activates its phonological form. Serial models (Bloem & La Heij's, 2003) assume that only the conceptual representation included in the stimulus passes activation to the lexical level. Our experimentation is too general in that it assumes that lexicalization does indeed occur in a cascade fashion. Further analyses are necessary to show whether phonological activation takes place along with lexical activation or whether semantically related lexical items are not activated at all. At least, a question could arise as to what extent lexical activation of conceptually related (semantically related) items is present to explain the retrieval of the target word. Further experiments are also necessary to place this naming retrieval of isolated words and words in context.

Finally, a possible interpretation of the data obtained in this study could be explained in these terms: conceptualization may operate at the same level as semantic activation, while phonological activation may operate at the same level as lexicalization. If that theory is true, consequences for L2 vocabulary teaching are not minimal.[3] In fact, the last decades have been particularly productive in pedagogical vocabulary studies (Schmitt, 1998, 2000). An important trend in this subarea suggests that words are framed in items of their relationships to other parts of the sentence (Aitchinson, 1994) or that words are built following syntactic and semantic networks, as the theory of collocations by McCarthy (1990). This has given rise to increasing attention to extensive reading to acquire new vocabulary in L2 (Coady, 1997; Meara, 1997) but always paying attention to the function of words in their syntagmatic context and paradigmatic context (semantic networks). From the data shown above, it is true that semantically related words have an impact on lexical retrieval. However, this impact is not as significant as the influence that phonologically related words have on accessing to lexical information. If that statement is true, then the theory defended by Vitevich *et al.* (1999) for speech perception, may equally work out for speech production. This theory states that the phonological link (neighborhood density) that articulates 'families' of words may be stronger than the semantic link that creates 'lexical families' ('semantic families').

The major consequences for language teaching would necessarily be connected with facilitating access to phonological information in the classroom. This new perspective in language teaching should therefore emphasize the spoken form of the word over the semantic content; however, this perspective has been addressed in previous studies (e.g. Waring, 1997). Materials should be designed accordingly, and instead of centering vocabulary teaching on practicing lexical families, they should encourage the exposure to phonological neighborhoods (following Luce and Pisoni's (1998) terminology). In fact, when Dupuy and Krashen (1993) or Coady (1997) emphasize the necessity of reading to acquire new vocabulary, they may be indirectly enhancing the acquisition of phonological patterns. However, further experimentation is needed to corroborate these latter statements.

What seems to be clear is that recently practiced lexical items are retrieved faster when a phonological stimulus is created than when a semantic stimulus is present. If these results are to be taken into account, then teaching methods should also be tested to see how much can be transferred to the EFL classroom. In that case, the difficulty would be assessing how much vocabulary has been acquired and how much can be retrieved, and to what degree acquisition and retrieval can have an influence on each other. Establishing the fine distinction between these two issues is challenging, but it is necessary to reach definitive conclusions.

Conclusion

In this chapter we have presented two experiments to demonstrate how information is passed from one level of representation (conceptualization) to another level (lexicalization) in speech production. The context is that of native speakers of Spanish in the EFL classroom. The results are conclusive in that there exists phonological overlapping of distractor words over target words. The experimentation proves the consistency of the Full-Cascade Model, but it is not conclusive as to explain whether the lexical activation of conceptually related words is ever triggered up. However, our observations support the notion that there is a cascade movement from the conceptual level to the lexical level and that this phonological activation takes place before lexicalization.

Further research is needed to confirm these results and to clarify other details. First, it is not clear whether phonological activation could be related to the semantic processing. New experiments could show whether there is some influence of spelling over phonology activation in retrieving lexical items. Second, applying the same protocol to a different population, namely L1 speakers and/or the study of lexical retrieval of recently practiced or already-acquired words, could shed more light on understanding the way conceptualization and lexicalization operate. In any case, these results are conclusive enough as to pursue a new line of research in the area of vocabulary teaching. Future research should concentrate on analyzing the effectiveness of teaching new vocabulary by means of using semantic families or rather exposing students to phonological networks. Some studies have assessed vocabulary learning measuring the size of the lexical families that learners are able to produce (Nation, 1990, 2001). However, it would be even more enlightening to examine the correlation between vocabulary learning and the acquisition of native-like pronunciation/perception.

Finally, a follow-up protocol is necessary in order to demonstrate the importance of phonologically-related networks on lexical activation. What has been defined here as being 'recently practiced' vocabulary might be seen as being far from being fully acquired, in terms of many SLA researchers (Thornbury, 2002). A long-term study should help understand how much of that vocabulary remains after initial instruction has taken place.

Notes

1. The target word is always chosen from a list of previously tested words that have proven to be new for the student. Prior to taking part in these experiments, participants had to fill out a series of questionnaires and perform tests in order to check the list of new words that were to be used in the experimental phase of the study.

2. Some authors prefer to use black and white pictures framed in different colors (e.g. green and red, to distinguish distractor from target pictures).
3. Richards (1976) defended that getting to know lexical competence should be a priority for L2 researchers as it can help foresee vocabulary learning difficulties as well as evaluate material design and testing.

Chapter 8
Concordances versus Dictionaries: Evaluating Approaches to Word Learning in ESOL

RACHEL ALLAN

Introduction

Over recent decades, the importance of vocabulary in gaining language proficiency has been highlighted. It is now widely accepted that there is a need for learners to acquire a core vocabulary of high frequency words as quickly as possible (e.g. Coady *et al.*, 1993: 225; Meara, 1995; Nation & Newton, 1997: 239). Alongside this is a wider awareness of the complexity of lexical knowledge, and the fact that we need to consider depth of knowledge in addition to breadth of vocabulary (e.g. Henriksen, 1999; Read, 2004). In other words, most learners need more than to simply recognize meanings – they need to know how to use the words appropriately to express their own meanings. This implies that word knowledge should extend to pronunciation, spelling, word form and its manipulation, register, and collocation (Nation, 1990: 31).

In this context, there seems to be a strong argument for explicit teaching of vocabulary in the classroom, with the aim not only of increasing depth of knowledge of core vocabulary, but also developing skills in our learners to help them find strategies for learning vocabulary autonomously. This is essential, given the extent of the English language lexicon, and the impossibility of teaching such a body of knowledge in a finite period of time. Explicit approaches to vocabulary learning are increasingly becoming a subject of empirical investigation (e.g. Barcroft, 2007; Cobb, 1997; Paribakht & Wesche, 1997); the study described here seeks to add to this growing body of research.

Research Question

The main question addressed by this study was whether vocabulary tasks using concordances in a 'data-driven learning' (DDL) style task as described below result in greater depth of lexical knowledge than similar tasks using dictionaries. It was hypothesized that the tasks using concordances would require greater depth of processing and would, therefore, lead to greater gains in the aspects of word knowledge tested, particularly collocation and use in context.

This study follows on from an earlier one, which indicated the value of concordance tasks at advanced level (CEFR level C1, Council of Europe, 2001) (Allan, 2006). The current study was applied to three levels of English language learner, intermediate, upper intermediate and advanced (CEFR levels B1, B2 and C1) in an attempt to see whether proficiency level influenced the effects of the different task types. It was hypothesized that use of graded corpora as described below would increase the accessibility of the concordances at B1 and B2 level, so that similar results could be anticipated at each level.

Concordances and DDL

The tasks using concordances in this study were based on 'data-driven learning' (Johns, 1988, 1991, 1994). DDL most typically refers to the use of a corpus of texts with concordancing software, to find answers to linguistic questions. In its purest form, the learners themselves use concordancing software, identifying and inputting their own target words, with examples from the corpus returned in a keyword in context (KWIC) format, with the target word in the middle of the line (see Figure 8.1). The learner can then sort these lines in a variety of ways to reveal patterns in meaning and usage. The learner is viewed as a 'research worker whose learning needs to be driven by access to linguistic data', whose role is to 'identify – classify – generalize' (Johns, 1991: 4) that data. In other words, learners themselves interact with the concordance and find answers to their questions about the target word by looking for patterns in it, categorizing them and deriving their own hypothesis, rather than relying on a teacher's intuition or research.

At a theoretical level, DDL is appealing in many ways. It is supported by current approaches within language teaching pedagogy, being inductive, learner-centered, using authentic language input and encouraging learners to 'notice' linguistic features. It can be viewed as a task-based approach with language as topic (Sheehan, 2005), and one in which 'learning by doing interacts thoroughly with learning by reflection' (Little, 1996: 210), a feature encouraging autonomous behavior. Not only does it use authentic input, but it is a 'pedagogical application of a research method' (Mishan, 2004: 222) – an authentic task in its own right. It would seem, then, to be an ideal method for lexical learning, providing multiple exposures to the word in context, while requiring learners to expend cognitive effort in identifying patterns and uses. It would seem to have great potential for increasing knowledge of collocations and contextual use of words.

BNC

1 Despite French government threats to prevent the <w NN1>*deal* going through, and criticisms by Belgium and Italy, few
2 effectively outside their day to day routine. A great *deal* has been said about the need to improve language skills
3 receiving the face value in local currency. The <w NN1>*deal* means the French bank will get some of the money it is
4 of the indigenous peoples; there was a great <w NN1>*deal* of theological questioning and guilt and struggle around
5 energy is nuclear. Normal stars contain a great <w NN1>*deal* of hydrogen, the lightest and most abundant substance

B2

1 he was sincere. We shared this interest. I knew a great *deal* about Italian wines myself, and bought large amounts
2 'He is rather unusual, perhaps. He has travelled a great *deal*, and seen much of the world. I suppose he is clever,
3 reported anywhere." Soon the two men shook hands. The *deal* was done. Wilson Argrow found Joe Roy Spicer in the
4 'of the highest importance' could he possibly have to *deal* with? I feared that the continued weight of misfortune
5 he answered. It was a difficult situation. The only way to *deal* with it was to use the direct method of shock. 'Where

B1

1 would still allow them to broadcast the show, but the *deal* meant that they were losing control of their most
2 with the big entertainment company Time Warner. The *deal* meant that she was now the boss of her own
3 her skills as a businesswoman when she signed a *deal* with a value of $60 million with the big
4 world and nobody can really explain it. So how can we *deal* with these changes? Handy tells us to forget about
5 on Chaos was clear, too: this book will help you to *deal* with the problem. Events in the years after 1987

Figure 8.1 Sample concordance lines on *deal* from the BNC (Data cited herein have been extracted from the British National Corpus, distributed by Oxford University Computing Services on behalf of the BNC Consortium. All rights in the texts cited are reserved.), B2 and B1 corpora. [These concordance lines are drawn from a variety of Penguin graded reader texts at levels 4 (B1) and 5 (B2), donated for research purposes by Pearson Education Ltd., and are reproduced here with permission, all rights reserved. (Titles cited: Evans, D., *Management Gurus & Women in Business*; Poe, E.A., *Tales of Mystery and Imagination*; Bronte, C., *Jane Eyre*; Grisham, J., *The Brethren*; Thornley, G.C. (ed.) *Outstanding Short Stories*.)]

Despite its numerous advantages, the difficulty with DDL lies in its initial inaccessibility. Learners are faced with large quantities of text which are not in sentences to be read from left to right, but snippets of text, with a central keyword, intended to be scanned from top to bottom. This can be extremely off-putting for a learner who is struggling to make sense of the language, and can lead to a great deal of initial resistance to DDL. In this study, learners used preprinted and presorted concordances of limited length, to answer questions which encouraged them to process the text in an appropriate way. This made the tasks more manageable for the learners, at the same time providing them with an induction into the principles of DDL.

Concordances with graded reader corpora

Even when using preconstructed tasks, the accessibility of the concordance will depend on the corpus used. A large corpus, like the British

National Corpus (BNC, 2001), which consists of 100 million words of running text, may contain the quantity and range of authentic texts required to reflect general language use, but it is extremely demanding to work with. While more proficient learners may be able to cope with this, those at an intermediate level, situated at B1 or B2 of the Common European Framework (Council of Europe, 2001), for example, are unlikely to be able to deal with the peripheral linguistic content of a search from the BNC or other large corpus. The B1 learner, for example, is described as being able to deal with 'high frequency everyday or job-related language' (Council of Europe, 2001: 26), while the B2 learner can deal with more complex and lower frequency language provided 'the topic is reasonably familiar' (*op. cit.*). As the sample concordance lines from the BNC shown in Figure 8.1, there is quite a high proportion of language on topics which are quite unfamiliar and far from everyday.

It has been suggested that grading the corpus, using 'limited and manageable' text sources (Gavioli & Aston, 2001: 244), might be a way of overcoming this problem. One such text source is the graded reader, as these contain a limited number of headwords and are designed to be appropriate to certain learner levels. In this study, two corpora of graded reader texts were constructed, one at B1 level, the other at B2 level. This meant that the ratio of known/unknown words was adjusted for learners with a more limited vocabulary, which would make them more able to work with the data. Looking at the following sample concordance lines from the graded corpora compared with the BNC illustrates this increased accessibility, as shown in Figure 8.1.

In the graded concordance lines there is no highly specialized or very infrequent vocabulary present. At times, the context gives very clear clues as to the meaning of the word, for instance, that when a deal is done, people shake hands (B2 line 3). Sentences are shorter; the lines include some complete sentences, and those that are cut off can be more easily predicted. Difficulties may still arise, for example in B2 line 4, from issues of style and register, but overall it is clear that the lines are much more manageable for learners. Although there is some compromise in that the range of text type available is more limited and has a fictional bias (although non-fiction is included), using a graded corpus of this kind would seem to go some way to overcoming the problems of inaccessibility for lower level learners.

Learner dictionaries

The learner dictionaries used as a comparative measure were monolingual English dictionaries, appropriate to the level of the group. As is common practice in many ESOL classrooms, such dictionaries are routinely supplied and referred to by learners in this research environment. Learner dictionaries have become increasingly sophisticated, containing a great deal of in-depth information about each headword, which is presented to the learner in an accessible manner. As such dictionaries are now based on very large corpora of texts, they provide the same kind of examples from real usage as we find in the concordances. Similarly, they are graded, with a limited number of words used as defining vocabulary. However, they differ from concordances in that the information from multiple examples has already been interpreted for the learner. While the learner may be given full information about the range of meanings and uses of a word, only very few illustrative examples are given. Concordances, on the other hand, require the learners to interpret multiple examples for themselves. The full range of meanings may not be present in the limited number of concordance lines learners work with, but it is contended that the information discovered about meaning and collocation will be more memorable as deeper processing is required (Craik & Lockhart, 1972).

To reflect classroom norms, the study used a range of up-to-date, level-appropriate dictionaries from Oxford University Press and Cambridge University Press. The tasks, as described below, asked learners to find specific information about certain words from their dictionary entries, to encourage them to exploit the full range of information given in the dictionary, not simply meaning.

Methodology

The methodology of this study was dictated to a large extent by the environment in which it was carried out, namely the Applied Language Centre (ALC) at University College Dublin. Owing to the longitudinal nature of the study, its participants needed to be committed to attending over a specific period, so students enrolled on ALC courses were used rather than volunteers. Thus, the components of the project had to be tailored to the needs of these students and achievable within the time constraints of their course. Teachers were also consulted in designing tests and tasks, to ensure their support in implementing them in class. Thus, tests and tasks are described below to explain their principles and samples are given in the appendices, but it should be noted that these were devised with a specific learner group in mind.

Participants

The participants were 58 adult learners of English, following a 10-week part-time English course at the ALC while residing in Ireland. They were of mixed nationality. At B2 and C1 level, the learners were preparing for Cambridge ESOL Examinations (at First Certificate and Advanced level), while B1 learners were following a general English course. Students were told at the outset that they would be asked to do some tasks and tests which had the dual purpose of helping them learn useful vocabulary, and as part of a project researching the effects of different ways of learning words.

Teachers attended an induction and were given clear guidelines for implementation of the study to reduce the potential for variability in the treatment in different classes. However, although teachers avoided specific treatment of the target words other than through the tasks, as these learners were living in an English-speaking environment, there were many opportunities for incidental word learning.

Target words

The learners involved in this study came from a diversity of backgrounds, and it was impossible to anticipate which words would be completely new to all of them; given that the study was taking place in a 'real-life' environment, with students preparing for exams, it would have been inappropriate to use pseudo-words. The emphasis of the study was therefore on depth of vocabulary knowledge (DVK). It was expected that some of the TWs would be already known to some degree by learners; the pretests aimed to establish how much was known about them, and the posttest would then measure any gains in depth of knowledge which had taken place. As the focus of the study was on gains in depth of word acquisition, target items were those with a high 'learning burden' due to multiple meanings and uses. This was balanced with their frequency level and usefulness to learners by referring to corpora of past Cambridge examination papers at the three levels, and consultation with course teachers. A range of word classes was included, with many straddling two word classes (e.g. trip *v.* & *n.*, cold *adj.* & *n.*). The 10 target items treated at each level are given in Appendix A.

Vocabulary tasks

The vocabulary tasks aimed to deepen knowledge of the words, their meanings, collocations and contextual use. Each task focused on two of the target words, asking a series of questions encouraging awareness of certain aspects of word knowledge, appropriate to the concordance or dictionary they were given as a resource. The tasks were intended to take 10–15 min, and to be carried out as pair work.

Concordance resources were limited to a maximum number of randomly selected lines. At C1 level the maximum number of lines given was 30, at B2 level on average 20 lines from the B2 graded corpus were used per target word, and at B1 level this was reduced to an average of 15 lines from the B1 graded corpus. These limits were set to ensure that learners did not feel overwhelmed by the text, as for less experienced users 'the risk of drowning in data is high' (Tribble, 1997: 2).

Samples of both a concordance task and a dictionary task are given in Appendix B.

Test 1: Cloze test

Two tests were constructed at each level, to be used as pre- and post-treatment tests. The first of these was a cloze test, on the basis that this would require production of the target word, potentially indicating knowledge of semantic meaning, an ability to spell it correctly and to manipulate its form according to the grammatical context. The type of cloze used was a selective deletion cloze, with one or two letters of the target word given.

Test 2: Word associates test

Following other recent longitudinal studies of increases in word knowledge (e.g. Greidanus *et al.*, 2004; Schmitt & Meara, 1997), the second measure adopted was a word associates test based on Read (1993, 1998). This is a measure of receptive word knowledge, whereby the student uses the stimulus (test item) to choose which words are associated with it. The version adopted followed the principles of Qian and Schedl's (2004) Depth of Vocabulary Knowledge Measure (DVK), with paradigmatic (synonyms) and syntagmatic (collocates) associations to ensure clarity as to whether changes in knowledge were connected with meaning or collocation. In this version, there is one stimulus word (an adjective) and eight potential associates, arranged in two boxes with four words in each. The left box contains words which may be synonymous to the stimulus word or an aspect of it, while the right box contains collocations. One to three of the answers in each box are correct, and there is always a total of four correct answers, though the balance of correct answers in the two boxes varies, thus overcoming the problem of guesswork when the number of correct answers is always the same.

This model was adapted in that a range of word classes were used as stimuli, not only adjectives. This had various implications for test design. The target words, as explained above, had been chosen in part because of their polysemy, with many of them polysemous across word classes. As the test needed to incorporate this aspect of polysemy, in the synonym box there is a mix of word classes. For example, *book* is used as a verb, *reserve*, and a noun, *novel*. Another implication for testing different word classes was the positioning of collocates, which was variable, for example, *book tickets, library book*. These features were highlighted in the instructions to the test, and the examples given in Figure 8.2 appeared in the instructions page to make this clear.

Heavy

| Easy | deep | Hard | high | wind | Rain | smoker | suitcase |

The four correct answers would be, from the left-hand box, the synonym *hard*, and in the right-hand box, the collocates *rain, smoker* and *suitcase*.

Book

| novel | bank | Envelope | reserve | newspaper | library | through | tickets |

Book can be used as a noun, *a novel*, or a verb, *to reserve*, so these are the correct answers in the left box. We talk about *a library book*, and *to book tickets* (for a plane, concert etc.), but we do not use *a newspaper book* or *book through*.

Figure 8.2 Examples of DVK test items

Procedure

Three classes at C1 level, three classes at B2 level and two classes at B1 level took part in the study. As the ALC is part of a University in an English-speaking country, most English language learners attending it are of at least B2 level or higher, and at the time of the study it was not possible to recruit a comparable number at B1 level. Each of these classes took the two pretests described above during the first two weeks of lessons. The classes were then designated as concordance group, dictionary group or control group (at C1 and B2 levels). The treatment groups (dictionary and concordance groups) carried out a series of five tasks appropriate to their level, based on dictionaries or concordances as described above, during lessons over a five-week period. The control group received no explicit tuition on the target words. At the end of this period, all groups took the two tests again over a two-week period. The project was carried out over a nine-week period, so that results could be distributed to the students in the final week of their course.

Quantitative Results

The results indicated that on average, gains were made on the target words in all treatment groups. A paired *t*-test was used to test the data, and results are shown in Table 8.1. When testing at $\alpha = 5\%$ level, there was

Table 8.1 Target word test results

	B1 Conc	B1 Dic	B2 Conc	B2 Dic	B2 Ctrl	C1 Conc	C1 Dic	C1 Ctrl
N	5	7	7	9	9	9	5	7
Cloze *t*-ratio	2.6*	5.5*	2.2*	3.5*	0.84	4.9*	2.2	−2.98*
DVK *t*-ratio	2.2	1.9	9.1*	4.1*	1.2	3.8*	1.8	−0.4

*$p < 0.05$.
Conc = concordance group; Ctrl = control group; Dic = dictionary group.

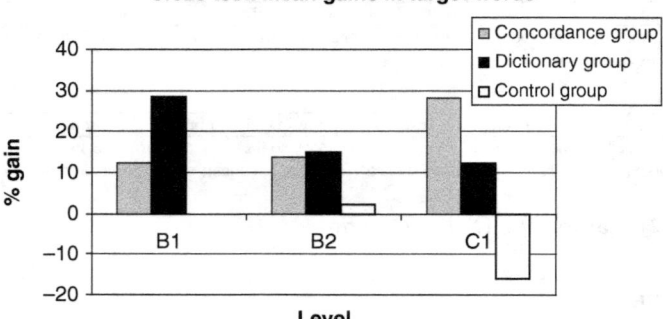

Figure 8.3 Gains in the target words achieved by the different groups on the cloze test

sufficient evidence to suggest a difference between the average pretest and average posttest cloze scores for all groups except the C1 dictionary group and the B2 control group. The C1 control group, interestingly, made significant losses. On investigation, this appeared to be due to lack of engagement in the test; as they had undergone no treatment, they did not see the value in a posttest. On the DVK test, again gains were found to be significant for all groups except the B1 and C1 dictionary groups, and both control groups.

Perhaps the most interesting aspect of the results is the difference in performance at different levels. This is evident in Figure 8.3, showing results on the cloze test. Gains among B1 and C1 learner groups show a mirror image, with the greatest gains evident in the concordance group in C1 learners, and in the dictionary group among B1 learners.

Among B2 learner groups, while gains on both tests and in both groups were found to be significant, the most dramatic gain is evident in Figure 8.4, in the concordance group on the DVK, suggesting that use of concordances was particularly effective in raising learners' awareness of synonymy and collocation at this level.

Learner Response

It was particularly interesting to assess learners' responses to the concordance tasks, as none of the learners had been familiar with concordances. As discussed above, concordances are not initially user-friendly, and I wanted to find out whether learners had been able to overcome this. To gather data on these questionnaires were issued to all teachers and learners involved.

The teachers working with the learners on the concordance tasks felt that learners had been interested in the tasks initially, as it was a novel

Concordances versus Dictionaries

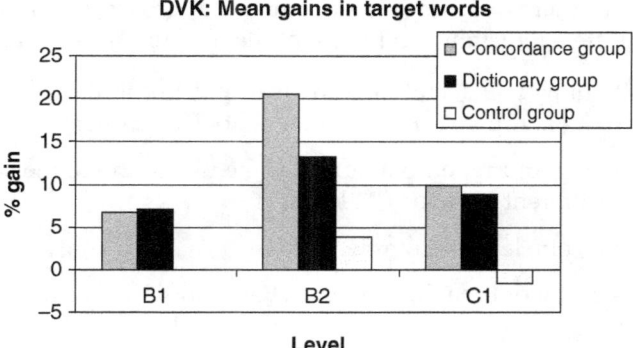

Figure 8.4 Gains in the target words achieved by the different groups on the DVK test

approach, but tired of them over the series, partly because they found the tasks time-consuming and difficult to complete in the time allocated. Teachers also commented on certain aspects of the tasks which contrasted with normal classroom activity, notably their predetermined, explicit nature, which may have made it difficult for learners to see a context for them, and the tendency for learners to carry out the tasks individually, rather than in pairs as instructed. At B1 level it was felt that more initial support, through a detailed induction into the concordances, may have led to improved results. However, the teachers felt that the tasks did raise awareness as intended.

Questionnaire results from the learners were quite mixed, suggesting that this approach is very much dependent on individual learning styles and preferences. Overall, the higher levels seemed to appreciate the value of the concordances more than the lower levels, as indicated in the comments below:

> It's good to learn words that naturally belong together but it's not a helpful way to expand your vocabulary knowledge (C1 learner)

This somewhat ambiguous statement indicates that the view that breadth of knowledge is what counts as 'vocabulary knowledge', although it indicates that the learner realizes the importance of the co-occurring words. Similarly, the learner below recognizes this, and adopts use of concordances for a particular purpose. Other learners at C1 level indicated that they found concordances most useful as a resource when writing, for the same reasons.

> I use concordances to see how a certain word is used, not to guess its meaning (C1 learner)

At B2 level, there was more resistance to the approach, but the comments below indicate a reluctant acceptance of the usefulness of the approach:

> I don't think I like that way of learning vocabulary but it's very demanding and involving so it may work (B1 learner)

> It's too long and repetitive but it can be useful to see the same word used in different contexts (B2 learner)

At B1 level, one learner commented:

> *If I have a lot of time this system is better for improve my vocabulary (B1 learner)

Most B1 learners agreed that the concordance tasks took too long, and indicated that they would prefer to see the words in a complete sentence. However, they all found the KWIC format helpful, and could understand the other words in the concordances, presumably due to the corpus grading.

Discussion

Results supported the underlying hypothesis of the project, that explicit word learning deepens vocabulary knowledge, as all treatment groups made greater gains than the control groups. They also indicated, however, that word gains were relatively small, and they showed the unstable nature of vocabulary knowledge, with many participants across groups and levels making losses on a few words, in accordance with other research findings (e.g. Meara & Rodriguez Sanchez, 1993).

The hypothesis I set out to test, that use of concordance tasks would result in deeper knowledge of the target words, is generally supported among C1 and B2 levels. The performance by B2 learners also provides support for the argument that use of graded corpora increases its accessibility. However, at B1 level, the results suggest the opposite, that the dictionary tasks resulted in greater word gains, at least in productive terms. The lack of significant gains in the DVK test suggests that neither task type has a great effect on knowledge of synonyms or collocations. In contrast to B2 level, at this level use of graded corpora did not appear to have had a positive effect.

These results raise a number of interesting questions for further investigation. The most obvious implication is that a lower proficiency level may result in less ability to identify patterns in data, suggesting that there is a threshold below which dictionary tasks are more appropriate. However, there are a number of other possibilities that should be considered.

On the concordance tasks, there is a question of whether the B1 learners found the quantity of data too difficult to deal with, although the level may have been appropriate, and whether more positive results might be achieved with less data. As concordances are an unfamiliar text type, it may have been that the learners were less able to orientate themselves within it, and required more induction before beginning the study. Another consideration regarding the concordances is that grading the corpus to B1 level may have resulted in oversimplification of language, providing impoverished data that was unable to supply learners with the information required.

Limitations of study

This was a small-scale study, and can only be indicative of results we may get in a larger study. Clearly, the study needs to adopt alternative control measures and be carried out among larger groups to provide robust data. This is currently being pursued at the ALC. One of the difficulties of replication in other environments is the desirability of tailoring the study to the learners' needs in order to make it useful to both participants and researchers. However, it is possible that the principles of the project could be followed, with its components adapted to make them suitable to a different learner profile. It would also be useful to include a more detailed qualitative element to the study, to gather information from the participants on their approaches to the task, and investigate their attitudes further.

Classroom implications

Given the limitations of the study and the need for further research, only tentative conclusions can be drawn. However, it does provide some evidence of the benefits of including short explicit vocabulary tasks using both dictionaries and concordances, both in terms of awareness raising of aspects of word knowledge, and lexical gain. Both approaches have their merits, and I would suggest that a combination is advisable, given the negative effect of repeating concordance tasks. However, it appears to be well worth introducing concordances, certainly at B2 and C1 level. Anecdotal evidence from teachers and learners suggests that they raise awareness of different aspects of word knowledge, and these initial test results suggest that they deepen that knowledge. Our experience in this study suggests, however, that they need to be used with care. An initial induction into what concordances are and how to use them will benefit learners, and short, focused tasks using a limited number of concordance lines, with a clear relevance to learners' needs are likely to be most successful in the early stages of their use. At B2 level, an appropriately graded corpus appears to be a useful tool in increasing accessibility.

For learners of intermediate proficiency, in contrast, this study suggests that developing skills in the use of learner dictionaries may bring greater rewards. If concordances are used, it is advisable to provide plenty of initial training, and keep the amount of data provided manageable. I would suggest that manageability can be usefully provided through a graded corpus, but it may be that grading the corpus to B1 level impoverishes the data too much, and grading to a B2 level may be more appropriate to retain the lexical richness required. I would propose that use of concordance tasks at this level may increase awareness of the complexity of lexical knowledge, and the need for depth as well as breadth of vocabulary knowledge, at an earlier stage of language proficiency. However, to state this with certainty, further research is required to investigate these issues.

Appendix A: Target Words

B1	B2	C1
attitude	badly	apart
habit	bear	benefit
plenty	carry	beyond
remove	comfort	bitter
rough	fall	condition
route	gloomy	distinct
serious	highly	entirely
take	praise	firmly
wide	rare	perceive
whenever	routine	pursue

Appendix B: Sample Tasks at B2 level

Concordance Task: Comfort

1   and playthings and was happy in the peace and *comfort* of the big house. Lara enjoyed her role of wife
2   our father had gone away, and was of great use and *comfort*, and Lady Lucas has been very kind, and
3   child will bring you and your wife great joy and *comfort*, and when she grows into a woman she will
4   decision. 'It's nothing to worry about, Mary,' *Andrew comforted* her. You won't feel any pain. I'll be in the
5   his hands to save her, and she seized him, feeling for *comfort*, cold now from the shock. 'He s dead,' she
6   about the room. Andrew smiled.'Don't worry!' *he comforted* them. He knew that this case would demand
7   to go on taking medicine!' It was surprising how *much comfort* this gave him. After the surgery, he went in to

8	ghost might rise before me. This idea, instead of *comforting* me, filled me with fear. At this moment, a
9	Collins could be forgotten, there was a great feeling of *comfort* everywhere -and by Charlotte's enjoyment,
10	remembered. A cold, empty letter, giving no word of *comfort*, and little information, except that she must not
11	he shouted at her. You only think about your own *comfort* when this terrible thing has happened to our
12	what he has done.' But as Elizabeth could not receive *comfort* from any such expectations, she did not
13	said, 'Follower, when and where are we going to rest?' '*Comfort*, answered Monkey, 'is for ordinary people, so
14	of my visit, of his great desire to see me, and of the *comfort* that he expected me to bring him. He began a
15	her name. During this time I made great efforts to *comfort* and cheer my friend. We painted and read
16	never see Dickie again. Her husband came over to *comfort* her. "Mrs. Greenleaf," Tom said softly, "I want
17	laid his hand on her knee. T will tell you one thing to *comfort* you. A week from now will bring the New Year.
18	thinner in the face. But Chris was always there to *comfort* and encourage him. By August, which was a

Article 1. *Comfort* can be used in two ways, that is as two different parts of speech. What are they?

Article 2. What kind of phrases might you use *to comfort someone*? (Look at lines 4 and 6)

Article 3. In what situations do you think you might need to comfort someone?

Article 4. In line 11, the speakers shouted 'You only think about your own comfort ...' What adjective could you use to describe someone like this?

Article 5. What kind of things are *of comfort* (line 9), or *give you comfort* (line 7) when you are worried or unhappy?

Article 6. Are there any *home comforts* that you miss, living in Ireland?

Dictionary Task: Comfort

Try to answer the following questions with your partner first, then use a dictionary to check and add to your answers.

1. *Comfort* can be used in two ways, that is as two different parts of speech. What are they?
2. Find two or more phrases using *comfort* in these two different ways:

Home comforts	comfort a baby

3. Which *home comforts* could you not live without?
4. When you are upset, who or what *comforts* you?
5. What *words of comfort* might you use to someone who was upset?

Chapter 9
Evidence of Incremental Vocabulary Learning in Advanced L2 Spanish Learners[1]

DIANA FRANTZEN

Introduction

Research suggests that much vocabulary learning takes place on an incremental basis. This has been found to be the case both for first language (L1) vocabulary learning (e.g. Deighton, 1959; Drum & Konopak, 1987; Herman *et al.*, 1987; Nagy *et al.*, 1985) as well as for second language (L2) vocabulary learning (e.g. Coady, 1993; Huckin & Bloch, 1993; Huckin & Coady, 1999; Parry, 1993; Schmitt, 2000). Drum and Konopak provided a colorful analogy when describing the incremental nature of L1 vocabulary learning, asserting that 'Access to word knowledge cannot be compared to an on/off toggle switch. A more appropriate analogy is the increasing luminescence of a rheostat' (1987: 79). Coady reported that 'The incidental acquisition hypothesis suggests that there is gradual but steady incremental growth of vocabulary knowledge through meaningful interaction with text, but there is little research as yet to illustrate how this occurs for either L1 or L2' (1993: 18).

The present chapter describes evidence of incremental vocabulary learning that was revealed incidentally, essentially as a by-product of a classroom-based study designed to investigate other vocabulary-learning phenomena. The original study was not designed to elicit these data, yet such evidence was exhibited by the answers provided on the testing instruments by the students who participated in the study. The data examined for the present chapter were gathered in a classroom experiment on vocabulary acquisition reported in Frantzen (1998, 2003). The original study was designed to determine whether previous exposure to words in a short story would enhance vocabulary learning while reading. It elicited data in two types of pre- and posttests (no-context and with-context) and their results were analyzed separately. Frantzen (1998) centered on vocabulary *learning*, and therefore discussed the students' performance over time on the no-context tests only. Frantzen (2003) focused on the students' *inferencing ability* when the tested words were supplied in context, thus, that study discussed the students' performance on the with-context tests. While investigating the two areas of focus in the other two articles, I came upon evidence of incremental vocabulary learning, and in light of Coady's (1993) statement, decided to examine the data more carefully to assess its nature and to determine the ways in which it manifested itself.

The research question that guided the analysis for the present chapter study was: What evidence of incremental vocabulary learning is revealed by advanced-level foreign language learners' performance over time on no-context and with-context vocabulary tests?

Method

The present chapter focuses on evidence of incremental learning (as evidenced in the students' answers on both sets of pre- and posttests), an element of vocabulary learning that was beyond the scope of the earlier articles. Information about the procedures and findings described in the previous articles will be presented here insofar as they are relevant to the present discussion. (For fuller discussions, see Frantzen, 1998, 2003.)

Participants

The participants were 11 students (10 female, one male; two were of Hispanic background) in an advanced (third-year) Spanish grammar class at a large public university in the Midwest.[2] Being an advanced-level grammar course, it provided an in-depth study of Spanish grammar and a vocabulary review. In addition, several readings were included in the course in order to allow for the examination of grammatical structures in context and to provide interesting topics for class discussion that would afford opportunities to practice grammar and vocabulary. The course was taught by the researcher.

Procedures

Two unannounced pretests were administrated during one class period. Test 1 (a no-context pretest) contained 40 Spanish words presented in an isolated-word format. The students were instructed to write the English meanings of as many of the words as they could. Test 2 (a with-context pretest) was administered immediately after Test 1; it contained 30 of the words from Test 1, but this time, they were presented in context. (The context was the Spanish short story in which the words appeared).[3] The students received a copy of the short story, which they had not read [similar to Appendix A in Frantzen (2003), except that the glossing had been removed], in which 30 of the pretest words had been underlined.[4]

The instructions indicated that they should write down the meanings of all the words they knew, as well as those whose meanings they could determine from the context. In addition, alongside these answers, the students were asked to write a brief explanation as to how they had determined the meaning of the words. After the administration of the two pretests, the short story was assigned as homework for the next class. Approximately four weeks later, the unannounced posttests were administered, also during one class period. Test 3 (the no-context posttest) tested a total of 50 words (the 40 original words plus 10 other words from the story). Test 4 (with-context posttest) tested these same words. For this administration, rather than providing a copy of the story again (which was deemed unnecessary at this point), the context for Test 4 consisted of sentences extracted from the story in which the words had been underlined, providing the sentences with the words right next to each tested word in order to make efficient use of the limited time available for taking the tests. (For the lists of tested words by test, see Frantzen, 1998, Figure 1; Appendix A [here] contains Test 4 as administered.)

Upon the administration of both the pre- and posttests, the researcher informed the students that these tests would not be used as part of their course grade, but asked them to complete them in earnest, as if they would receive a grade. None of the tests was returned to the students.

When the story was assigned as homework for the next class, as with the other readings assigned for class, the instructor (researcher) instructed the students to read the story and prepare the questions that accompanied the story in the textbook where it appeared. The instructor focused the class discussion on the story's content, attempting not to focus undue attention on the tested words.

Frantzen (1998) investigated whether pre-exposing students to tested words before they read a short story containing the words would result in significantly more learning of the pre-exposed words as compared to other words from the story to which they were not pre-exposed. The results of that study indicated that the pre-exposure had been valuable because the students learned a significantly higher percentage of pre-exposed words than non-pre-exposed words.

For the present chapter, students' successful learning of the tested words' meanings was not the focus; instead, partial learning that was exhibited in stages was of interest as well as successful learning that had been preceded by a stage of lack of knowledge. Because this evidence occurred incidentally – it was not intentionally elicited – the quantity is not large. Nonetheless, tracking the students' answers on the pre- and posttests revealed some patterns of vocabulary-learning behavior that suggest they had made incremental gains in vocabulary knowledge during the interim between the administration of the pretests and the posttests.

In the following sections, several types of incremental learning exhibited by the students' answers will be presented and discussed.

Results and Discussion: Evidence of Incremental Learning

Recall that the third-year Spanish students who participated in the study took two sets of pre- and posttest vocabulary tests, with an intervening stage during which they read the story which contained the tested words. The incremental gains manifested themselves in various ways.

Use of approximations

In several instances, students supplied words on the pre- and posttests that, although incorrect, approached the actual meaning of the word. These close-but-incorrect answers are often referred to as 'approximations'.[5] For example, when one student supplied 'form of transportation' for the word *guagua* (bus),[6] this answer was identified as an approximation.

Approximations only account for a small percentage of the total number of incorrect answers on all four tests but did appear on both the no-context and with-context tests (see Appendix B). Not surprisingly, the students supplied a greater number of partially/nearly correct answers on the tests in which the context helped steer them in the direction of the meaning: 4.79% of all errors on the no-context tests were approximations as compared to 20.68% of the errors on the with-context tests.

The majority of the approximations that appeared on Test 3 (the no-context posttest) show a relationship to the story. Two illustrative examples involve the target words *sato* and *moscones*. On Test 3, two students supplied 'breed' for *sato* (mongrel, mutt), and for *moscones* (large flies), students supplied five different 'insect-like' words: bugs, wasps, insects, moth and mosquitos. Neither of these tested words had yielded any of these approximations – or any other approximations, for that matter – on Test 1, the no-context pretest. The word *sato* was used in the story to describe Tedy; his lack of a pedigree was pointed out and contrasted with the good breeding of the family's other dog. These students apparently remembered that *sato* had been used in reference to breeding but had not recalled the lack of *good* breeding intrinsic to its meaning. As for *moscones*, in the story, Tedy was described as a dog that enjoyed chasing butterflies and contemplating *moscones* with iridescent wings. By their insect-related answers, the students showed they had learned the insect-like aspect of the word but had not yet zeroed in on the exact meaning. (See Appendix B for a complete list including these and other examples of approximations provided as answers on both the no-context and with-context tests.)

In all, students supplied 13 approximations on Test 1 (no-context pretest) and 15.5 on Test 3 (no-context posttest). While both sets of approximations indicate partial knowledge of the words, those on Test 1 showed the partial knowledge students had before taking the pretests and before reading the story; those on Test 3 not only indicate the partial knowledge yielded on Test 1 but, in addition, reflect partial knowledge they had picked up from reading the story for the class. Eight of the thirteen approximations on Test 1 were followed on Test 3 with correct answers. It is therefore possible that at the time of Test 1, some of these students had already partially learned them; some combination of factors – the pre-exposure of the vocabulary tests, the reading of the story, and/or discussing it in class, and so forth – seems to have helped them learn the words more fully. Thus, at the time of the pretest, these words appear to have been on the verge of being known more fully, again lending support to the assertion by many researchers that much L2 vocabulary learning takes place in increments (Coady, 1993; Huckin & Bloch, 1993; Parry, 1993; Schmitt, 2000).

Although the number of approximations used throughout is very small, tracking the students' use of approximations over time revealed two patterns or tendencies: For some students (3 of the 9) if an approximation appeared prior to Test 3, it tended to be followed by a correct translation on Test 3. However, for the majority of the students – the remaining eight – approximations tended to be followed by incorrect answers. Thus, for some students, the approximation appeared to be temporary stops on the way to the final destination of accuracy. The other students seemed satisfied to have a general or approximate understanding for the words they did not know, within the context of the present study's design.

Some guesses do not remain viable

Evidence of incremental learning also emerged when students supplied answers on subsequent tests that suggested they realized that some of their previous guesses were not correct. This knowledge manifested itself as follows: whereas some students were willing to hazard certain guesses on Test 1 (the first no-context test), once the context (the story) had been provided, in many instances, the original wrong answers were not supplied again. This behavior suggests an awareness that their original answers were no longer viable. This occurred in two patterns which will be discussed below.

(1) *Reliance on 'synforms' and faulty morpheme analysis becomes a less common strategy.* Another indication of incremental learning involves errors that can be attributed to faulty morpheme analysis and/or an inappropriate association with similar-looking English or Spanish words. Analysis of the incorrect guesses on the no-context tests indicated that the students' primary strategies were to associate a word with one that resembles an

English or Spanish word or to analyze a word in terms of roots and affixes, which is similar to what Haynes (1984) found. Haynes used the term 'mismatches' for incorrect translations of similar-looking Spanish or English words; Laufer (1988, 1991) called them 'synforms' ('similar lexical forms')[7]; Huckin and Bloch (1993) refered to them as 'mistaken IDs'. Two examples of incorrect associations with an English word were a guess that *palo* 'stick' meant 'pale' and that *sato* 'mutt' meant 'sated' or 'satisfied'. Two examples of incorrect associations with another Spanish word were a guess that *alambre* 'wire' meant 'shining' (*alumbrante*) and that *gallina* 'hen' meant 'cookie' (*galleta*). (See these and additional examples of confusion with English or Spanish words in Appendix C.)

Several of the students' incorrect guesses involving synforms on no-context tests show evidence of what they knew about Spanish morphology, although this knowledge was often misapplied due to faulty morpheme analysis. For example, the word *ladrido* 'bark (of a dog)' yielded wrong answers that all appear to – but do not – have the same root (*ladr-*): the similarity is only superficial. Two students guessed that *ladrido* meant 'robber' or 'thief', which is '*ladrón*'; another student guessed that it meant 'brick', which is '*ladrillo*'. Two others made related guesses and equated the *-ido* of *ladrido* with the past participle ending *-ido* and thus guessed 'burglarized' and 'bricked', respectively. Additionally, two students guessed that *gemido* 'moan' meant 'twin', apparently confusing it with *gemelo*, and another analyzed the word as a past participle, as in the previous example – because of the *-ido* – guessing it meant 'twinned'.

Five students guessed on Test 1 that *arrobado* 'entranced'/'enraptured' meant 'robbed' (or something related: 'stolen', 'to be robbed', 'thief'), associating it with the word *robado*. Four of these same students made similar guesses on Test 2 when the story was supplied, even though the context made these guesses illogical. Three of these four students did make incremental gains with regard to this word after Test 2, however, because they did not make these guesses again on either of the subsequent posttests: neither on the no-context posttest nor on the with-context one. In fact, they each made no attempt to define this word on Test 3. Even though they had not learned the word's meaning yet, their answers indicated that they had learned that it did not mean 'robbed'. Then, on Test 4, two students supplied other incorrect (but logical) guesses in the blank and one student left it blank. (One student stuck with the word 'robbed' both on Tests 3 and 4 and thus demonstrated no incremental learning on this word. Frantzen (2003) referred to this type of behavior as 'Oblivious Certainty'.) Appendix C contains numerous other examples of faulty morpheme analysis and/or confusions with English or other Spanish words.

It is not surprising to find that, on tests with an isolated-word (no-context) format, the students would rely on their knowledge of similar-looking English and Spanish words or would resort to attempted morpheme analysis for their guesses because, in the absence of a context, this is the best strategy to employ given that little else is available to call upon for increasing the likelihood of a correct response. In fact, on Test 2 when students were asked to infer the meanings of these same words using the context of the story in which they appeared, the majority of the previously cited examples and of those in Appendix C disappeared. This behavior suggests that the students realized that these answers were no longer viable. When context was supplied, morpheme analysis became a much less used strategy. Occasionally, however, as in the previously cited example of *arrobado*, some of these Spanish- or English-related guesses remained, despite the fact that the words were used in contexts that did not support these meanings.

This pattern of behavior among the students in the present study – that of *not* providing an answer after having supplied a wrong answer previously – is an indication of incremental vocabulary learning. Recognizing that what one thought to be correct is not correct is an important step on the way to learning a word's meaning(s) because it opens up the possibility that a correct answer will eventually replace the incorrect one. Indeed, in some cases, they learned the correct meanings subsequently. When one of their participants provided no answer after previously supplying an incorrect answer, Huckin and Bloch (1993) cautiously speculated that this could be evidence of incremental learning: 'This may not seem like much of an improvement, but if it indicates awareness of a possible misidentification, it could be the kind of incremental change that Nagy *et al.*, and others, have claimed to be typical of vocabulary growth' (p. 172). The frequency of this kind of behavior in the present study, especially considering the instances when a correct answer was eventually supplied, provides clear evidence of incremental learning so that it no longer needs to be the matter of speculation that it was for Huckin and Block. The examples in this section give further evidence to support previously cited research that much L2 vocabulary learning takes place in increments.

(2) *Advanced-level learners can accept multiple meanings of a polyseme.* A new finding was revealed in the examination of the way some of the participants dealt with polysemes. On Test 1, students occasionally supplied English equivalents for the tested words whose meanings, while correct, were not the meanings of the words in the context of the story. (These types of words are called polysemes or homonyms.[8]) Three tested words fell into this category and are presented in Figure 9.1: *pata*, *tapa* and *deshacerse*. (In the examples, the meanings provided in the second column are the ones supplied by the students on Test 1; the meanings in the third column are the meanings of the words in the story.)

Significantly, none of the students who had supplied these meanings on Test 1 supplied them on any of the subsequent tests, apparently because they recognized that the context of the story had ruled out these

Spanish word	English meanings supplied on Test 1	Meaning of word as used in the story
pata	duck	paw
	'luck' (slang)	
tapa	snack	top (e.g. lid)
	appetizer	
deshacerse	to fall apart	to get rid of
	to come undone	

Figure 9.1 Use of polysemes

meanings. Although the students did not always learn the story-context meanings, they did learn that these words had other meanings and that the answers they had supplied on Test 1 were no longer appropriate. In the present study, the participants' discarding of polysemous meanings once they realized that the context did not support them contrasts with the pattern among Bensoussan and Laufer's (1984) and Huckin and Bloch's (1993) participants. Bensoussan and Laufer reported that 'in the case of a polyseme, the student knows one of its meanings and does not abandon this meaning even when it is wrong in context' (1984: 22). Similarly, Huckin and Bloch reported that 'where polysemy is involved, learners who know only one meaning of the word will try to stick to that meaning even in the face of negative context cues' (1993: 169). Although the numbers are relatively small here (both number of students and number of polysemes under consideration), one possible explanation for the difference between the present findings and those of Bensoussan and Laufer, and Huckin and Bloch is the level of L2 proficiency. The participants in Bensoussan and Laufer's study were first-year students; the participants in Huckin and Bloch's were at the intermediate level; in the present study, the students were at the advanced level (in a third-year [sixth-semester] course). Proficiency level seems to be a factor since these researchers found that their beginning- and intermediate-level students exhibited an attachment to one meaning of a polyseme despite context clues that didn't allow it whereas the advanced-level students in the present study were able to reject the meanings they had supplied on the no-context pretest when faced with the contexts.

Further examination was necessary to rule out the possibility that the students already knew both meanings and simply recalled the story meaning when they had the story to refer to. For one of these polysemes (*deshacerse*), one student provided the meaning accurate for the context (to get rid of) on Test 2 and she did indicate prior knowledge when she explained on Test 2 how she had determined this word's meaning. For the other student, his nonanswer on Test 2 shows that he did not have prior knowledge because he could not figure out its meaning when provided with the context. As for *tapa*, both students who had supplied the polysemous 'snack' or 'appetizer' on Test 1 indicate no prior knowledge of the correct meaning in this context: in one case, the student did not provide an answer and, in the other, the student provided a wrong answer which she had inferred from the context. In the case of *pata*, both students who had provided a polyseme on Test 1 provided the correct 'paws' on Test 2. It appears that they did not have prior knowledge, however, because both provided explanations indicating that the context had helped them determine the word's meaning: one student wrote, 'I could figure out that it meant some part of the dog, and paws sounds similar'; the other wrote, 'It has to be a body part of a dog'. In sum, evidence for the three words discussed above suggests – with the one exception, for one student, with *deshacerse* – that the students who supplied the non-story polyseme initially only knew the meanings they had supplied on Test 1.

Conclusion

The students who participated in the study described here made incremental gains in vocabulary knowledge, which manifested themselves in various ways: (1) by their use of approximations which showed partial knowledge of a word's meaning and (2) by the fact that, while they had not always yet learned a word's meaning, many times they showed evidence of an awareness that some of their previous incorrect answers (e.g. those resulting from faulty morpheme analysis, synform errors, and misinterpretations of polysemes) were no longer viable once they were presented with the context of the story. Unlike the findings in previous research (Bensoussan & Laufer, 1984; Huckin & Bloch, 1993) where lower-level learners held a firm attachment to one of the meanings of a polyseme, the advanced students in the present study did not similarly cleave to one meaning; instead, they demonstrated acceptance of multiple meanings of a polyseme. Thus, this analysis has revealed that advanced-level students are capable of differentiating between multiple meanings of a polyseme. These findings not only support L2 vocabulary research that suggests that much vocabulary acquisition occurs incrementally (Coady, 1993; Huckin & Bloch, 1993; Parry, 1993; Schmitt, 2000) but also support Schmitt's affirmation that 'not only is vocabulary acquisition incremental, but it is incremental in a variety of ways' (2000: 120). And, although evidence of steady incremental growth Coady (1993) called for was not revealed in the present analysis, clear evidence of incremental gains in vocabulary knowledge was documented.

Notes

1. Earlier versions of this research were presented at the following conferences: The 14th World Congress of Applied Linguists, Madison, WI, July, 2005 and the American Council on the Teaching of Foreign Languages conference, Baltimore, MD, November, 2005.
2. Although there were 13 students in the class, two had to be eliminated from the study because they were absent for the administration of one or more of the testing instruments.
3. The story – 'Tedy' – by Lupita Lago (in *Repase y escriba: Curso avanzado de gramática y composición*, Dominicis & Reynolds, 1987) is narrated by a woman reminiscing about Tedy, one of her family's dogs. The dog, though well loved by the narrator and her brother, was considered useless by their overly practical mother. This story has been reproduced in Frantzen (2003), Appendix A. Readers who do not know Spanish may wish to refer to my English translation of the story in Frantzen (2003), Appendix B.
4. Only 30 of the words on Test 1 were included on Test 2 because of the time limitations.
5. This usage of the term 'approximation' is similar but not identical to 'approximation' as one of the L2 learner strategies defined by Tarone (1980). The key difference is that in her usage, the learner knows that the word he/she has used is not correct but is satisfied that the word is close enough. In the present context, we do not know whether – and cannot assume that – the learners who used approximations knew they were wrong; in fact, it would be reasonable to assume they were striving to give fully correct answers.
6. The sentence in which *guagua* (bus) occurs appears in Appendix A (sentence 39). Translation: 'It seemed strange to my brother Beto and me not to see his wet little nose at our side when we got off the bus'.
7. Most of Laufer's examples involve intra-language confusions (in this case, in English), but this term can also be used for incorrect associations between words of different languages.
8. As been pointed out in the field of semantics, determining whether an individual word is a polyseme or a homonym can be problematic (Leech, 1974: 228). Leech provides the following definitions: homonymy: 'two or more words having the same pronunciation and/or spelling' (p. 228); polysemy: 'one word having two or more senses' (p. 228). Leech explains that if that the meanings of the word are related (usually assumed to be related historically but can be related psychologically, perhaps by means of metaphoric transfer), then those meanings are generally accepted to be polysemes; if they are not related, then they are considered homonyms. Although the definitions appear to be clearcut, in actual practice, determining whether two words are polysemes or homonyms is not always easy (Leech, 1974: 228–230). Two of the examples discussed here are probably better classified as homonyms rather than polysemes (*tapa* and *pata*). However, the decision was made to use the term polyseme here because some researchers use polyseme as a term encompassing both polysemes and homonyms as defined by Leech. For instance, the examples identified as polysemes in Bensoussan and Laufer appear to be of both types (1984, Appendix II, p. 29).

Appendix A: Copy of Test 4 (with-context posttest)

Write the English equivalents of the following underlined words in the contexts provided (from the story 'Tedy'). If you are not sure of a word's meaning, but can make a reasonable guess, do so. If you have no idea, leave it blank. The sentences are *not* in chronological order. You will have <u>15</u> minutes to do this exercise.

_____1.	El cuerpecillo blanco y café parecía aún más frágil, y temblaba con una mezcla extraña de alegría y <u>pavor</u>.
_____2.	Le fascinaba perseguir mariposas, contemplar arrobado los <u>moscones</u> de alas tornasoladas que zumbaban en el bochorno espeso de la tarde, jugar al juego interminable de convertirse en trompo viviente tratando de capturar su propio rabo.
_____3.	A mi hermano Beto y a mí nos extrañó no ver a nuestro lado su <u>hociquito</u> húmedo cuando bajamos de la guagua al volver del colegio ...
_____4.	Princesa es mansa, pero es muy grande, y su <u>ladrido</u> profundo puede asustar a cualquier intruso.
_____5.	De éste, quedó sólo un <u>hoyo</u> semiseco, relleno hasta más de la mitad con hojarasca y cascajo.
_____6.	Los perros de raza fina se conocen porque de <u>cachorros</u> tienen las patas muy gordas.
_____7.	Cuando mi padre la compró, había un pozo exiguo en el centro del <u>mangal</u>...
_____8.	La <u>alarma</u> surgió cuando llegó la noche.
_____9.	Por eso Princesa, aunque era una gran danesa de rancia <u>estirpe</u>, no lo parecía ...
_____10.	No se usaba tampoco cuando yo era niña, la <u>poda</u> cruel de orejas y rabos que es hoy ritual obligado para algunas clases de perros.
_____11.	Este cuento de Lupita Lago, una escritora contemporánea, expone la crueldad, tal vez inconsciente, a que pueden llegar algunos <u>seres</u> de inteligencia limitada.
_____12.	Beto bajó con certero tino la <u>vara</u> de tumbar mangos ...
_____13.	... y se criaba una multitud de <u>gallinas</u> para no tener que comprar huevos ni pollos.
_____14.	Y un perillo como Tedy era a las claras un <u>trasto</u>.
_____15.	Pasó el sábado y <u>amaneció</u> un domingo radiante.
_____16.	... los amigos eran una fuente <u>inagotable</u> de plantas, perros y gatos.

(*Continued*)

_____ 17.		Por eso un día–esto lo supe después–mi madre le pidió a Gerardo que <u>se deshiciese</u> de Tedy.
_____ 18.		... y se criaba una multitud de gallinas para no tener que comprar huevos ni <u>pollos</u>.
_____ 19.		Cuando logramos romper el alambre, Tedy saltó, como saltan esos muñecos de las cajas metálicas de juguete mientras se toca la música con una <u>manigueta</u>.
_____ 20.		El resto del terreno lo compartían un <u>naranjal</u> y una arboleda de mangos que era la envidia de la comarca.
_____ 21.		Y este cachorro no dejaba dudas de que era <u>sato</u>, por las patas delgadas y el cuerpecillo endeble, que temblaba lastimosamente al menor susto.
_____ 22.		A mi madre le encantaba que hubiese gente a comer, porque esto le daba la ocasión de de sacar el <u>mantel</u> bordado de hilo ...
_____ 23.		La <u>tapa</u> no encajaba bien, pero estaba asegurada con un alambre.
_____ 24.		Y este cachorro no dejaba dudas de que era sato, por las patas delgadas y el cuerpecillo <u>endeble</u>, que temblaba lastimosamente al menor susto.
_____ 25.		Cuando mi padre la compró, había un pozo <u>exiguo</u> en el centro del mangal, pero él decidió que nos hacía falta agua de la mejor calidad, y tras excavar un pozo artesiano un poco más allá ...
_____ 26.		¡Viene del <u>pozo</u> seco!
_____ 27.		Le fascinaba perseguir <u>mariposas</u>, contemplar arrobado los moscones de alas tornasoladas que zumbaban en el bochorno espeso de la tarde, jugar al juego interminable de convertirse en trompo viviente tratando de capturar su propio rabo.
_____ 28.		... no me pasó por la mente nada malo, simplemente quería que le encontrase otros <u>amos</u>.
_____ 29.		Los perros de raza fina se conocen porque de cachorros tienen las <u>patas</u> muy gordas.
_____ 30.		Armados de un <u>palo</u> largo con un gancho en la punta ...
_____ 31.		La tapa no encajaba bien, pero estaba asegurada con un <u>alambre</u>.
_____ 32.		Le fascinaba perseguir mariposas, contemplar <u>arrobado</u> los moscones de alas tornasoladas que zumbaban en el bochorno espeso de la tarde, jugar al juego interminable de convertirse en trompo viviente tratando de capturar su propio rabo.
_____ 33.		Le fascinaba perseguir mariposas, contemplar arrobado los moscones de alas tornasoladas que <u>zumbaban</u> en el bochorno espeso de la tarde, jugar al juego interminable de convertirse en trompo viviente tratando de capturar su propio rabo.

(*Continued*)

_____34.	Y este cachorro no dejaba dudas de que era sato, por las patas delgadas y el cuerpecillo endeble, que temblaba lastimosamente al menor <u>susto</u>.
_____35.	Y después de concentrarse escuchando los gemidos, dictaminó con voz de <u>perito</u>: ¡Viene del pozo seco!
_____36.	En el centro del pozo, semihundido en la mezcla pantanosa de hojarasca y piedras, había un <u>latón</u> abollado y herrumbroso.
_____37.	No he explicado aún que no vivíamos en la ciudad, sino en las <u>afueras</u>...
_____38.	Le fascinaba perseguir mariposas, contemplar arrobado los moscones de alas tornasoladas que zumbaban en el bochorno <u>espeso</u> de la tarde, jugar al juego interminable de convertirse en trompo viviente tratando de capturar su propio rabo.
_____39.	A mi hermano Beto y a mí nos extrañó no ver a nuestro lado su hociquito húmedo cuando bajamos de la <u>guagua</u> al volver del colegio...
_____40.	Princesa es <u>mansa</u>, pero es muy grande, y su ladrido profundo puede asustar a cualquier intruso.
_____41.	Le fascinaba perseguir mariposas, contemplar arrobado los moscones de alas tornasoladas que zumbaban en el bochorno espeso de la tarde, jugar al juego interminable de convertirse en <u>trompo</u> viviente tratando de capturar su propio rabo.
_____42.	Le fascinaba perseguir mariposas, contemplar arrobado los moscones de alas tornasoladas que zumbaban en el bochorno espeso de la tarde, jugar al juego interminable de convertirse en trompo viviente tratando de capturar su propio <u>rabo</u>.
_____43.	Armados de un palo largo con un <u>gancho</u> en la punta...
_____44.	Gerardo era un peón desmañado, rayando en <u>retrasado</u> mental...
_____45.	El latón es viejo y él está todo lleno de <u>óxido</u>.
_____46.	Habíamos cogido cuatro o cinco mangos, cuando un <u>gemido</u> apagado llegó a mis oídos.
_____47.	Gerardo era un peón <u>desmañado</u>, rayando en retrasado mental...
_____48.	Beto bajó con certero <u>tino</u> la vara de tumbar mangos...
_____49.	El gemido era ahora un <u>aullido</u> que taladraba los tímpanos.
_____50.	El resto del terreno lo compartían un naranjal y una arboleda de mangos que era la envidia de la <u>comarca</u>.

Appendix B: Approximations Supplied on Tests 1-4

Word (English meaning in story)	Test 1 (no context)	Test 2 (with context)	Test 3 (no context)	Test 4 (with context)
afueras (outskirts)	–	outside-country, country	country	country
alambre (wire)	–	rope, something like a rope or chain, fastener	–	rope
amo (master, owner)	–	–	–	guardians
cachorro (puppy)	–	domestic animals, dog, type/kind of dog, type of dog or animal		mutt (dog), type of species of dog
comarca (region)	–	community	*comunidad* [community]	neighborhood, community
deshacerse (to get rid of)	to undo (something)	–	–	–
endeble (weak, frail)	–	scrawny, skinny, unnourished, fine	fine	scrawny, fine
estirpe (lineage)	–	kind of dog, fine breed[a], blue blood	–	pure breed[a]
gallina (hen)	goose, rooster	chics, roosters, *tipo de animal para la comida* [type of animal for food]	goose, rooster	roosters
gemido (moan)	–	type of sound, it's something like noises of complaint, noise, loud noises, shouts, crying, bark, sound	crying	yelp, howl, screem, crying, cry

(Continued)

Word (English meaning in story)	Test 1 (no context)	Test 2 (with context)	Test 3 (no context)	Test 4 (with context)
guagua (bus)	small motorcycle, public transportation	form of transportation, *coche* [car]	–	–
hociquito (little nose/snout)	little mouth	Little mouth	–	–
latón (drum)	milk carton	bucket[b], winch, type of box, box, carton	box	box, *cubeta* [bucket][b]
mangal (mango orchard/mango grove)	–	orchard, mango tree, field	mango tree	mango tree, orchard, fruit orchard
manigueta (handle, crank)	–	Knob, key	–	key
manso (tame, meak)	–	–	–	timid
mantel (tablecloth)	table top	placemat	–	–
mariposas (butterflies)	–	–	bugs	bug
moscones (large flies)	–	type of insect, horseflies, an insect	bugs, wasps, insects, moth, mosquitos	wasps, moths, bugs (mosquitos)
palo (stick)	bat	[not included on test]	–	–
pavor (fear, fright)	–	[not included on test]	–	anxiety, vulnerable
sato (mutt, mongrel)	–	*corriente* [common]	breed	a poor specimen

Note: Answers supplied are verbatim (including spelling errors). Remarks provided in square brackets are comments or clarifications added by the author.
[a] 'Breed' by itself was accepted as correct.
[b] *Latón* can mean 'bucket', but not as used in the story.

Appendix C: Vocabulary Errors on No-Context Tests: Confusion with English or Spanish Words and/or Use of Faulty Morpheme Analysis

Word	English meaning in story	Students' guesses	Likely Spanish word (if any) with which confused
afueras	outskirts, suburbs	outside, outdoors	*afuera*
alambre	wire	shining◆	*alumbrante*
amo	master, owner	love	*amor, amar*
arrobado	entranced	robbed[a], stollen[a], to be robbed, thief	*robado*
cachorro	puppy	hat◆	*gorro*
camarca	region	brand	*marca*
deshacerse	to get rid of	to undo◆	*deshacer*
endeble	weak, frail	indelible◆	*endeleble*
espeso	thick, dense, heavy	weight[a]	*peso*
		mirror[b]	*espejo*
estirpe	lineage	tight◆	*estrecho*
		stirrup◆; stripe	–
gallina	hen	cookie◆	*galleta*
		gallon◆	*galón*
gemido	moan	twin, twinned	*gemelo*
guagua	bus	bark ('ruff, ruff')◆	*guau guau*
ladrido	bark [of a dog]	robber, thief◆, burglarized◆	*ladrón*
		brick◆, bricked◆	*ladrillo*
manigueta	handle, crank	maniquin◆ [sic]	*maniquí*
manso	tame	great size[b]◆	*inmenso*
mantel	tablecloth	mantle◆	–
mariposas	butterflies	shellfish◆	*mariscos*
		daisies◆	*margaritas*

(Continued)

Word	English meaning in story	Students' guesses	Likely Spanish word (if any) with which confused
palo	stick	pale[a]	–
pavor	terror	favor◆	*favor*
		fervor[b]◆	*fervor*
pozo	Well	turkey◆	*pavo*
rabo	Tail	rabid◆	–
		rabbi◆	*rabino*
sato	Mutt	sated, satisfied[b]	–
seres	Beings	series◆	*series*
surgir	to arise	suggest	*sugerir*
		to happen	*suceder*
susto	Fright	a thing that sustains something◆; food◆	(?*sustento*)
tapa	top, lid	tape	–
trasto	worthless object	dish	*traste* (in *lavar los trastes*)
trompo	top [toy]	trick	*trampa*
vara	rod, pole, stick	various	*varios*

Note 1: All examples, except those noted, appeared on Test 1, the no-context pretest.
Note 2: ◆ = *Not* guessed again on any of the subsequent tests.
[a]Also on Test 3.
[b]Only on Test 3.

Part 3
Materials Design and Strategies for Vocabulary Teaching and Learning

Chapter 10
Conspicuous by Their Absence: The Infrequency of Very Frequent Words in some English as a Foreign Language Textbooks

JIM LAWLEY

Introduction

In the 1980s, statistics from the computerized analysis of a corpus of native-speaker English (the COBUILD corpus) showed that: the most frequent 700 words of English constituted 70% of English text; the most frequent 1500 words constituted 76% and the most frequent 2500 words of English, 80% (Willis, 1990: 46). More recently much larger corpora have pointed to the same basic reality (see e.g. Schmitt, 2000: 73): the figures show that a relatively small number of English words make up a very high proportion of what is said and written in English, and strongly suggest that being good at English involves being good at understanding and using these words. They show too that as we move down the frequency list, words become much less frequent very quickly:

> The 700 most-frequent words cover 70% of text, but coverage begins to drop rapidly thereafter. The next 800 words cover a further 6% of text and the next 1000 words cover 4%. If we are talking about the 2500 most-frequent words in English, however, no learner is likely to get very far without needing to express and understand notions and functions carried by words at this level of frequency. (Willis, 1990: 47)

Key Issues

In view of these observations one would not expect EFL textbooks to avoid these high-frequency words. Yet some of these words such as *seek*, *issue* and *likely*, for example, do not appear to feature in books used in secondary schools in the early stages. In other cases, *by*, for example, the word itself appears, but its most frequent use (discussed below in this section) is often avoided. In general, the textbooks used in this sector do not seem committed to encouraging the study of the most-frequent English words. It is true of course that frequency cannot be the only criterion for vocabulary selection, and as Sinclair and Renouf (1988: 157–158) point out, no-one would wish 'to imply that there is an identity between the worlds of the learner and the native speaker'. Nevertheless, the exclusion or under-representation of such words needs to be carefully justified since students will be constantly encountering them in any authentic native-speaker speech or writing to which they are exposed, and understanding such speech or writing will be made very difficult if they do not know them.

One reason for avoiding these words appears to be that they are considered 'difficult'. Lewis comments:

> The most-frequent "words" are frequently items previously regarded as structural and, ironically, words of low semantic content. These largely delexicalized words are highly frequent precisely because they often have several meanings, and their pattern profiles are extremely complex. Mastery of words like *to, with, have* is considerably more difficult than mastering a vocabulary item with higher meaning content: *accident, soot, slump.* (Lewis, 1993: 109)

Indeed, a glance at the *Collins Cobuild English Dictionary* (CCED), an EFL learners' dictionary, shows that while the entries for a handful of these words, such as *her, yes* and *I*, occupy less than a quarter of a page, suggesting that they are straightforward words to define and exemplify, most of the very high-frequency words in English take up much more space. The word *by*, for example, which according to the Cambridge International Corpus (Schmitt, 2000: 72) is the 19th most frequent word in the English language, has many different meanings and uses and fills nearly a whole page in the CCED.

But this argument overlooks the fact that one meaning of these high-frequency words is often more frequent than all the other senses combined (Sinclair, 1991: 19). Sinclair and Renouf (1988: 157–158) point out that in the case of *by*, for example, over 50% of the uses correspond to the sense covered in the *Cobuild Dictionary* by the definition 'If something is done **by** a person or thing, that person or thing does it' (CCED, 1995: 223). This sense is adequately covered in one very short and easily understood paragraph in the dictionary. So in fact, according to Lewis (1993), complexity of profile cannot plausibly be used as an excuse for not showing learners the most frequent senses of the most-frequent words. Lewis does not seem justified either when he observes that as one moves down the frequency scale: '[...] the words are easier to learn, and any L2 = L1 equivalence, which students almost inevitably make, is more likely to be accurate [...]' (Lewis, 1993: 109–111). Certainly, there is nothing complex about the profile of the sense of *by* discussed above and the speakers of many major languages will find a very obvious L2 = L1 equivalence. Indeed, examination of the 660 most-frequent English words as identified by the Cobuild project (see list in Lawley, 1996: 111–115) suggests that the great majority of these words have obvious equivalents in other major languages.

Spanish Secondary School Students' Knowledge of these Words

In a recent experiment, conducted at a secondary school in Spain with a view to writing this chapter, a group of 20 17- and 18-year-old *Bachillerato* students preparing for the university entrance examination, most of whom had studied English at school for at least eight years, were asked to give mother tongue equivalents of 20 words taken from the list of the 660 most frequent English words. The 20 words were: *seem, road, against, likely, allow, however, feel, rule, seek, hit, issue, job, large, step, towards, main, fear, perhaps, foreign* and *actually*. These words were chosen at random from the list of the 660 most frequent words except that words which were identical (e.g. *idea*) were deliberately excluded.

The student participants were told that some of the English words had more than one meaning but that they were only being asked to write one equivalent word. In the event, it turned out that out of a total of 400 possible correct answers, an aggregate score of only 108 (27%) was achieved.

It could be objected that these words were not contextualized in the test and that context would have helped students to understand them. However, it is worth noting that it is precisely these very high-frequency words which often supply the context that would help students work out the meaning of less common words. Each word has an obvious equivalent in Spanish and students were only asked to provide these equivalents; the students' inability to say that *road* means *calle* and *foreign* means *extranjero*, for example, strongly suggests that they simply did not know what *road* and *foreign* mean.

In conversation, the students' teacher was surprised to learn that many of these words are in fact such high-frequency items in native-speaker English. He was sure that many of them do not appear with corresponding frequency in the textbooks his students use during their school careers; indeed, his impression was that some do not appear at all. He also suggested that these textbooks often made little explicit provision for the systematic recycling of key vocabulary items or for the intentional learning of vocabulary. The expectation of the textbook writers, he suggested, seemed to be that students would 'pick up' vocabulary by contact with texts (written and spoken) in English.

The test was repeated once with very similar results with students of the same age at another school in a different region of Spain. The experiment was then abandoned since teachers in other Spanish schools who use different textbooks reported that the results would doubtless be very similar and for the same reason: students do not know many of these words because they do not feature prominently and frequently enough in the textbooks they use. Indeed, examination of textbooks widely used by Spanish children studying in the four-year *Educación Secundaria Obligatoria* (ESO), aged between 12 and 16, suggest that they are unlikely to meet words such as *should*, *might* and *rather* until the later stages. Since these are mainstream, international textbooks, it seems probable that Spain is by no means unique in this respect. Nor is the problem confined to textbooks used in secondary schools: the word *by*, for example, in its most frequent sense (discussed above) is associated with the passive voice, which many internationally used textbooks do not introduce until the third or fourth year of study. In general, as López-Jiménez (Chapter 11: 156) suggests, the selection criteria for the vocabulary presented in EFL textbooks are not specified, and these materials lack systematicity in this important respect.

The Collins Cobuild English Course

What materials can teachers offer their students if they want them to study the most frequent senses of the most frequent words from the very outset? One obvious solution for teachers would be to use a textbook with a lexical syllabus; that is, a book which takes these words and their central patterns of usage as its syllabus, giving them special attention and systematically recycling them. Such a book, the *Collins Cobuild English Course* (CCEC) by Jane and Dave Willis, a three-level course was published in 1988. The CCEC described itself in the following terms:

> The CCEC represents a major advance in the teaching of English. It is based on the research findings of the COBUILD project at Birmingham University – the same research which produced the acclaimed Collins Cobuild English Language Dictionary. It focuses on what the real English students will encounter and need to use in today's world.

> There are three levels, taking students up to pre-First Certificate standard.

> Book 1 is for the false beginner adult learners. In all, 15 units will provide about 100 h of class work, at the end of which students will be able to cope confidently with a very wide range of straightforward situations.

> (1) The syllabus covers the most useful patterns of 700 of the most-frequently used words in English.
> (2) Special sections on 'Grammar Words' and the 'Grammar Book' appendix highlight those very common words which are used to build vital structures.

(3) Students discover recurring features of the language by analyzing samples of real English.
(4) From the outset, students listen to native speakers talking spontaneously on topics which are relevant to adults worldwide.
(5) The reading texts are taken from a wide variety of authentic sources.
(6) Early oral and written tasks are very simple, becoming more challenging in later units, so that students use the language in contexts which become gradually more demanding. Activities focus in turn on accuracy and fluency (Willis & Willis, 1988: back cover blurb).

The writing of, and thinking behind, the CCEC is described in detail by one of its authors in *The Lexical Syllabus* (Willis, 1990); this book discusses in depth both the syllabus and the methodology employed. In fact, since the Cobuild project had already identified the most frequent words, the key question remaining was the methodological question: How are students to acquire this knowledge of the most common words in their most common patterns? By way of example, Willis discusses in detail how the CCEC sets about equipping students with the knowledge of one of these words: *way*.

'Each of the two main categories of meaning for the word **way** is the focus of an exercise in CCEC Level 1:

> 78 **Ways of saying numbers**
>
> 78a a How do you say telephone numbers in your language?
>
> b Look at the numbers on the right.[1] What are they? What about 1989 for example? Could it be a telephone number, or a date, or car number? How would you say it if it was a date? One thousand nine hundred and eighty-nine? ... One nine eight nine...? Discuss with your partner how you could say the numbers. How many different ways can you find and what do they each mean?
>
> • Tell the class
>
> 78c c Bridget and David talked about the same numbers. Did they think of the same things as you?
>
> Write down the things David and Bridget thought of.

In addition to the uses of **way** in the rubric for this activity:

Ways of saying numbers.

and:

How many different ways can you find ...

A recording of native speakers doing the task contrasts the American way of saying dates with the British way. Inevitably the word **way** will feature a good deal in the exchanges in the classroom between teacher and learners, and among learners.

> How many ways did you think of?
> Yes that's another way.
> We got three ways.
> etc.

(Willis, 1990: 34)

It is worth noting that Willis' use of 'inevitably' here in fact begs the question. *Ways* and *way* are not strictly speaking necessary in the sentences he cites:

> How many did you think of?
> Yes that's another.
> We've got three.

Indeed, it might be argued that the versions just quoted – without *way*(s) – are in fact more natural. The very presence of *ways* as the first word in the title of this section establishes it as basic to all that follows. Paradoxically, when it is quite clear to all involved in a language event that they are talking about *ways*, the word itself may become redundant. Proficient speakers in fact often avoid repeating a word in the way illustrated by Willis. Moreover, Willis points out on numerous occasions that students need time to assimilate new language and that it is unreasonable to expect them to start using words they have only just encountered (Willis, 1990: iv, 22–23, 24–25, 69). In the light of these reflections it seems rather less than 'inevitable' that students will be using *ways* at this stage.

Willis emphasizes that *way* is a very common and therefore very important word, and that it appears frequently during the course; in exercises, rubrics and reading and listening texts. Yet he quite frankly admits that all this exposure is no guarantee of 'intake'.

> We can never be sure when, or even whether, input will become part of the learners (sic) behavior. Indeed the very concept of *input* is a misleading one. Input implies intake, and there can never be any guarantee that learners will take in the language that they hear. (Willis, 1990: 22–23)

Willis' position seems to be that while we cannot be sure that students will have incorporated the word into their repertoires by the end of the course, they will certainly have had plenty of opportunities to do so. This is a very honest position; more honest, second-language learning research suggests, than that of the advocates of Presentation – Practice – Production methodology which, Willis (1990: iii) points out, gives a more or less entirely spurious impression that something has been learned. Nevertheless, spurious or not, this is an impression that many learners and teachers like to have, and the CCEC's resolute refusal to provide it may go some way toward explaining its lack of commercial success. There is also an inconsistency in Willis' position here. On the one hand, he suggests that the analytic lexical syllabus contained in the CCEC has a 'high surrender value', in contrast to the 'low surrender value' of a synthetic structural course:

> If you give up such a course (a traditional structural course) after say one hundred hours, you will have learned very little that will be of use to you. Your grammar will be very limited and may be missing major categories like the passive, and many of the modals. (Willis, 1990: 42)

In contrast, he points out, in the frequency-driven lexical syllabus the most important words and the most central patterns of usage are present from the very early stages. Yet, as we have just seen, elsewhere Willis quite frankly admits that even the abundant exposure offered by the CCEC is no guarantee of 'intake'. It might in fact be the case that the lexical syllabus has an even lower surrender value than the traditional synthetic structural syllabus which, as Willis concedes, is at least likely to give 'good control over the limited grammar [...] learned' (Willis, 1990: 42).

Certainly, students and teachers are likely to feel that the former get plenty of contact with natural English but they may sense uneasily that they are in fact not retaining as much as they should or would like. The psychological need that both learners and teachers have for immediate 'tangible' results is itself also a classroom reality, and one that perhaps the authors of the CCEC did not bear sufficiently in mind.

The authors of the CCEC espoused a task-based methodology, yet it may be that there is an irreconcilable contradiction between a lexical syllabus and a task-based methodology. The lexical syllabus insists on the commonest words in their commonest patterns, on the grounds that this is what students most need to learn. But in the task-based syllabus, as the name implies, and Willis underlines, the emphasis is on the real-world outcome of the task not on the language used to achieve it. Students are free to use any language they like – indeed are *encouraged* to use any language they like – to perform the task. There is then simply no way of ensuring that they are in fact making use of the most common words in their most common patterns in order to perform them.

In fact, the authors seem torn between their role as promoters of a lexical syllabus which leads them to want to specify the language students will learn and use and their role as designers of task-based material in which they want to leave students free to perform tasks and solve puzzles with any words they like. Occasionally, the difficulty of trying to do two contradictory things at once shows. In Level 2, for example, students are told: 'here are some other words which are used in the same way as **thing** category 3'. They are then shown sentences like this:

	fact		living in London is more expensive
The	point	is	transport's easy in Central London
	trouble		it's difficult to park your car
	problem		shopping is such fun, you spend too much
			you can find whatever you want

(Willis & Willis, 1988: section 195)

Students are then instructed 'to make up five sentences and try to remember them'. It's difficult to see why students should be required to remember these sentences (For how long? one wonders, and, to what end?), and difficult to avoid the impression that what the authors really mean is '[...] and try to retain the structure'.

In short, it's true that in the CCEC the learner is 'exposed to a carefully constructed sample of the language which contains the most common important features of the language as a whole, and (that) all of these features (are) highlighted for the learner' (Willis, 1990: 70), but it's also true that it's easier to take a horse to water than it is to make it drink.

It is worth noting too that, like most international mainstream general-purpose EFL coursebooks, the CCEC requires for its successful completion a teacher, fellow students (for the many pair- and group-work activities), and access to the cassettes. There is relatively little provision for self-study activity. Most of the workbook activities require guidance and feedback from the teacher; the reference sections at the back of the book make little provision for the type of interactive study which would enable students to self-evaluate. Allwright and Bailey comment:

> [...] some modern communicative textbooks [...] can be quite useless to learners [...] if, for instance, they are trying to study independently, or to catch up on a lesson they have missed. Learners may come to see such materials as generally unhelpful, and as reason for feeling they are never going to succeed as learners. (Allwright & Bailey, 1991: 163)

Clearly if students cannot study a course outside as well as inside the classroom then the time when they can learn from it will be greatly reduced.

The CCEC is now out of print, and it is not easy to envisage how a textbook that attempts the same task could be made to work in demanding EFL classrooms such as, for example, those found in the secondary sector in Spain. The question arises then: is there another way in which all these essential high-frequency words can be studied from the very first stages of an EFL course?

Bilingual Word Lists

We have already noted that the most-frequent English words often have simple L1 = L2 equivalences which suggests that one obvious solution would be to provide bilingual word lists in which high-frequency words are presented in small groups for easy learning. For example, for basic-level Spanish speakers:

> area = *área*
> road = *carretera, calle*
> air = *aire*
> city = *ciudad*
> ground = *suelo*
> centre = *centro*
> country = *país*

Such bilingual word lists were widely used in foreign language learning – in the 1960s and 1970s, for example. In those days it was usual to group words in semantic clusters; for example, words for different fruits such as *apple, peach, pear, orange, cherry, plum* and *banana* would be studied in the same session. Research by Higa (1963), however, showed that such groupings made learning harder:

> One may infer from these experimental results that the present-day textbook writer's practice of introducing semantically closely related words in the same lesson is causing more "difficulty" than facilitation. Perhaps the textbook writer today is too theme-oriented, i.e. to every lesson regardless of its length, he has a tendency to give a title such as "In a restaurant," "Family," or "School" and attempts to tell some kind of story. In a lesson titled "Family," for instance, many kinship terms are introduced all at once such as *father, mother, brother, sister, uncle,* and *aunt* in their foreign equivalents. It would seem that, in order to reduce the amount of interference in word learning, this practice may be corrected in favor of teaching words of little semantic relationship in the same lesson. (Higa, 1965: 173)

As a result of further research (Tinkham, 1997), however, thematic clustering has been put forward as an approach that seems better than learning either completely unassociated words or semantic clusters:

> [...] while there was strong and consistent evidence that semantic clusters are learnt with more difficulty than unrelated sets, the evidence that thematic clusters are learnt more easily than unassociated sets [was] generally positive... (Tinkham, 1997: 161)

As an example of thematic clustering Tinkham (1997: 141) offers: *frog, green, hop, pond, slippery, croak*. The words *area, road, air, city, ground, centre, country* in the sample material above are also offered as an example of thematic clustering.

On the subject of word lists in general, Schmitt comments:

> [...] teaching new words in class may not be the most efficient way of handling vocabulary. It is probably more productive to assign students homework that introduces them to new words, such as word lists or reading, and then elaborate, expand and consolidate these words in the classroom. (Schmitt, 2000: 145)

Moreover, Schmitt (Chapter 3: 30–31) observes that '[...] a form-meaning link is the minimal specification for knowing a word, and being able to use it in any practical way. It therefore makes sense to encourage learning form-meaning links as the initial step of vocabulary learning.'

Meanwhile, in a recent, valuable literature review, Serrano van der Laan (2008: 5) concludes that 'there is [...] a considerable body of research that has found that decontextualized list learning is actually more conducive to learning vocabulary than contextualized learning'. Serrano van der Laan (2008: 8) also notes the importance of respecting students' preferred learning styles, pointing out that rote learning is prevalent in many non-English-speaking academic cultures, and arguing that it is more productive to use it as a resource rather than to try to impose new learning styles that clash with learner expectations. In this context she cites Nation (2001: 383) who points out the importance of what he calls 'environmental analysis'; the discovery of preferred study methods which propitiate learning.

Conclusions

Certainly, the psychological appeal of comprehensive word lists is hard to deny and the reasons for their appeal are worth examining. Learning from such lists is a straightforward, reassuringly repetitive process: students need waste no time struggling to understand the mechanics of new exercise types, but instead can concentrate all their mental energy on the new language they are trying to learn. They can learn independently of a teacher and other students; as a result, there will be more times when they can study. Moreover, such lists make it possible for them to quantify and therefore to take satisfaction in their progress. Since the most-frequent words can be taught first, study time will have 'a high surrender value'.

The CCEC endeavored to provide a rich learning environment in which the most frequent words were systematically recycled. It might prove to be the case that once students have learned the high-frequency words in bilingual word lists, the abundant authentic materials which nowadays are readily available throughout the world in the form of newspapers, magazines, books, DVDs, CDs and on the internet will instead form that rich learning environment. Once students have mastered the most frequent words they have a better chance of being able to understand authentic English and can choose texts which particularly interest them. Such texts might help them learn more about the central patterns of usage of these words. Schmitt (Chapter 3: 36) comments '[...] the initial learning of a word is likely to establish only its form-meaning connection, and perhaps a bit of knowledge of its grammatical characteristics, including morphology. But this is not enough to know a word well, and so additional exposures are necessary to start promoting acquisition of the contextual facets of word knowledge'. For that vital initial step, however, bilingual word lists would provide a language-learning tool which is easy to provide yet currently unavailable and which at least some students might like to make use of.

Acknowledgments

I am most grateful to Marta Serrano van der Laan of the Language Center at Politecnico di Torino (Italy) for a number of highly instructive conversations about teaching and learning vocabulary.

Note

1. These numbers to the right are not reproduced here. The numbers, given in a variety of fonts, are: 22, 0, 1989, 3.14, 748, 22756, 10.12 and 021 3370452.

Chapter 11
The Treatment of Lexical Aspects in Commercial Textbooks for L2 Teaching and Learning

MARÍA DOLORES LÓPEZ-JIMÉNEZ

Introduction

From the point of view of the L2 teacher, many textbook writers regard textbooks as a tool that saves teachers time (Acklam, 1994; Freebairn, 2000; Greenall, 1984; O'Neill, 1982; Richards, 1993; Studolsky, 1989; Tice, 1991). Therefore, textbooks may be described as: (1) the starting point for the class and for the teacher that should lead to creative and spontaneous improvisation, adaptation and interaction; (2) a springboard for ideas to react to current trends in applied linguistics; (3) a resource bank for teaching materials and ideas; (4) a potential syllabus; and (5) a reference for grammar and vocabulary without suppressing the teacher's creativity.

Despite these positive views, textbooks have also been criticized. Sheldon (1987) claims that some of the problems associated with textbooks reside in their design. In other words, the presentation and recycling of new vocabulary together with the selection and grading of texts rarely appear in the L2 course rationale. Moreover, textbooks seldom indicate whether they are based on a needs analysis or whether they have been piloted before their publication. Educators are generally dissatisfied with the absence of answers to students' needs and interests in textbooks (Lawley, 2000; Richards, 1993; Swan, 1992).

Swan (1992) criticizes textbooks' distorted image of students by the inclusion of texts that do not reflect their interests. According to Lawley (2000), this absence of idiosyncratic aspects of a certain readership is due to economic reasons, since it is more profitable to publish one single book that might be used in many countries than it is to design one that incorporates the specific teaching context in each country. In other words, the lack of these cultural idiosyncrasies leads to a homogenizing process (Ariew, 1982, cited in Richards, 1993). On the contrary, nonnative teachers and those with little experience usually praise textbooks, sometimes unjustifiably.

This uncritical praise considers the decisions made by textbook writers superior to those of teachers (*reification*) (Richards, 1993). However, teachers sometimes become too involved in the teaching/learning process due to textbooks' weaknesses (Lawley, 2000; O'Neill, 1982). Lawley (2000) asserts that textbooks often force students to depend on the teacher, since what is to be done with the textbook might not be readily apparent to them. As a result, teachers spend more time in class explaining how the textbook should be used than they do explaining what students should be doing. Furthermore, some textbook writers point out the negative effects on L2 teaching/learning caused by the publishing industry. Greenall (1984), for instance, warns of a lack of credibility in textbooks due to practical reasons, such as the publication of as many textbooks as possible. Textbooks have also been criticized for ignoring the most recent findings in applied linguistics (Bruton, 1997; Hutchinson & Torres, 1994; Sheldon, 1988). For example, failure to consider up-to-date research on L2 lexical acquisition typically results in the unsystematic selection and presentation of vocabulary (Sheldon, 1988). Tice (1991) also notes the lack of variety in the content and the types of activities, the presence of inappropriate or unbalanced syllabi and boring or limited topics.

Lexical Aspects in Commercial Textbooks for L2 Learners: Selection, Presentation, Practice, Recycling, Learning Strategies and Glossaries with L1 Translation Equivalents

Over the past 30 years, vocabulary has become increasingly important in L2 teaching. There has been an increase in the number of pedagogical materials from the publishing industry that address vocabulary. This can be evidenced by 'a website search using the words "grammar" and "vocabulary" at three major ESL publishers which found twice as many grammar books as vocabulary books at Heinle & Heinle [...] but also equal numbers at the University of Michigan Press [...] and Houghton Mifflin [...]' (Folse, 2004: 28). Although foreign-language teachers understand the central importance of vocabulary, their concerns now center on what and how to teach this vocabulary.

Regarding what vocabulary to teach, word lists based on frequency of use were popular during the 20th century. However, the high frequency of a lexical unit does not necessarily reflect its usefulness. A low-frequency lexical unit might be vital if it is the only one that conveys that particular semantic value and cannot be easily replaced with other lexical units. Other factors such as culture, needs and proficiency level (Gairns & Redman, 1986) should be considered. Word lists may contain lexical units that, due to cultural ethnocentricity, are not relevant to students' needs. In the same way, students' needs may conflict with their language proficiency level. Sometimes, textbook writers have to face the problem of designing technical material (e.g. business English) in an L2 for low-level students. Gairns and Redman (1986) argue that it is not easy to reconcile students' need for highly technical vocabulary together with their inability to manage basic grammatical structures. They state that in current practice preference is given to students' proficiency level over their needs.

Turning attention to concerns about how to teach vocabulary, some of the most common ways in which the meaning of new items is explicitly presented in textbooks are the use of synonyms, antonyms, L1 translation equivalents, written explanations, definitions and visual techniques. The use of synonyms and antonyms might be useful when teaching passive vocabulary. However, finding a synonym in the student's L2 may have some drawbacks, that is, very few words are totally equivalent and the possible L2 equivalent might be an unknown word to the L2 student (Lewis & Hill, 1985). On the contrary, in the case of antonyms, sometimes it is not enough to provide the opposite of a new item, but it is necessary to illustrate the contexts in which the opposite functions as a real antonym of the new item. For example, a new item like 'sour' might be contrasted with 'sweet' as in 'sugar is sweet and lemons are sour' (Gairns & Redman, 1986: 74). Nevertheless, the same opposite relationship does not apply in 'sweet wine' versus 'sour wine'. With regard to the use of L1 translation equivalents, it is sometimes argued that it might prevent the student from developing an independent lexicon in the L2 (Thornbury, 2002). In addition, when translating into the student's L1 there may not be a one-to-one translation equivalent between the L1 word and the L2 word. He also adds that the L1 translation does not allow the student to be in contact with the L2. Conversely, research has shown that translation into the student's L1 may increase vocabulary retention in the L2 when compared to the use of pictures only as a presentation technique (Lotto & de Groot, 1998). More recently, Folse (2004) states that research should tackle questions such as whether the value of L1 translations is as effective for higher-proficiency students as it is for lower-proficiency students and whether translation is more effective with certain words (e.g. concrete nouns, one-word verbs as opposed to multiword phrasal verbs or adjectives). Other presentation techniques such as written explanations and definitions expose L2 students to the target language and they are more demanding from a cognitive point of view (Thornbury, 2002). However, providing a definition alone may often be inadequate as a means of clarifying meaning when presenting new words. Thus, contextualized examples to clarify the limits of the L2 word may be needed. Finally, visual techniques found in textbooks mainly include photographs and drawings. They are particularly useful for the teaching of concrete vocabulary (e.g. food, furniture, etc.) and semantic fields related to places, professions and occupations, descriptions of people, actions and activities (e.g. sports and verbs of movement) (Gairns & Redman, 1986). As far as implicit ways present meaning in textbooks are concerned, many textbook writers resort to written texts. Hulstijn (1992) showed that L2 students were able to retrieve the target words whose meanings had been guessed from context better than those whose meanings had been given explicitly to students. Other authors (Haynes & Baker, 1993; Schatz & Baldwin, 1986) state that context clues are very limited and unreliable predictors of word meaning. It may be the case that the assumption that context clues are very useful when guessing the meaning of an unknown L2 word comes from a flawed analogy with L1 acquisition (Folse, 2004).

Another dimension to take into account is vocabulary practice. In general, research on the types of exercises that increase the retention of L2 vocabulary has been limited. Some of the factors that should be considered in the analysis of different types of exercises/activities include depth of processing, attention and number of attempts needed for retrieval. The learning model based on depth of processing (Craik & Tulving, 1975) claims that learning is greater when deeper processing is needed. Sciarone and Meijer (1995) conclude that fill-in-the-blank exercises do not contribute to learning vocabulary more significantly than conversational practice. Nevertheless, these researchers do not call for the inclusion of conversational practice and the abandonment of controlled exercises. Hulstijn (1998) examined the advantages of writing words over encountering them in a reading passage in their retention. It was found that the students who had to use the target words in a letter retained a greater number of words than the students who were asked to read a letter with the target words in it and the students who read a letter with the target words in it and then did a fill-in-the-blank exercise with the same words. In a similar study, Laufer and Hulstijn (1998) concluded that the students who were asked to write a composition in which they had to use 10 target words that were accompanied by explanations and examples obtained better retention scores on the immediate posttest than the other two groups. The first group received a text with the boldfaced target words and their translation into the students' L1 in the margin of the text followed by multiple-choice comprehension questions. The second group took a test that included the same text and the same comprehension questions. Instead of the target words, this group had a word list that they had to use in order to fill in 10 blank spaces. Each word from the list appeared with a translation and an explanation. The results in Hulstijn (1998) and Laufer and Hulstijn (1998) can be justified and interpreted in the following way (Folse, 2004): first, writing a letter using a number of words already provided requires a deeper level of processing than either receiving input that contains the target words or completing a fill-in-the-blank exercise with the target words [the first and second tasks in Laufer and Hulstijn's (1998) study]; second, writing a letter with a number of words already given draws the student's attention to the use of each word within the context of each letter and not within isolated sentences, and it also makes the student interact with the same word more than once (having multiple encounters with the same word); third, the fact that the student has to write a letter using certain words makes the student focus on them. Nonetheless, in Folse (1999) the activities in which the students produced original sentences with the vocabulary provided did not cause a greater retention of the number of words when compared to a fill-in-the-blank exercise. Folse (2004) argues that the number of times that a student must use a word is the most important factor in depth of processing.

Regarding exercise/activity typologies (Cervero & Pichardo Castro, 2000; Gómez Molina, 2004; Morante, 2005; Oxford & Scarcella, 1994; Thornbury, 2002), their effectiveness in the retention of L2 vocabulary in long-term memory still needs to be addressed in experimental studies. Furthermore, researchers rarely specify if their proposals are valid for the teaching/learning of *one*-word lexical units and *multi*-word lexical units (e.g. lexical collocations) or only for *one*-word lexical units, taking into account that the knowledge of *multi*-word lexical units (e.g. collocational knowledge) does not evolve in parallel to the rest of the lexicon (Gitsaki, 1996).

Another aspect that should be considered when teaching vocabulary in an L2 is that learning a lexical unit is a gradual process in which memory, review and repetition play an intrinsically important role. Thus, vocabulary recycling becomes a key factor in that process. Some psychologists (Craik & Lockhart, 1972; Craik & Tulving, 1975, cited in Nation, 1990) argue that repetition is not an important factor in learning the L2 vocabulary, but rather the type of attention paid to the word, for example, oral repetition is not as efficient when compared to remembering the written form of a word. Brown (1993) did not find any connection between the learned words and the number of times that they appeared in a text. However, a correlation between the words and their frequency of use was observed by Nation (2001: 74, 76). Nation claims that repetition carries quantitative and qualitative benefits to vocabulary learning: 'repetition is essential for vocabulary learning because there is so much to know about each word that one meeting with it is not sufficient to gain this information, and because vocabulary items must not only be known, they must be known well so that they can be fluently accessed'. Nation (2001) distinguishes among intervals, types and number of exposures. Pimsleur's (1967) memory hypothesis suggests that the intervals between the different repetitions ought to increase over time. Studies like those of Seibert (1927), Anderson and Jordan (1928), Seibert (1930) and Griffin (1992) conclude that one tends to forget more immediately after the first encounter with a word and that does not occur after further encounters. Learning by repetition not only depends on the intervals of the reencounters, but also on the nature of the repetition itself. More elaborate repetitions, such as expanding the meaning of a lexical unit while including some lexical collocations, brings greater benefits compared to successive repetitions that contain the same information with respect to the first encounter (Stahl & Fairbanks, 1986).

With regard to the relation between the number of encounters and learning an L2 lexical unit, no fixed number seems to exist. Saragi *et al.* (1978) estimate that repetition accounts for 20% of all the factors that influence the learning of a new word. In their study, the researchers used a text but did not inform the participants that they were going to be tested on the new vocabulary. The researchers concluded that the participants needed 16 or more repetitions to incorporate a word into their lexicon. Kachroo (1962) calculated that seven or more encounters with the same word in the textbook were needed so that the majority of the students could learn it. However, half of the words appeared only once or twice in the textbook and were not acquired by the majority of the class. Paribakht and Wesche (1997) point out that the probability of learning a new word after only one encounter is between 5% and 10%. Likewise, in a recent work by Tomlinson (2008) (*cf.* Arnold & Rixon, 2008; Dat, 2008) he states that in spite of the effective number of exercises provided for students to practice new vocabulary within every unit, the need for recycling the language being taught is overlooked in textbooks. O'Dell (1997) advises that textbooks should recycle vocabulary exhaustively.

As to the influence that some teaching approaches exerted on L2 vocabulary teaching, an interest in vocabulary learning strategies and an emphasis on the exclusive use of the L2 in the classroom can be attributed to communicative approaches over the past 25 years. Among the central factors behind the emergence of studies on vocabulary learning strategies, Schmitt (1997) mentions the following: the idea that the student's actions rather than his/her aptitude constituted a decisive factor in the success/failure of learning an L2, the discovery that students use more learning strategies with vocabulary than with other language learning activities (e.g. listening comprehension or oral presentations) (Chamot, 1987), the nature of the lexicon as a component makes it possible to define strategies more precisely, and the importance attached to the study of vocabulary among students themselves (Horwitz, 1988).

With the emphasis that communicative approaches placed on the exclusive use of the L2 in the classroom, glossaries with L1 translation equivalents have remained relegated. However, several empirical studies (Chun & Plass, 1996; Grace, 1998; Hulstijn, 1993; Knight, 1994; Laufer & Shmueli, 1997; Prince, 1996) have shown the superiority of bilingual dictionaries when learning an L2. Knight (1994) studied dictionary use while reading. One of the questions that she addressed in her study was whether there was a significant difference between reading comprehension scores for students who used a dictionary (in this case, the subjects had to provide a written definition or an L1 translation equivalent of the target word) and those who did not use it. The findings of her study showed that subjects who used a dictionary not only learned more words but also achieved higher reading comprehension scores than those that did not have a dictionary and had to rely on context clues. In addition, the results demonstrate that low-verbal ability students obtained higher scores than high-verbal ability students. The low-verbal ability students looked up words in the bilingual dictionary, whereas the high-verbal ability students used context first and then their dictionaries to check their guesses. Luppescu and Day's study (1993) shows similar results. Half the students they tested were allowed to have access to a bilingual dictionary while reading the text, whereas the rest were not. They concluded that the use of a bilingual dictionary helped students achieve higher scores on a test administered at the end of the reading task. Recently, Lawley (this volume, Chapter 10: 154) points out that bilingual word lists help students save time when learning new words as they do not need to understand the mechanics of new exercise types and they also help students learn independently of the teacher and other students.

In the development of L2 learners' communicative competence *multi*word lexical units, that is, lexical collocations play an important role. In the next sections, a definition of the concept of lexical collocation will be provided together with the main types and reasons for teaching and learning lexical collocations in an L2.

Lexical Collocations

In teaching *multi*word lexical units, the concept of lexical collocation has acquired greater importance during the past 15 years. In the present study, we follow Higueras' (2004: 71) definition, as it effectively combines different points of view, such as, psychological and semantic perspectives, frequency of use, combination preference and combination restrictions:

> a type of lexical unit (Higueras, 1997; Lewis, 1993), a psychological unit for native speakers of a language (Benson *et al.*, 1986), constituted by two lexemes (Mitchell, 1971) that frequently co-occur, and which show a typical relationship between both (Koike, 2001). Collocations are partially compositional since the base retains its original meaning; however, the collocate takes up a special one when it appears with the base (Castillo Carballo, 2001; Corpas Pastor, 1996; Koike, 2001). Collocations also show combinatory preferences and restrictions imposed by usage and norm (Corpas Pastor, 1996: 76; Zuluaga, 2002: 106). Such preferences and restrictions might come from our world knowledge or they might be due to idiosyncratic reasons related to individual languages.

There are different types of lexical collocations, such as:

(1) noun *subject* + verb:
English: blizzards rage, bees sting
Spanish: ladrar un perro, estallar una guerra

(2) verb + noun *object* (verb + preposition + noun):
English: squander a fortune, burst into tears
Spanish: poner a prueba, entablar amistad

(3) adjective + noun/noun + adjective:
English: weak tea, rough estimate
Spanish: éxito fulgurante, fuente fidedigna

(4) noun + preposition + noun:
English: a colony of bees, a pack of dogs
Spanish: un banco de peces, un enjambre de abejas

(5) verb + adverb:
English: affect deeply, apologize humbly
Spanish: desear fervientemente, negar rotundamente

(6) adjective + adverb:
English: sound asleep, strictly accurate
Spanish: estrechamente ligado, rematadamente loco

Over the last 30 years, growing attention has been given to the processes by which students learn vocabulary. Beginning in the 1970s, Levenston (1979) pointed to the need to study how collocations are learned. However, it was not until the 1990s when empirical studies in this area began to proliferate. Among those, there are studies on the accuracy with which students of different L1s use English collocations (Aghbar, 1990; Aghbar & Tang, 1991; Arnaud & Savignon, 1997; Bahns & Eldaw, 1993; Channell, 1981; Fayez-Hussein, 1990; Nesselhauf, 2003) and studies on the development of collocational knowledge (Ghadessy, 1989; Zhang, 1993). Overall, the previous literature indicates that (a) there is a lack of collocational knowledge on the part of L2 learners of English; (b) collocational knowledge does not evolve parallel to the rest of the lexicon; (c) the knowledge of lexical collocations does not evolve parallel to that of grammatical collocations[1]; (d) it is necessary to teach the concept of collocation and explicitly teach those collocations which are different in the student's L1 and L2 in order to avoid mistakes caused by L1 transfer; (e) factors like idiomaticity, frequency and formality influence the development of collocational knowledge; and (f) deficiencies in collocational knowledge are attributed in part to the excessive emphasis on grammar and the practice of free selection of L2 vocabulary in detriment to the principle of idiomaticity. However, these conclusions are tentative since the authors referred to above do not explicitly state the selection criteria used in their studies nor do they offer a methodology to teach lexical collocations in an L2 based on language and learning theories (Higueras, 2007: 92).

Reasons for including collocations in L2 teaching

Lewis (1997a: 32) states that since words are rarely used alone, it makes sense to teach them in those patterns in which they typically appear. Corpas Pastor (1996) shows that collocations help learners improve the comprehension and production of certain texts and registers, given that certain collocations only appear in specific language varieties. Hill (2000: 49–62) justifies the teaching of collocations in the following way: (a) in the mental lexicon, the collocation is the strongest force in the creation and comprehension of texts; (b) the lexicon is not arbitrary, that is, to a certain extent, the choice of a lexical unit is predictable. Therefore, the knowledge of certain collocations helps predict the type of words that appear together. For example, if we think about the verb *have* within the context of a liquid, the most likely combinations that might surface include *tea, coffee, milk, mineral water, orange juice* and so on, but not *engine oil, shampoo, sulphuric acid,* etc.; (c) roughly 70% of what we hear, decide, read or write forms part – to a greater or lesser extent – of fixed expressions. Thus, it is not enough to know a great number of words, but it is also necessary to have an adequate collocational knowledge; and (d) teaching collocations solves one of the main problems that many students experience. Put differently, an adequate understanding of collocations would help students avoid nonnative-like grammatical usage, which originates in their being unaware of the existence of collocations. This lack of collocational competence makes students create longer utterances in order to express the content of the collocation that they do not know. With respect to this point, Morgan Lewis (2000: 16) claims that collocations often express complex ideas in a simple and precise way, thus helping students avoid longer productions that might not reflect the same idea with the same precision level.

Reasons for including collocations in L2 learning

Nation (1990, 2001) claims that the knowledge of a word would remain incomplete for students if they are not aware of its collocational combinations. It could be argued that learning lexical collocations in an L2 may bring certain benefits to students from the productive and the receptive points of view of word knowledge due to their noncompositional nature, apart from encouraging learner autonomy.

First, the encoding of meaning in L2 lexical collocations (productive knowledge) may be problematic (Brown, 1974; Cowie, 1978; Hussein, 1990;

Mackin, 1978; Martin, 1984), as they have acquired a certain degree of idiomaticity. Castillo Carballo (2001: 136) states that L2 learners employ target-like use of collocations when choosing the base, but they do show nonnative-like variation with the collocate itself as it takes up a special meaning when it appears with the base. Lewis (1993: 82) also stresses the important role of collocations in the creation of meaning. For example, it is impossible to explain the meaning of the verb *to bark*, without referring to the word *dog*. Likewise, the meaning of the verb *to bark* is not complete only with the collocational combination *dogs bark*, but also with the following collocations: *dogs bark, pigs grunt and ducks quack*. In justifying the learning of collocations in an L2, McCarthy and O'Dell (2005: 6) claim that collocations are often the most natural way of expressing something in a language (*smoking is strictly forbidden* is more natural than *smoking is strongly forbidden*) and they carry a greater degree of precision in expressing a notion (*It was very cold and very dark* could be expressed as *It was bitterly cold and pitch dark*).

Second, the decoding (receptive knowledge) can also be problematic for L2 learners in cases of intense semantic specialization of the collocate. For example, in the Spanish collocation *dinero negro* ('black money') the adjective refers to the illegal way in which the money has been obtained, not to its color.

Finally, given the arbitrary nature of collocations (i.e. collocations show preferences and restrictions due to idiosyncratic reasons related to individual languages), learning lexical collocations in an L2 plays an important role in encouraging learner autonomy (Woolard, 2000). According to Woodlard (2000: 35), learning collocations in an L2 mostly consists of students noticing and recording them, so teachers should provide students with enough resources to explore texts for themselves.

The Study

The present empirical study analyzed 24 textbooks (TBs) for teaching English and Spanish to speakers of other languages at different proficiency levels: 12 EngTBs and 12 SpaTBs. Each set of textbooks included four books from three levels: beginning, intermediate and advanced. All textbooks were designed for nonintensive language study.

The goals of the study were to compare the treatment given to (a) the selection and presentation of new vocabulary (*one*-word lexical units and lexical collocations) in EngTBs and SpaTBs at different levels; (b) vocabulary practice (*one*-word lexical units and lexical collocations) in EngTBs and SpaTBs at different levels; and (c) other lexical aspects such as vocabulary recycling, vocabulary learning strategies, and the inclusion of vocabulary lists with L1 translation equivalents at the end of the textbooks.

Instruments

The 12 EngTBs and 12 SpaTBs analyzed were aimed at young adults (16–18) and adults (18 and older) and were published between 1997 and 2007 by European and North American publishers. For admission as data in the present study, the textbooks were required to have explicit vocabulary sections not shared with any language skills (e.g. reading or writing). An additional requirement was for the textbooks to include at least three skills besides the grammatical and lexical components.

The different vocabulary exercises/activities were analyzed following a typology based on the relative degree of control over the answer: (a) *mechanical exercise*: explicit comprehension of the lexical item is not necessary; there is only one correct answer (e.g. completing a word with the missing vowels and/or consonants); (b) *closed exercise*: a greater degree of comprehension of the target vocabulary is needed, and there is still only one option or valid answer (e.g. fill-in-the-blank exercises); (c) *open activities*: students are required to understand the target vocabulary, and there are various possible options and various valid answers and there may or may not be explicit information gaps[2] (e.g. question-and-answer activities based on the target vocabulary, giving a definition of a word); (d) *communicative activity*: there is an open answer and/or a lexical choice that is necessary to complete the activity, along with explicit information gaps; the instructions ask students to interact with each other to achieve a predetermined final outcome which may not be reached individually (e.g. writing advertisements in pairs using the vocabulary provided); and (e) *ambiguous exercise/activity* is a single exercise or activity which contains features of more than one of the previously mentioned categories.

Results

The results of the first part of the analysis (selection and presentation of vocabulary) show that the selection criteria for the vocabulary to be taught were not (explicitly) identified in most of the textbooks under scrutiny. Only two of these textbooks acknowledge the sources of the vocabulary included in them. These sources are 'The Cambridge International Corpus', 'The Cambridge Learner Corpus' and '*Frecuencia de uso y estudio con especial aplicación a la enseñanza del español como lengua extranjera,* H004/2000'.

In terms of vocabulary presentation, in the SpaTBs the percentage of presentation (both explicit and implicit) of *one*-word lexical units is greater than in the EngTBs (71.94% vs. 23.08%, respectively). The tendency of the textbooks analyzed is to reduce the percentage of vocabulary presentation at the advanced level (22.5% in the advanced EngTBs and 65% in the advanced SpaTBs) compared to the percentage presented at the intermediate level (39.58% in the intermediate EngTBs and 75% in the intermediate SpaTBs) (see Figure 11.1).

The Treatment of Lexical Aspects in Commercial Textbooks 167

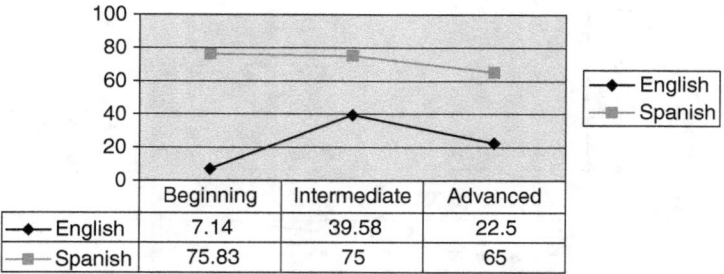

Figure 11.1 (Explicit and implicit) presentation of *one*-word lexical units

On the contrary, the techniques used in the EngTBs to present *one*-word lexical units are less varied than the techniques found in the SpaTBs (see Figure 11.2).

In the SpaTBs there is a higher percentage of presentation of lexical collocations than in the EngTBs (25.83% vs. 12.15%, respectively). However, as the proficiency level of the EngTBs increases, the percentage of textbooks that (explicitly and implicitly) introduce lexical collocations increases too (4.17% in the beginning EngTBs, 12.5% in the intermediate EngTBs and 19.75% in the advanced EngTBs), while the opposite occurs in the SpaTBs (35.83% in the beginning SpaTBs, 25.3% in the intermediate SpaTBs and 16.35% in the advanced SpaTBs) (see Figure 11.3).

Regarding the second object of this study (vocabulary practice), in both EngTBs and SpaTBs, the percentage of closed exercises (47.97% and 57.24%, respectively) and open activities (33.36% and 33.08%, respectively) that were intended for practice of *one*-word lexical units is higher than the percentage of mechanical exercises (14.15% and 1.53%, respectively) and communicative activities (0.09% and 4.88%) (see Figure 11.4).

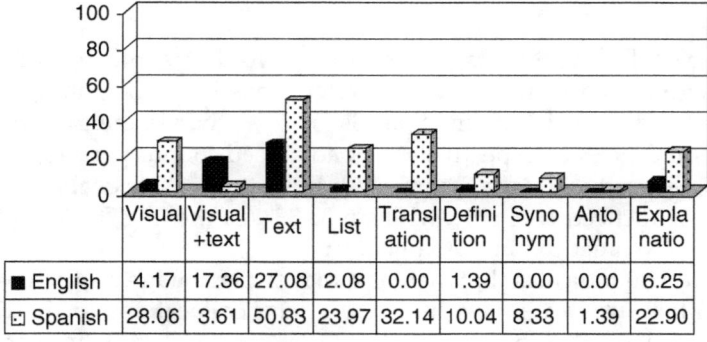

Figure 11.2 Presentation techniques for *one*-word lexical units

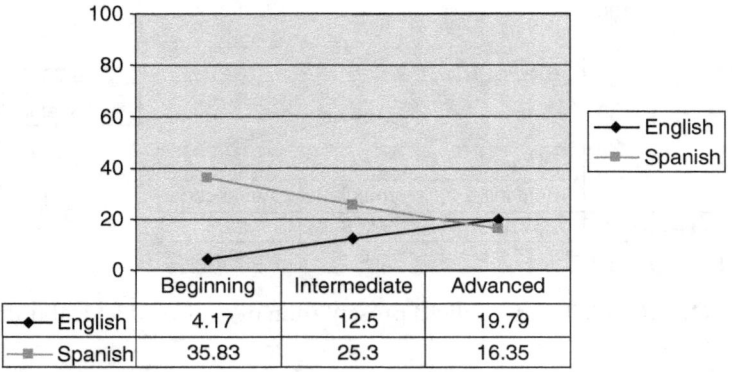

Figure 11.3 (Explicit and implicit) presentation of lexical collocations

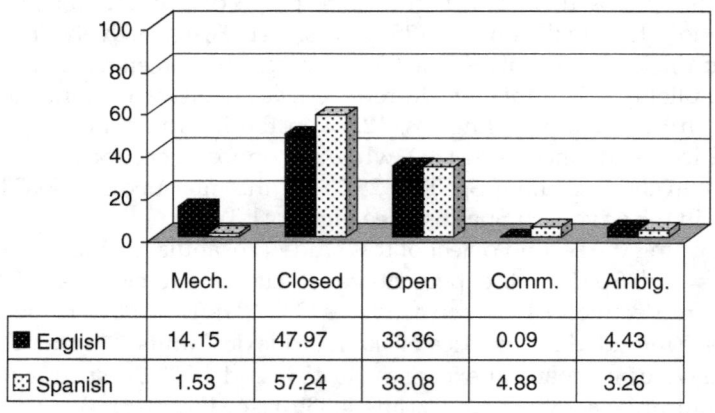

Figure 11.4 Practice of one-word lexical units

There is a lower percentage of teaching units that (explicitly and implicitly) include the practice of lexical collocations in the beginning EngTBs (45.14%) and in the beginning SpaTBs (51.41%) than in their intermediate (64.26% and 59.38%, respectively) and advanced counterparts (57.29% and 59.52%, respectively) (see Figure 11.5). In the SpaTBs, lexical collocations were not practiced explicitly, while in 83.33% of the EngTBs lexical collocations were practiced in an explicit way.

Figure 11.6 indicates that there is a higher percentage of teaching units that contain *adjective + noun* and *verb + noun* collocations in the EngTBs (48.03% and 61.76%) and the SpaTBs (56.87% and 42.72%) when compared to other types of collocations.

The Treatment of Lexical Aspects in Commercial Textbooks 169

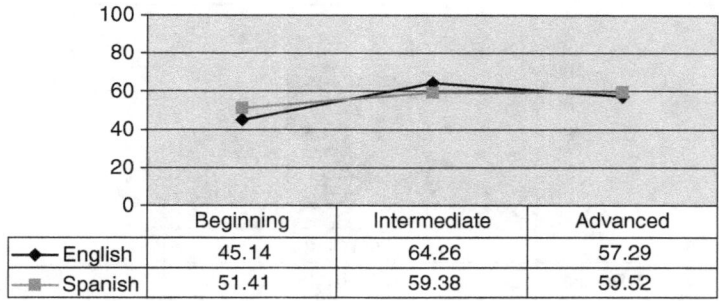

Figure 11.5 (Explicit and implicit) practice of lexical collocations

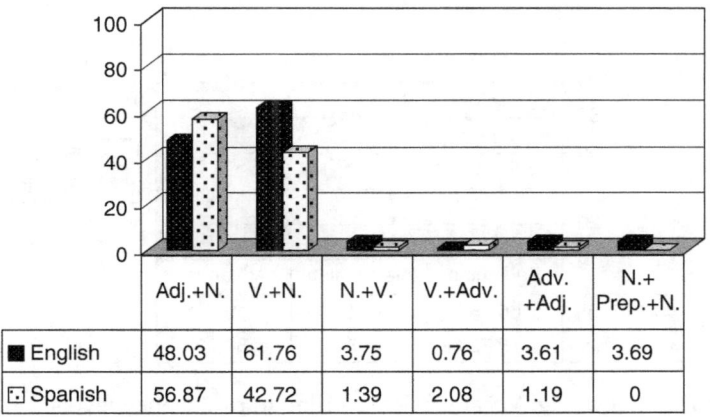

Figure 11.6 Types of lexical collocations

Lastly, with respect to the final object of the study (other lexical aspects), the percentage of teaching units/sections that recycle vocabulary in the EngTBs (66.81%) doubles that which was found in the SpaTBs (32.6%) (see Figure 11.7). In the case of the SpaTBs, an increase in the textbooks' proficiency level correlates with an increase in the number of teaching units/sections in which vocabulary is recycled (18.75% in the beginning SpaTBs, 25% in the intermediate SpaTBs and 54.05% in the advanced SpaTBs). In the advanced EngTBs, there are fewer units/sections (48.33%) containing recycled vocabulary than in the beginning and intermediate EngTBs (68.75% and 83.33%, respectively) (see Figure 11.8).

The percentage of sections that contain vocabulary learning strategies in the EngTBs (11.6%) is slightly over three times higher than that found in the SpaTBs (3.82%) (see Figure 11.9).

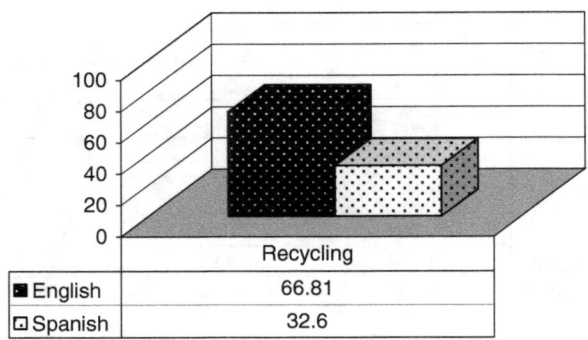

Figure 11.7 Recycling: Vocabulary in Eng TBs vs. Sp TBs

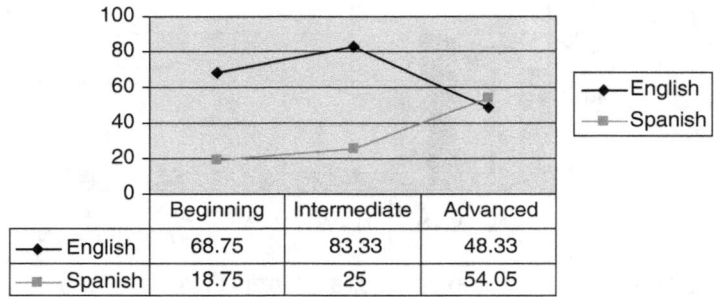

Figure 11.8 Recycling: Vocabulary according to proficiency levels

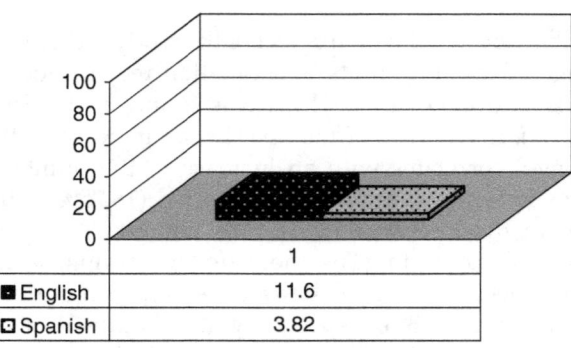

Figure 11.9 Vocabulary learning strategies

The Treatment of Lexical Aspects in Commercial Textbooks 171

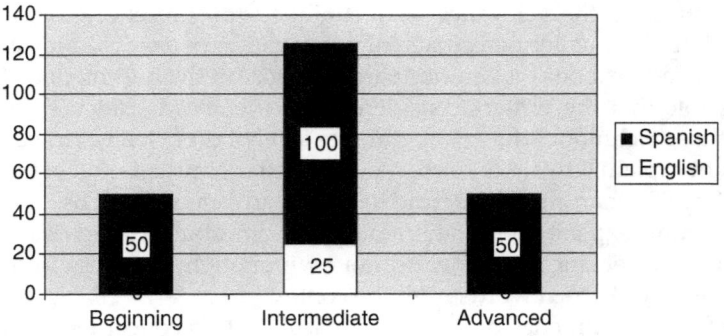

Figure 11.10 Vocabulary lists with translations into the student's L1

Glossaries with L1 translation equivalents at the end of the textbooks are more frequent in the SpaTBs (50% in beginning SpaTBs, 100% in intermediate SpaTBs and 50% in advanced SpaTBs) than in the EngTBs (0% in beginning EngTBs, 25% in intermediate EngTBs and 0% in advanced EngTBs) (see Figure 11.10).

Discussion

The results obtained from the analysis of the 24 textbooks under scrutiny indicate that vocabulary selection criteria appeared in only 8.33% of the textbooks. It is possible that the textbook writers might have used the principle of free selection for the vocabulary taught in the other textbooks.

It is difficult to explain the smaller percentage of presentation and the less variety of techniques for presenting *one*-word lexical units in the EngTBs. One might speculate that the greater variety of presentation techniques in the SpaTBs might be due to their places of publication. Slightly over half the SpaTBs, that is 58.33%, were produced by US publishers to be used as Spanish-language textbooks for L2 learners of Spanish in the United States. With respect to the EngTBs, 16.66% of the EngTBs (2 out of the 12 EngTBs) were adapted to the local context. The titles specify that they were intended for non-compulsory secondary education in Spain (16–18-year-olds) ('New Results for Bachillerato 1', 'New Impact 1° Bachillerato'), while the rest of the EngTBs are global textbooks and could be used in either ESL or EFL classrooms. Considering that foreign language students' oral contact with the target language is most often limited to the classroom and they rarely have the opportunity to clarify the meaning of new vocabulary outside the classroom, it is likely that the writers of the SpaTBs published in the United

States stressed the relevance of techniques for presenting vocabulary. Regarding the smaller percentage of presentation of *one*-word lexical units in advanced textbooks when compared to those at the intermediate level, it is possible that the writers considered that advanced students no longer need those techniques due to their higher level of proficiency. However, this does not explain why there is less new vocabulary presentation in the beginning EngTBs than in the intermediate and advanced EngTBs. As Nation (1993) claims explicit presentation of the new vocabulary is advisable at the beginning level since students do not own enough resources to infer the meaning of unknown words from the context.

As far as the practice of *one*-word lexical units is concerned, there is an imbalance in the number of mechanical exercises, closed exercises, open activities and communicative activities. Closed exercises are the most frequent ones whereas communicative activities rarely appear in the EngTBs and the SpaTBs analyzed. In terms of (explicit and implicit) practice of collocations, the tendency in the analyzed textbooks is to include more lexical collocations in intermediate and advanced textbooks than in beginning textbooks. Hill (2000) considers that the intermediate level is the starting point for the teaching of collocations that contain words that students have already learned as isolated words, whereas Higueras (2004) and Castillo Carballo (personal communication, 2009) state that explicit collocations should be taught from the beginning level. Thus, it seems that there is no consensus with regard to the starting point for the teaching of these combinations. Gitsaki (1996: 31) criticizes the lack of scientific rigor in L2 collocation teaching with respect to what and how many collocations should be taught, how to practice them, and the level at which they should be introduced. Unlike the EngTBs, lexical collocations in the SpaTBs are not practiced explicitly. Empirical studies have shown that it is necessary to teach collocational phrases explicitly, at least those that are different in the students' L1 and L2 (*cf.* Nesselhauf, 2003). Only one of the EngTBs in which lexical collocations are explicitly practiced is a publication for the local Spanish context ('New Impact 1° Bachillerato'). However, the description of this textbook does not specify whether its selection of the lexical collocations included was based on L1 versus L2 differences. On the contrary, *verb + noun* and *adjective + noun/noun + adjective* collocational combinations are the most frequent types in the EngTBs and the SpaTBs, a situation which reflects the frequency with which they occur in both languages (Koike, 2001).

With regard to other lexical aspects, vocabulary recycling is clearly insufficient in the SpaTBs. Research has shown that seven or more encounters with the same word are necessary for a new lexical item to be retained in long-term memory. Nevertheless, the textbooks do not expose students to different encounters with the same item. In the case of vocabulary learning strategies, their presence is anecdotal in both the EngTBs and the

SpaTBs. Thus, learner autonomy is not promoted. Finally, the scarcity of glossaries with L1 translation equivalents in the EngTBs may be due to economic reasons and the influence exerted by communicative approaches. According to Lawley (2000), it is considerably more profitable to publish a textbook that can be sold in many countries than to adapt the same book to a local context. In addition, communicative approaches emphasized L2 use in the classroom in detriment to L1 use. However, as it was pointed out in the literature review, recent empirical investigations have shown that the use of bilingual dictionaries is conducive to L2 learning.

Conclusions and Pedagogical Implications

To conclude, the majority of the EngTBs and SpaTBs analyzed for this study lack systematicity regarding vocabulary selection as the selection criteria used are not specified in the description of most textbooks. Furthermore, it seems that economic benefits are given preference over pedagogical ones in the majority of the EngTBs. For that reason, in the EngTBs, translations into the students' L1 are nonexistent, besides the scarce presence of glossaries with L1 translation equivalents. The interest of publishers might have been to send the greatest number of textbooks into the market, thus ignoring the students' L1. Finally, the writers provide a rather traditional treatment of vocabulary in the textbooks studied as they do not seem to have taken into account the results of recent empirical studies on vocabulary acquisition in an L2. In the EngTBs and SpaTBs, vocabulary practice is mainly comprised of closed exercises adapted from traditional teaching methods and learner autonomy is hardly promoted. In the EngTBs, the students' L1 is ignored whereas in the SpaTBs vocabulary is hardly recycled and lexical collocations are not explicitly practiced.

In spite of the increased attention given to L2 vocabulary teaching over the last three decades, there is still a great deal of room for improvement as regards the design of vocabulary teaching techniques in L2 textbooks. In EngTBs and SpaTBs, vocabulary selection criteria should be given more consideration and should be explicitly identified to avoid selection based on intuitions. More explicit presentation of new lexical items is advisable in beginning EngTBs. There is a need for explicit practice of lexical collocations in SpaTBs and, in the case of EngTBs, differences between the L1 and the L2 should be pointed out to L2 learners when lexical collocations are explicitly practiced. Reducing vocabulary recycling might provide students with more opportunities for new vocabulary to be introduced; however, due to the nature of vocabulary acquisition, recycling must be present in SpaTBs more frequently. Finally, a larger presence of vocabulary learning strategies should also be included in EngTBs and SpaTBs.

Acknowledgments

The author is greatly indebted to Dr Christián Abello Contesse for his invaluable comments.

Notes

1. Grammatical collocations are phrases that contain a base word (noun, adjective, verb) followed by a preposition or a grammatical structure formed by an infinitive or a subordinate clause (Benson *et al.*, 1986: IX). For example, *decide on a boat* meaning 'choose (to buy) a boat', has a grammatical collocation, namely '*decide on*'.
2. According to Richards and Schmidt (2002: 257), in a communicative act between two or more people an information gap constitutes 'a situation where information is known by only some of those present. In communicative language teaching it is said that in order to promote real communication between students, there must be an information gap between them, or between them and their teacher. Without such a gap the classroom activities and exercises will be mechanical and artificial'.

Chapter 12
A Second-generation CALL Vocabulary-learning Program ADELEX: In Search of a Psychopedagogic Model[1]

CARMEN PÉREZ BASANTA

Introduction

There is great deal of consensus amongst applied linguists to say that for a long time vocabulary teaching has not received enough attention and has been downplayed in the field of second language acquisition. Traditionally, teachers and researchers have prioritized the teaching of grammar, functions and phonology at the expense of vocabulary teaching (Pérez Basanta, 1999). Until 20 years ago or so, it was not generally acknowledged that lexical competence lay at the heart of communicative competence and hence was crucial to EFL teaching/learning. From a pedagogic perspective, the most influential cause was the interest in vocabulary and its developments by some applied linguists. To bring back some opinions of that time, we might recall Widdowson's (1978: 115) words: '... lexis is where we need to start from, the syntax needs to be put to the service of words and not the other way round'. And Wilkins (1972: 111) went even further in his highlighting of the importance of vocabulary in his much-often remark: 'Without grammar very little can be achieved, without vocabulary nothing can be achieved'. However, the real trigger was Richard's seminal paper 'The role of vocabulary teaching' (1976), which in the light of the findings concerning a deeper understanding of the nature of vocabulary in both the fields of linguistics and applied linguistics, raised the issue that the teaching of vocabulary should be redefined to fit into the way we design our syllabi. At the end of the 1980s, the so-called Lexical Approach (Lewis, 1993; Willis, 1990) highlighted the importance of teaching vocabulary and promoted the emergence of many studies devoted to prove the essential role of vocabulary in the acquisition of a second language. As Jiménez Catalán claims (2002: 149), over the last

20 years, research on the process of learning and teaching vocabulary in L2 has moved from a marginal to a privileged position in studies in second language acquisition. To us, vocabulary is absolutely essential for the acquisition of a second language and, therefore, it should be an important part of syllabus/curriculum design. In short, lexis is at the heart of language acquisition.

We can now affirm that in the last two decades vocabulary has been gaining momentum and there are now a great deal of approaches to vocabulary teaching and an abundance of instructional and testing techniques to choose from. Amongst them, CALL applications have had a major influence in vocabulary acquisition current trends. In fact, technological advances in the way of multimedia language input (text, sounds, DVDs, etc.) and resources from the web (online dictionaries, thesauri, concordancers, lexical databases, back-grammars and other tools) alongside exposure to authentic comprehensible input provided by the Internet have also contributed to the support and design of instructional materials. In line with this, Watts (1997) advocates the use of multimedia CALL applications as 'they provide exploratory learning environments in which digital sound, image text and video components are fully integrated through computer platforms and placed under the direct control of users who are able to follow individual pathways through data stores' (1997: 2). Therefore, the next section will be devoted to reviewing computer-assisted vocabulary learning and will suggest some principles for the design of CALL applications, focusing on the basic tenet underlying a second-generation lexical program entitled 'ADELEX: Assessing and developing lexical competence through web-based learning' (*cf.* Pérez Basanta, 2003b, 2004, 2005, 2006b).

Vocabulary and CALL

Vocabulary learning has always been a popular subject in CALL programs, especially in the early stages of CALL (1980s) when vocabulary learning could be easily integrated into CALL (Ma & Kelly, 2006). According to Goodfellow (1995) citing Jung's review of CALL materials (1988) 'vocabulary as a topic came top amongst the software packages he [Jung] reviewed'. The earlier vocabulary activities were very simplistic and mechanic – text reconstruction, gap-filling, speed-reading, multiple choice and vocabulary games, easily integrated into multimedia commercialized packages (Levy, 1997). These are known now as first-generation CALL programs. Later on in the 1990s and very much in accord with the growing interest in vocabulary acquisition and the new theories in vocabulary teaching and learning, technological advances (hypertext, glossing, digital LMS, online dictionaries, corpus resources, etc.) brought about a second-generation of computer-assisted vocabulary learning applications whose main objective was the design of CALL programs focusing on the possibilities that the computer offers for the access, selection and processing of lexical knowledge. Amongst these computer-mediated applications we can mention:

(1) *LEXICA* (1994), a program which in words of its designer tries 'to help learners enhance their ability to acquire vocabulary, by promoting awareness of semantic and/or formal features among target lexical items, by making use of mental associations that can be generated using these features, later memorization and productive retrieval of items' (Goodfellow, 1994: 219).

(2) *CAVOCA* (2000) – Computer-Assisted Vocabulary Acquisition – developed by Groot (2000) at the University of Utrecht is intended for the acquisition of 500 key words for ESP university students. Although the number of words (500) had very little to do with vocabulary at the tertiary education level, the model for the acquisition of those words draws on solid psycholinguistic principles structured in three stages: (a) Noticing words taking into consideration their different traits: grammatical, morphological, syntactic, stylistic, collocational and others. (b) Storing words by means of word associations and nets. (c) Consolidating word meaning and form by encountering them in different contexts. In fact this psycholinguistic model might help to firmly anchor the word and facilitate its acquisition.

(3) Ma and Kelly's *WUFUN* (2006) draws on 'the current research findings of vocabulary acquisition and CALL, aiming to help Chinese university students to improve their learning of English vocabulary, particularly that with which they experience most difficulty. It is argued that vocabulary should be learned explicitly as well as implicitly; learners need to be trained to become good learners, for example by being instructed in useful learning strategies, to enable them to learn vocabulary more efficiently and effectively' (Ma & Kelly, 2006: 15).

(4) *ADELEX* – Assessing and developing lexical competence through WebCT – (*cf.* Pérez Basanta, 2003b, 2004, 2005, 2006b) was developed at the University of Granada and its overall objective was to improve lexical competence amongst students of English Studies drawing on lexical aspects from the fields of lexicography, lexicology, semantics and discourse analysis, corpus linguistics, and it also tried to profit from the advances of new technologies to maximize virtual learning. All in all, activities have been designed to expand word knowledge, collocations, idioms and lexical phrases and encourage the use of metacognitive strategies such as the use of online dictionary look-up, lexical databases and other linguistic resources on the web (2003b).

The origin of this lexical project is a research study which attempted to measure the lexical size of students of English Studies at the University of

Granada (Pérez Basanta, 2005). In short, its findings showed that their lexical dimension fell short for their academic and social demands. As a result, a further study was undertaken to develop a web-based course that would improve the vocabulary levels of university students (2003b, 2004, 2006b). This project obtained several national and European prizes.

Thus, the thrust of ADELEX is based on the following hypothesis:

> Being lexical competence one of the most important aspects of communicative competence and thus essential in SLA, and in the light of the empirically proven lexical shortcomings of students of English Studies (Pérez Basanta, 2006b), we proceeded it on a dual front, on the one hand, it has been thought that a pedagogical treatment targeted to enhance learners' lexical competence – word knowledge, collocations, idioms and formulaic sequences – might be highly beneficial; while on the other, we sought a computer-mediated methodology which might develop learner autonomy through self-access and interactive learning – administered through the newly launched ***Campus Virtual Andaluz***. Overall, this learning experience within the framework of constructivism should be informed by relevant psycholinguistics hypotheses, based on a solid lexicological investigation and carried out by virtual learning via a digital platform (WebCT). Alongside this, Internet might provide not only motivation but free access to a rich bank of authentic, content-rich and comprehensible materials. We also count on the use of a variety of instructional strategies such as autonomy, hypertextuality, interaction and cooperative learning through LMS (Learning Management System), the new technological developments in corpus linguistics and computational linguistics for the exploration and selection of materials.

Although we cannot discuss and further compare the merits and limitations of these programs, what they undoubtedly share is the idea of 'situating vocabulary learning in context instead of treating it as an isolated activity, as was the case before' (Ma & Kelly, 2006: 16). Another important facet of the last two is to give learners as much freedom as possible in choosing what to learn and how to learn.

However, a first argument often deployed against computer-mediated lexical environments is the need to tackle 'the complexity of processes involved in vocabulary-learning by capitalizing on theories of the structure of the mental lexicon' (Goodfellow, 1995: 223). Another criticism is that they lack a pedagogical basis and they are more technology-driven than psycholinguistics or pedagogy-led (Brennan *et al.*, 2001). In other words, new digital learning lacks 'guiding principles to inform their design, and that there is a requirement for a more fundamental level of discussion' (Goodfellow, 1994: 1). Likewise, Poel and Swanepoel (2003: 173) argue that vocabulary instruction 'has often been decided more by gut feeling, common sense or the trendiness of certain approaches than by theoretically, empirically and/or pragmatically motivated and design criteria'. This is the reason why in ADELEX we wanted to challenge both objections by first establishing relevant psycholinguistic hypotheses concerning lexical processing in computer-mediated courses, and then looked into key pedagogic factors of web-based learning and their close connection with constructivism and why Language Management System (LMS) such as WebCT might be the best way of delivering online learning.

Psycholinguistics and Lexical Acquisition in a Computer-mediated Environment

Over the last two decades or so there has been a burgeoning interest in the way in which lexical knowledge is internalized. It is widely accepted now that the more we know about vocabulary acquisition from a psychological perspective, the more teaching and learning will benefit from it. However, applied linguistic scholars have been reluctant to take on board psycholinguistic insights (Meara, 1997). To Meara (1997), one of the reasons applied linguistics literature on vocabulary acquisition has moved so slowly as a field is due to the fact that psycholinguistic work has in fact been ignored. Thus, this section attempts to highlight the most relevant psycholinguistic hypotheses concerning the mental processes individuals go through when acquiring words which, by extension, have far-reaching implications for the teaching of vocabulary in a web-based environment. What we really want to do in this section is to analyze how CALL can provide effective lexical processing. Owing to paper length restrictions, we will just concentrate on three of the most relevant hypotheses: The *imaginability or dual-processing*, the *context availability* and the *depth-of-processing* hypotheses.

(1) The 'imaginability hypothesis' or 'dual-coding theory' (Paivio, 1986; Plas, 1998) assumes that subjects perform better on concrete words than on abstract nouns on the grounds that the semantic memory consists of two separate but interlinked systems, a subsystem of verbal concepts and a system of visual concepts. In line with Poel and Swanepoel (2003: 187), we strongly believe that 'visual material supports the verbal information and supports the comprehension of a lexical item'.

Granting this assumption, creating mental images through multimedia materials and Internet can facilitate recall and so numerous studies have looked into the beneficial effects of multimedia on developing lexical acquisition showing that computer-mediated programs can certainly be useful for learning vocabulary (Al-Seghayer, 2001; Brett, 1998; Groot, 2000; Hulstijn, 2000; Laufer & Hill, 2000; Nicolova, 2002).

(2) Many teachers are led intuitively to believe that context-embedded input is crucial, arguing that there is no real grasp of a word until students have performed some mental contextualization. The answer to this could be the 'context availability' hypothesis (Morton, 1969; *cf.* the logogen hypothesis) which suggests that words encountered in contextual information are more accessible and ultimately more firmly established in the mental lexicon. To Morton (quoted in Singleton, 1999: 84): '... any context which increases the probability of words in a generation situation would be expected to lower their threshold of recognition'. Hence, if presenting and learning words in context is a vital factor for word learnability (Sternberg, 1987), web-based instruction might be particularly suitable for the design of real-like activities intentionally devised to build bridges between the classroom and the real world. It goes without saying that Internet has the advantage of offering an almost limitless bank of authentic materials in a way that the numbered pages of coursebooks cannot (Pérez Basanta, 2003a).

(3) Craik and Tulving (1975) in their 'depth-of-processing (DOP) hypothesis' reveal that something absolutely crucial in vocabulary acquisition is the kind of activity the brain requires at the moment learning occurs. The central idea of DOPH is that 'deeper analysis of a stimulus leads to a more persistent memory trace, with "depth" referring to a greater degree of semantic involvement' (Segler, 2001: 23). This leads us to another issue directly related to L2 lexical acquisition: the importance of learner personal involvement (Channell, 1988). In line with Channell's ideas, we construe that in lexical acquisition one of the most decisive factors is the active role of the learner. This process is affected by several factors, amongst which motivation is a crucial one. Thus, if learner interest and motivation go hand in hand, then the Internet may have something to offer which other approaches lack. The fact that students can work at their own pace and engage in both short- and long-term 'discovery' learning tasks and projects (Thorne & Thorne, 2000) would seem to provide a solid foundation on which to tackle the perennial problem of involving and motivating students. As it is widely acknowledged (Warschauer, 1996) that the Internet is a very motivating factor, we can conclude that web scenarios are particularly apt for developing vocabulary.

In the preceding discussion, we have tried to argue that although perhaps there is no 'best' way about how to approach vocabulary in an absolute sense (Poel & Swanepoel, 2003), there seems to be a clear consensus about the benefits of creating positive conditions for facilitating imaging and concreteness, providing contextual variables and fostering deeply cognitive processing. Thus, in the design of ADELEX we have attempted to provide multimodal environments for offering visual component (graphics, animation video, pictures) and audio as well; embedding activities in genuine socio-cultural contexts, and designing task-oriented learning for fostering deep processing of words.

The Search for a Pedagogic Model: Virtual Learning and Constructivism

Similar to any other mode of teaching and learning a language, web-based learning is only worthwhile when it is guided by sound pedagogical principles which are girded up by theoretical notions of language learning and acquisition (Pérez Basanta, 2006a). Beyond doubt it is essential for online instruction that course design is developed with due regard for sound theory of teaching/learning. In fact, efforts have been made to ensure that ADELEX is based on state-of-the-art techniques and on strong and, where appropriate, innovative theoretical lexical considerations. As mentioned before, we very strongly believe that web-based contents should not be technology-driven, but pedagogy-led. But despite years of CALL instruction, technology seems to be driving pedagogy and there is still a shortage of literature that addresses the specific issue of a coherent web pedagogy (Jasinski, 1998; Knupfer, 1993). We entirely agree with this view and strongly believe that teaching and learning associated with online delivery must be sustained by a sound web pedagogy which in turn should contribute to any judgement about the effectiveness of web-based education.

Although to date there is no definitive paradigm yet to the design of learning methodologies, there is an increasing interest in several critical issues that concern the effectiveness of the instructional design in virtual learning. First and foremost, these issues involve the promotion of autonomy (*distance learner and learner autonomy*), the participation in real-like learning environments (*authenticity of materials and multimedia*), the ability to cope effectively with different types of information in a holistic way (*hypertextuality* as opposed to linear and atomistic learning), the cooperation with other members of the community by participating in well-organized synchronous and asynchronous discussions (Web communication tools), and the provision of interactivity (*human mediation and online resources*). In this vein, it is quite striking to see the affinities between virtual learning and constructivism. Some even suggest that the come-back of constructivism is due to its obvious affinities with web-based pedagogy.

> It is probably no accident that constructivism is gaining popularity and momentum at the same time interactive, user friendly computer technologies are becoming widely available. The computer offers

effective means for implementing constructivist strategies that would be difficult to accomplish in other media. (Driscoll, 1994: 376)

In fact, comparing the pedagogic lines of web-based and constructivist paradigms, we have found a close parallel which could be summarized as follows (Pérez Basanta, 2006a):

Constructivism	*Web-based learning*
Construction of learning through meaningful activities	Authentic and multimedia materials
Emphasis on big concepts not sequential and atomistic knowledge	Hypertextuality
Collaborative learning	Web communication tools
Coaching and scaffolding	Human mediation and interaction
Learner's responsibility	Distance learning and learner autonomy

Thus, the rest of this section intends to develop a framework for the establishment of effective distance-learning constructivist scenarios.

(1) *Promotion of learner autonomy*: One main objective of virtual learning is to implement a methodology which will develop learners' autonomy through self-access and distance learning. For many years now a growing list of authors (Benson, 2000; Benson & Voller, 1997; Holec, 1981, 1988) have foregrounded the importance of promoting learner autonomy in ELT. Likewise, numerous studies have underscored the role that the web might play in fostering learner independence (Healey, 2002; Motteram, 1997) as learners have to make their own choices and thus take more responsibility over their own learning. In this sense, e-Learning seems to increase students' responsibility (Benson, 2000) as

> [it] has the potential to raise the stakes for learning of all kinds by offering an unprecedented level of autonomy to self-paced and self-directed learners. If the outcome is a learning process that is led by learner demand rather than by supply-driven force-feeding, this will be to the benefit of all parties, from individuals to organizations to societies. (Bowles, 2004: 90)

In addition, learner autonomy through an online methodology can help learners to work at their own pace while engaging in both short- and long-term 'discovery' learning tasks (Thorne & Thorne, 2000). Not surprisingly, most researchers admit now that enhancing students' vocabularies largely rests on their personal investment of time, effort and attention (Hilton & Hyder, 1995).

(2) *Participation in real-like learning environments through authentic materials*: As mentioned before, the aims of online virtual learning, very consistent with constructivist paradigms, are to make students active participants in the construction of new knowledge through hands-on activities, reflection and critical learning (Kearsley & Shneiderman, 1999), in contrast with some traditional learning in which they act as mere recipients of knowledge. Therefore, there is the underlying idea of engaging learners in meaningful activities. through tasks-based learning.

It follows from this that, for instance, in terms of syllabus design, there are primary differences between language learning via the web and conventional classroom learning. It is widely acknowledged that distance learning imposes some requirements on syllabus design. One of the most salient is that the syllabus should not be product-based – that is, a mere list of contents – but process-based – that is, an inventory of activities (White, 1995). The pedagogical goal of the teaching through ICT is to improve performance by participating in interaction. Here the computer acts as a participant and it can well be argued that our learners work interactively with the computer (Chapelle, 1997). It is also interesting to note that in this task-based approach learners build up knowledge by engaging in some sort of interaction. Again the pedagogical theory behind web-based learning is constructivism (Zahorik, 1995).

Moreover, if presenting and learning words in meaningful contexts is a vital factor for word learnability (Sternberg, 1987), web-based instruction might be particularly suitable for the design of real-like materials intentionally devised to build bridges between the classroom and the real world. Undoubtedly, the Internet has the advantage of offering an almost limitless bank of authentic resources and content-rich information input both in themselves as well as in the visual images and sounds that often accompany them in a way that the numbered pages of coursebooks cannot.

(3) *Web communication tools*: Online delivery facilitates new and exciting modes of communication between learners and teachers. It is particularly noteworthy of the promotion of interactivity through communication tools in courses delivered by means of digital platforms. In fact, WebCT provides the assistance of computer-mediated communication (CMC) for replicating the interactions of the classrooms. E-mails, discussion forums, chats and whiteboards are beginning to offer a new environment for promoting interaction in an asynchronous or synchronous way. In this vein, discussions or forums between student–teacher, student–student(s) and teacher–student(s), student-to-student and students-to-teacher communication around topics and questions relative to your course provide the tools for collaborative

learning, whose ultimate objective is to enhance linguistic interactivity and social learning. This is also a central tenet of constructivism for which learning is considered a social process in need of constant encouragement, support, feedback and opportunities for practice. Perhaps it should be noted here that research work is just beginning to investigate the implications of online support via communication tools on learning a second language. In fact, research carried out in our project has proven that LMS (Language Management System) was highly beneficial (Pérez Basanta, 2004).

(4) *Human mediation and interaction*: Much of the theoretical underpinnings of web-based learning revolve around the concept of 'interactivity'. As Brennan *et al.* (2001, Internet) states there are two sources of interaction:

> This term can be used to refer to levels of engagement with computer-based learning resources, everything from sitting and receiving information and activities with the learner ostensibly in 'control'; through to collaborative relationships with others online in a constructed environment where the learner pursues interests and ideas with some scaffolding of support.

Hence, interaction is organized in two different modes: (a) interactive activities (assignments, self-tests and quizzes) for the provision of on-the-spot feedback, and (b) human mediation or 'scaffolding' which according to McLoughlin and Marshall 'is a form of assistance provided to a learner by a more capable teacher or peer that helps the learners perform a task that would normally not be possible to accomplish by working independently' (2000: Internet). Following from this definition, the most important way of digital scaffolding is offered by LMS insofar as it offers learners human support and coaching in their online learning experience.

Presumably, one big advantage of web-based learning, as a revolutionary medium, is the possibility of providing learners with interactional feedback, in the way of human coaching and/or interactive activities. In line with this, if feedback points to positive relationship with performance in any language skill, it has proven to be particularly beneficial and favorable in learning vocabulary (Nation, 2001).

(5) *Hypertextuality*: Nelson, who originally coined the term 'hypertext' defines it as 'non-sequential writing' (Nelson, 1987). Seemingly, the hypertextual world of the world wide web is a gestaltic and holistic learning experience in contrast with atomistic and sequential on-the-ground learning. In fact, online environment enables learners to move independently among associative nets of information through hypertext to construct their own experiences and hypertextuality is thus an embodiment of constructivism as Jonassen, Mayes and

McAleese eloquently express in this quotation: 'acquiring knowledge from hypertext requires the user to engage in constructivist learning processes' (1993, Internet). Therefore, hypertext requires active readers insofar as the reader creates their own individual texts and experiences (Webb, 1996).

Although there is very little work on hypertextuality and the way it affects learning, we wish to claim here its beneficial effects on vocabulary acquisition. The underlying assumption is that, as there is widespread evidence now that frequency plays a large part in word intake, hypertextuality can offer students the possibility of increasing word encounters through multiple semantically related texts. In this respect, Jenkins and Dixon (1983) have argued that you need between 6 and 12 encounters to learn a word.

Throughout this section we have analyzed main principles behind web-based environments and constructivism. We can conclude that there is no clear division between the two areas but overlapping themes and issues. This makes us think that constructivist views run *pari passu* with virtual learning (Driscoll, 1994) and in the final analysis, we are totally convinced that the solution to the search for a web pedagogy lies in the conjunction of the two approaches.

Conclusion

In the first part of this chapter we briefly reviewed the important role that lexis plays in SLA. There seems to be now a great deal of consensus among researchers and teachers that lexical competence is an essential component of communicative competence. Second, we were concerned with some literature on CALL vocabulary programs. Third, in view of the lack of psycholinguistic thinking concerning vocabulary acquisition and the mental lexicon, we discussed the most relevant hypotheses and their implications in web-based learning. This was followed by the search for a CALL efficacy model to ensure the quality of online learning environments. This model was found in a constructivist philosophy of learning whose principles go hand in hand with assumptions behind virtual learning and effective instructional design.

Note

1 This chapter is part of an R&D project (Ref: HUM2007-61766/FILO) entitled 'ADELEX: Assessing and Developing Lexis through New Technologies'. The project is financed by the Spanish Ministry of Education & Science.

Chapter 13
Word Associations as a Vocabulary Teaching Strategy in an Advanced L2 Reading Class

ZORANA VASILJEVIC

Introduction

A significant dilemma in applied linguistics research concerns the techniques of vocabulary instruction in an L2 class. While some researchers (e.g. Nagy & Herman, 1987; Nation, 1990) see guessing from context as the most effective way of vocabulary learning, others (e.g. Kelly, 1990; Sökmen, 2000) argue that learners are more likely to benefit from systematic vocabulary instruction. One of the most commonly offered arguments in favor of implicit vocabulary learning is the number of words that learners encounter in L2. The average educated native speaker is thought to have a vocabulary of around 20,000 base words that have been acquired at the rate of 2–3 words per day (Nation, 2001). Although second language learners' rate may keep pace with that of native speakers, reaching the vocabulary size of native speakers is hardly an achievable goal. The gap is simply too big, as most non-native speakers (NNS) have limited time at their disposal and limited exposure to the foreign language. Computer analysis of language corpora shows that about 80% of the individual words in most written English texts are members of the 2000 most-frequent word families. Therefore, it has been argued that explicit instruction should focus on the 2000 most frequent words, and that the primary strategy for dealing with low-frequency words should be to teach learners to infer word meaning from context (Nation, 1990, 2001). Experimental data from several studies, however, raise questions about the effectiveness of this approach. First, due to factors such as distance between L1 and L2, lack of linguistic proficiency, and insufficient contextual clues, students seldom guess the correct meaning (Kelly, 1990; Pressley *et al.*, 1987). Furthermore, even when students infer word meaning correctly, the retention rate is usually low. It has been found that learners need between 5 and 16 repetitions of a word for learning to occur (Salling, 1959; Saragi *et al.*, 1978).

The arguments presented above suggest that there is a place for direct vocabulary instruction at all levels of language proficiency. Learning a foreign language to advanced level of proficiency, however, involves the acquisition of many thousands of words. Therefore, it is important to consider ways in which instructional programs might foster the integration of such a large number of lexical items. This is a complex question and one that can only be answered adequately when we specify the type and level of the learner, the goal of learning and the specific learning context.

The central aim of this study is to assess the efficacy of semantic link-based instruction in the development of vocabulary knowledge in a foreign language instructional context. The study will focus on advanced learners who have a limited contact with the target language.

Semantic links are relationships between words that make up the semantic network by which lexical knowledge is represented in the mind of the language users, be they native speakers or language learners. They can be classified into two basic categories: context-independent links in which lexical items are related to other words in the language (also referred to as word associations), and text-based lexical links where the semantic links are defined in relation to other words in the text. The present study will focus on the first type of semantic links – context-independent word associations.

Word associations are believed to reflect the semantic organization in the human mind. Psycholinguistic studies have found that words in the minds of adult native speakers tend to be semantically organized, and that these links are strong and long lasting (Postman & Keppel, 1970; Read, 1993). The evidence from both native and non-native speakers suggests that a shift from phonological to semantic associations is closely related to the level of integration of the target word in the mental lexicon.

Word association tests have mainly been applied to vocabulary assessment to examine the level of maturity of an individual entry in the mental lexicon, the mechanics of individual word acquisition and the development of lexical networks in second language reading (Read, 1993; Schmitt & Meara, 1997). Little research, however, has been done on word-association-based instruction and vocabulary growth in L2.

This study is an attempt to critically examine word association as a vocabulary teaching strategy in terms of its effects on vocabulary growth, text comprehension and the interaction between students in class. The point of departure for the present study was an observation – which is confirmed in the literature (e.g. Bahns & Eldaw, 1993; Hill, 1999; Koosha & Jafarpour, 2006) – that L2 learners often have particular problems with word combinations, even at a relatively advanced level. Bahns and Eldaw (1993), for example, found that for advanced students, collocations present a major problem in the production of correct English. These problems can be attributed to two major sources. One is students' tendency to carry over semantic patterns from their L1 to their L2 production. The other is inadequate emphasis given to semantic links in L2 instruction.

L1 interference is considered one of the major causes of L2 learners' errors (Gabrys-Biskup, 1992). Given the presence of an established, L1 conceptual and semantic system, L2 learners, in particular adult learners, may tend to rely on this system in the process of acquisition of L2 vocabulary.

In the L1 mental lexicon, each lexical entry is represented on two levels: *the lemma* and *the lexeme* (Levelt, 1989). Lemmas involve semantic and syntactic knowledge, that is, knowledge of a word's basic meaning, part of speech, grammatical properties and its pragmatic and stylistic features. Lexemes contain morphological information and formal (phonological and orthographic) specifications about a lexical item. Meaning and form are highly integrated within each entry in the mental lexicon enabling automatic access to all information once the entry is opened.

The presence of the existing semantic and lexical system of L1 inevitably affects lexical acquisition in L2. Lexical development in L2 is believed to go through three basic stages (Jiang, 2000). At the initial stage, also known as the formal stage, L2 items exist as purely formal entities. There is no semantic or grammatical information associated with an L2 entry and with the lemma structure being empty, both receptive and productive use is mediated through L1 translation equivalents.

The second stage is the L1 lemma mediation stage where the content of L1 lemmas is attached to L2 lexemes. L1 lexical forms cease to play a crucial role in L2 word use, and the direct connection between L1 lemma and L2 lexical form results in a higher degree of automaticity in the use of L2 words.

The final stage is the integration stage where semantic and syntactic information of L2 lemmas is attached to L2 lexemes. Only at this stage does lexical representation and processing follow the pattern of L1. L2 lexemes will be directly associated with other L2 lexemes, both being directly related to the respective lemma knowledge.

While in principle any L2 word can reach the third stage, in practice that is often not the case. Despite high motivation, for some learners lexical development ceases before they reach native-like proficiency. Jiang (2000) hypothesized that the reason for lexical fossilization may be only partial integration of semantic and syntactic information into the lexical entry. As learners tend to rely on the preestablished conceptual/semantic systems of L1, L2 items are often acquired as purely formal entities. While exposure to highly contextualized input may provide additional information about a word to the learner, given the presence of the L1 lemma in the lexical entry, the input may also be strengthening the link between L1 lemma and L2 lexeme and, consequently, slowing down or even blocking the integration of L2 lemma information into the entry. As a result, whenever there is no complete overlap in semantic and grammatical specifications between L2 words and their L1 translations, lexical errors in L2 production are likely to occur.

The above outlined model of L2 lexical development has some important pedagogical implications. Even with sufficient exposure and metacognitive knowledge of language rules, errors in language production may occur because the relevant lexical information is stored outside the lexical entry. Errors in word choice and usage cannot be eliminated as long as the learner relies on conscious recollection of lexical links between the L1 and L2. In conclusion, if L1 intervention leads to lexical fossilization, then vocabulary instruction should aim at minimizing the reliance on L1 and encouraging meaning interference. The development of word associations seems to be a prerequisite for full integration of lexical entries and therefore, it should be one of the primary objectives of explicit instruction.

However, despite the fact that word associations are both indispensable and problematic for foreign language learners, they have been neglected by both conventional approaches, such as the Grammar Translation Method and the modern approaches, such as the Communicative Approach. As Lewis (2000) points out, the reason why many students fail to make any perceived progress is simply because they have not been trained to notice which words go together. Students' knowledge of word associations and collocations in particular lags far behind their knowledge of vocabulary in general (Bahns & Eldaw, 1993). This knowledge, however, is essential to full communicative mastery of the target language.

The current study was developed on the assumption that instruction that exploits stable semantic links in the language (i.e. links that are not limited to any particular context) would enable learners to acquire lexical properties beyond the basic meaning or specific context, and consequently result in better quality of vocabulary knowledge. It is hypothesized that instruction that exploits semantic networks beyond the sentence level can help learners overcome the difficulties mentioned above and develop vocabulary similar in size and quality to that of native speakers.

Method

The effect of semantic-link-based instruction on vocabulary learning was assessed by comparing three vocabulary teaching conditions: word associations (WA), explicit definitions (ED) and inferencing from context (IN). Each treatment was considered to promote a different aspect of lexical competence.

As associations of a word to a large degree reflect the various meaning systems that the words fit into (Nation, 2001), instruction through word associations was expected to help learners gradually acquire a set of features that make up the meanings of words. The potential limitation of this approach is that while it provides valuable information on the semantic and syntactic properties of the word, these properties are acquired incrementally. The word's form–meaning link cannot be established as quickly as in the Explicit Definition method.

In the Explicit Definition treatment learners are asked to select the correct definition for each of the target words from a list of possible choices. The Explicit Definition method draws on the core sense of a word. The advantage of this approach is that it enables learners to quickly and reliably match a new word form with the meaning and related concept. The potential disadvantage is the limited information learners gain about the network of associations between the target words and other words in a language and consequent potentially stronger reliance on L1 mediation.

The Inferencing method is a contextualized approach to vocabulary teaching where learners are asked to 'discover' the meaning of new words by utilizing various contextual clues. This method enables learners to learn the target word associates in the specific context. By examining contextual clues, learners build their awareness of how the word is actually used. The downside of the Inferencing approach is that it gives a less definite meaning of the target word, it can be time consuming and it is an intrinsically error-prone process. Limited proficiency in L2 and interference from L1, often prevent learners from recognizing the relevant contextual clues and inferring word meaning correctly.

Participants

The experiments were conducted with advanced learners of English in Japan. The students were at the high-intermediate level with TOEIC scores of 700–800 (TOEFL 540–570). They attended EFL classes twice a week for a total of 3.5 h (105 min of listening and 105 min of reading) for a period of 18 weeks. Vocabulary acquisition was examined in reading class for two reasons. One is that medium-to-low frequency words tend to occur more often in written than in spoken language. Written texts are more likely to contain the words that advanced learners may not be familiar with. The other is the premise that reading provides more opportunity to study context, form hypotheses and infer the meaning of unknown words (Li, 1988), the conditions necessary in order to evaluate objectively the effectiveness of the Inferencing method. Totally, 12 participants were enrolled in the study. Overall, 10 students completed all the stages of the experiment.

Reading Materials

Four magazine articles were selected from the English-medium weekly magazines *Time* and *The Economist*. The decision to use authentic material was made on the grounds that the organizational structure of texts like these facilitates top-down processing and enables the learner to use global contextual clues (Haynes, 1984; Young, 1993). Authentic material also ensures that contextual clues are not exaggerated or reduced.

Choice of Test Items

In all, 60 target words believed to be new to the students were selected from four magazine articles, forming four sets of 15 items (five words in each learning condition). The test was done with real words rather than imaginary words or blanks to reduce as far as possible the element of artificiality in the test. All target words were content words. Target items were presented in the same grammatical class as they occurred in the article, so the list included nouns (22), verbs (21), adjectives (16) and adverbs (1). The words are listed in Appendix I.

In order to identify the words that students are less likely to be familiar with, Nation's *Vocabulary Profiler* was used as a guideline. The program analyzes a sample of text and classifies the words into four frequency bands: the first thousand words (K1), the second thousand words (K2), an academic word list (AWL) and off-list words; that is, all the words that do not belong to any of the first three categories. *Vocabulary Profiler* does not distinguish between different parts of speech and different meanings of the same word type. It was assumed that students were most likely to have difficulty with AWL and low-frequency off-list items. Out of the 60 target words, 47 (78.3%) were off-list items, 11 (18.3%) were on AWL, one word (1.7%) was classified as K2 and one word as K1 (1.7%). K1 and K2 words (*to bar* and *spell*) were included in the study, because it was believed that these specific items would be new to the students. While most students are likely to know *bar* used as a noun (=pub) and *spell* used as a verb (as in 'spell your name'), it was anticipated that a majority of the participants would not be familiar with the usages in the texts [*to bar* = to forbid; *spell* (n.) as in 'magic spell'].

Study Format

The study consisted of four parts:

(a) a pre-test;
(b) reading treatment;
(c) practice tests;
(d) a post-test.

Pretest

The pretest assessed learners' receptive knowledge of the target items by having them translate the English L2 word into the Japanese L1. The English words were presented without context. The time allocated for the task was 15 min.

Reading treatment

The reading treatment was designed as an intensive reading program, which involved a close study of short texts with deliberate attention being given to the lexis, grammar and discourse of the text. The students were presented with four magazine articles followed by comprehension activities: open-ended comprehension questions, true and false questions, referencing and inferencing tasks and paragraph summaries.

Practice tests

Each reading treatment was followed by two practice tests. Practice tests were not used for vocabulary assessment, but as a vocabulary teaching tool. Their main purpose was to encourage learning, not to measure learners' knowledge of the target words. Each test consisted of three sections: a multiple-choice explicit definition test (EDT), a word association test (WAT) and a test of lexical inferencing from context (INT). All three parts of the test were developed to enable systematic, formal vocabulary instruction and an effort was made to create the conditions that would be most conducive to learning. (For test samples see Appendix II.)

The Word Association tests were designed to strengthen knowledge of word meanings, knowledge of the words the stimuli were associated with and knowledge of the collocations in which they occurred. The study adopted the test format developed by Read (1993). For each of the target words, a list of four context-independent associates and four distractors was given. Following Read's (1993) study, all distractors were chosen on the basis that they had no semantic link with the target word, and no attempt was made to create distractors by using words that had some orthographic or morphological relation to the target form. In order to reduce the probability of guessing, an attempt was also made to select associates which were not obviously semantically related. The learners were asked to select paradigmatically or syntagmatically related words. (In the instructions, test-takers were advised to look for words that go together or have similar meaning.) The participants were also instructed to leave the questions open if they did not recognize the word. The number of possible associates was fixed at four, and the participants were informed of that. As noted by Read (2000: 185), if test-takers are not informed of the actual number of associates, they may stop at two or three responses. As the word may have various meanings, careful consideration was given to ensure that the associates were related to the sense of the target word in the text. In order to ensure the reliability of the test, two English teachers (native speakers) were asked to review the items to check whether they agreed on the associates for each item. Where there was disagreement, the items were revised.

The Explicit Definition tests consisted of a multiple choice of four possible definitions for the target words. As definitions were given in L2, they had to be lexically and syntactically simple enough for the learner to understand them. Therefore, all entries in the multiple choice test were taken from the *Oxford Advanced Learner's Dictionary (OALD)*. *OALD* was chosen because it had been used extensively in class and was therefore familiar to the participants in the study. The definitions were given in the forms of synonyms or paraphrase. For the words with multiple senses, a definition was given for the sense that appeared in the text. Effort was made to ensure that all distractors and the correct answers were of the same part of speech as the target item, but unrelated in meaning.

The Inferencing test (INT) was more open-ended than the EDT and WAT. All participants in the study received training in strategies for inferring word meaning from context as a part of their regular course work. The instruction included practice in recognizing word functions within sentences, practice in word formation (analysis of roots, prefixes and suffixes) and practice in recognition of the cohesion techniques of English texts (discourse markers, referencing and restatements). During the instruction, special attention was given to the differences in application of cohesive techniques in English and Japanese. While the two languages share some cohesive devices, such as demonstratives and ellipsis, others are language specific. For example, while in English cohesion is often established through pronouns, synonymy, selection of a more general term and use of the definite article, Japanese displays a tendency toward repetition of the same words, full noun phrases, or elliptical structures (Rittershofer, 1987). It was felt important that the learners were made aware of these differences.

Procedures

As the tests were not intended for assessing learners' knowledge of the target words, but rather as a vocabulary learning strategy, each practice test was done twice, and the learners were given feedback on their performance. Wrong answers were corrected to prevent the learning of incorrect meanings and the model answers were provided to the students in writing. For EDT and WAT words, feedback consisted of correct definitions and appropriate associates. For the INT, where answers were less clear cut, the students were given 1–2 possible substitutes for the target words in the specific context, and the relevant contextual clues were pointed out if necessary.

Practice tests and feedback for all four articles were administered to the learners at equal time intervals in order to reduce the possible effect of treatment proximity on test results. The repetition of the tests and feedback was expected to draw students' attention to new words, increasing the chances of them being learned. Drawing on the well-established findings of the superiority of spaced over massed repetition (Griffin, 1992; Pimsleur, 1967), the first practice test was given immediately after the reading treatment, with feedback provided in the following week. The second practice test was distributed to the learners a month later, again with feedback provided a week after that.

Post-tests

Several important methodological considerations had to be taken into account when the posttests were designed. First, an effort was made to ensure that the post-tests were not an exact repetition of what occurred in the course. If the post-tests were the same as the practice tests, learners could rely on episodic memory, making it more difficult to assess the effectiveness of the experimental treatments and consequently reducing the validity of the study. Second, the results of the post-tests had to be comparable to the pre-test. Different test formats often result in different degrees of test sensitivity. Therefore, a translation component was included in the post-test as well. Third and most important, the post-test had to be relevant to the goals of the study. As the main purpose of this study was to examine how the different treatments affect receptive and productive learning and whether word associations can lead to vocabulary learning beyond a simple definition or the specific context, it was important to test both learners' understanding of the target words and their ability to use them in new contexts. Therefore, the test could not be limited to translation of individual words in isolation. In order to evaluate the effectiveness of the experimental treatments and assess the amount of learning that took place, in addition to the translation task, the learners were asked to generate sentences using the target words. This test format was selected on the grounds that it offered greater opportunities for simultaneous assessment of several aspects of word knowledge. Generating sentences tests both understanding of the concepts and the ability to use the target words in new contexts appropriately. The time allocated for usage posttest was 30 min. All the tests were done with pen and paper.

Data Analysis

One point was assigned for each correctly translated item on the pre- and the post-test. In order to ensure reliability of the study, students' responses were examined by two independent raters. One native speaker of Japanese and one native speaker of English, both bilingual, served as raters. Where there was a disagreement, the responses were reexamined by the raters.

In the usage test, sentences were rated for the quality of description and the usage of grammatical forms. Each correct sentence was awarded one point. No points were awarded for sentences which clearly showed that the learner did not understand the target word or confused it with a similar one, and only half a mark was awarded for the sentences where a context was not specific enough to indicate understanding. Half a mark was also deducted if there were errors in the inflectional or derivational forms of the target word or collocations. No marks, however, were taken off for sentence level grammar errors, such as tense, spelling of other words and so on. To ensure objectivity of the assessment, each sentence was rated by two native speakers of English. Where there was a disagreement, the sentences were reexamined by the raters.

Interrater reliability was established by the calculation of Pearson's product–moment correlation coefficient, a common measure of correlation between two sets of interval data. The statistical significance of the difference between the pre- and posttest scores was established through a Wilcoxon signed-rank test, a nonparametric alternative to *t-test* for correlated samples. The usage and translation scores were compared across conditions using Friedman's two-way analysis of variance, a non-parametric method form comparing group means.

Results

Pre-test

The results of the tests showed that the majority of the target items were not known to the students and the known–not known ratio distributed fairly evenly across the three learning conditions. Of the 20 target items for each learning condition, the mean numbers of unknown words were as follows: Word Association (WA) 2.26/20; Explicit Definition (ED) 1.67/20; and Inferencing (IN) 1.92/20. The results of the pretest with mean values and standard deviations are summarized in Table 13.1.

Table 13.1 Translation pretest: Learner performance by instruction condition and articles by raw scores

Article	Word associations		Explicit definitions		Inferencing from context	
	Mean	SD	Mean	SD	Mean	SD
#1	0.42/5	0.67	0.83/5	0.83	0.50/5	0.67
#2	0.42/5	0.85	0.42/5	0.51	0.00/5	0.00
#3	0.75/5	0.87	0.17/5	0.39	0.67/5	0.65
#4	0.67/5	0.83	0.25/5	0.45	0.75/5	0.75
Average mean	0.56/5	0.81	0.42/5	0.61	0.48/5	0.65
Overall mean sum	2.26/20	1.65	1.67/20	1.37	1.92/20	1.56

Table 13.2 Translation posttest: Learner performance by instruction condition and articles by raw scores

Article	Word associations		Explicit definitions		Inferencing from context	
	Mean	SD	Mean	SD	Mean	SD
#1	3.17/5	1.75	3.67/5	1.83	3.00/5	1.28
#2	4.17/5	0.94	3.92/5	1.16	2.25/5	1.48
#3	3.50/5	0.97	3.20/5	1.32	3.10/5	1.52
#4	4.00/5	1.10	4.18/5	0.60	3.18/5	1.17
Average mean	3.71/5	1.27	3.74/5	1.32	2.88/5	1.38
Overall mean sum	14.84/20	4.85	14.97/20	4.80	11.53/20	4.20

Post-test (translation)

The effectiveness of the different vocabulary treatments was evaluated by examining students' performance on the translation and the usage post-tests. The mean and standard deviations for the translation posttest can be found in Table 13.2.

The average mean scores across the articles show differences in the effectiveness of the three learning conditions. By the end of the treatment, the students were familiar with around 74% of the target words presented under WA and ED conditions and only 57% of the target words introduced under the Inferencing condition. The Inferencing condition also had the lowest mean scores in all four articles suggesting that this strategy may be the least effective for vocabulary instruction of adult learners in formal settings.

Post-test (usage)

The analysis of the results on the usage posttest followed the same procedures as the translation posttest. The means and standard deviations were calculated for each instruction condition and each article individually. The summary of the results is provided in Table 13.3.

The results provide positive evidence regarding the effects of vocabulary treatment conditions on the growth of word knowledge. In all conditions, however, the gains were modest when compared to the results of the translation posttest. The average mean scores across the articles suggest significant differences in the effectiveness of the three learning conditions. By the end of the treatment, the students were familiar with around 52%

Table 13.3 Usage post-test: Learner performance by instruction condition and articles by raw scores

Article	Word associations		Explicit definitions		Inferencing from context	
	Mean	SD	Mean	SD	Mean	SD
#1	2.25/5	1.76	3.29/5	1.88	1.54/5	1.29
#2	3.12/5	1.30	2.79/5	1.53	1.29/5	1.01
#3	2.20/5	1.06	1.92/5	1.21	2.07/5	1.50
#4	2.91/5	1.44	2.54/5	1.31	2.27/5	1.55
Average mean	2.62/5	1.44	2.64/5	1.54	1.79/5	1.36
Overall mean sum	10.48/20	4.90	10.54/20	5.37	7.17/20	3.88

of the target words presented under the WA and ED conditions and only 36% of the target words introduced under the IN condition, showing that the latter method was again the least effective.

Pre-test–Post-test differences (translation)

The effectiveness of the three instruction conditions was assessed by comparing the results in the pre-test and the translation post-tests. Of interest was the number of items learners acquired during the treatment and possible differences between the instruction conditions. On average, 14.97 (74.8%) of the target words were acquired in the ED treatment, 14.84 (74.2%) in the WA condition and 11.53 (57.6%) in the IN condition. The figures indicate no significant difference in the effectiveness of ED and WA methods when the goal of vocabulary instruction is the recall of word meaning. Inferencing was not found to be as successful as explicit instruction.

Six students had the best results under the ED treatment, three students under the WA condition and one student benefited most from the IN method. These results indicate that the latter may not be the most effective way of vocabulary teaching for adult learners in formal settings where the exposure to the target language is limited.

The statistical significance of the pre-test–post-test differences on the translation test was examined through the Wilcoxon signed-rank test. Pairwise comparisons were carried out for each learning condition (Table 13.4).

Pre-test–Post-test differences (usage)

No usage pre-test was administered, so a direct comparison of pre- and post-test usage performance is not possible. The effect that the vocabulary

Table 13.4 Wilcoxon signed-rank test (pre-test–post-test differences by instruction condition (translation))

	ED pre-test–post-test (transl.)	WA pre-test–post-test (transl.)	IN pre-test–post-test (transl.)
Z	−3.064[a]	−2.984	−3.061
Asymp. sig. (2-tailed)	0.002	0.003	0.002

[a]Based on negative ranks.

treatments had on the growth of the students' productive vocabulary knowledge was examined by comparing the results on the usage post-test with students' scores on the translation pre-test. The mean and the standard deviation were calculated for each learning condition and each article individually as well as a total. The summary of data is presented in Table 13.5.

Compared to the results of the translation post-test, the gains were more modest, but still evident. The best results were obtained under the Explicit Definition treatment where the students acquired around 44.3% of the target words. Under the Word Association condition, 41.1% of the target words were acquired. Only 26.3% of the words presented under the Inferencing condition were learned by the subjects. The average number of words acquired by the subjects was 22.3 (37.2%). Seven subjects had the best results under the ED treatment, and for three subjects the WA condition was the most effective. These results were in line with earlier studies (Hulstijn, 1992; Kelly, 1990) which indicate that the IN method may not be a suitable method for classroom instruction in ESL settings where exposure to L2 is limited.

Table 13.5 A comparison of translation pre-test scores with usage post-test scores: Learner performance by instruction condition and articles by raw scores

	Word associations		Explicit definitions		Inferencing from context	
Article	Mean	SD	Mean	SD	Mean	SD
#1	1.83/5	2.16	2.46/5	1.69	1.04/5	1.47
#2	2.70/5	1.52	2.37/5	1.55	1.29/5	1.01
#3	1.45/5	0.99	1.75/5	1.29	1.40/5	1.26
#4	2.24/5	2.11	2.29/5	1.19	1.52/5	1.53
Average mean	2.05/5	1.75	2.21/5	1.43	1.31/5	1.30
Overall mean sum	8.22/20	5.68	8.87/20	5.10	5.25/20	3.66

Table 13.6 Translation pre-test – usage post-test differences by instruction condition

	Translation test		
	Translation pre-test – usage post-test scores		
	Explicit definition	Word association	Inferencing from context
Z	−3.061[a]	−2.669	−2.847
Asymp. sig. (2-tailed)	0.002	0.008	0.004

[a]Based on negative ranks.

The statistical significance of the results was tested through the Wilcoxon signed-rank test. Pairwise comparisons were carried out for the pre-test–post-test differences for each condition. In all instances, the observed z exceeded the 1.96 critical value ($p < 0.05$ nondirectional). The summary of the results is provided in Table 13.6.

Post-test performance: Translation versus usage

The effects of the treatments on vocabulary knowledge were further as expected, differences in students' performance on the two post-tests were noticeable in all articles and all learning conditions. The average number of learned items per article was significantly lower when acquisition was measured by the ability to use the target words. When results of the tests are converted into percentages it becomes clear that regardless of the treatment, the scores on the usage test were approximately 20% lower than the scores on the translation post-test (21.8% for WA, 22.1% for ED, 21.8% for IN). The difference in the results can be attributed to the nature of the task – the recall of word meaning on a translation test places less demands on the learner than sentence production.

The Usage and Translation results were compared across Conditions using Friedman's two-way analysis of variance. The difference between pre- and posttest scores for the Translation task were significantly better than that on the Usage task [chi-square (5) = 28.09, $p < 0.000$]. Follow-up pairwise comparisons were carried out for the pre-test–post-test differences for each condition and compared across the Usage and Translation responses. All tests are two-tailed. For the Explicit Definition condition Translation Difference – Usage Difference = −2.91, $p = 0.004$. For the Word Association condition: Translation Difference – Usage Difference = −2.94, $p = 0.003$. For the Inferencing condition: Translation Difference – Usage Difference = −2.59, $p < 0.01$.

Discussion

Students' performance on both posttests suggests positive effects of vocabulary treatment on lexical development. Owing to the complexity of the task, for all three conditions the scores on the usage test were lower than the scores on the translation test. On both the translation and the usage test, the best results were obtained when the students were provided with explicit definitions of the target words. The differences between ED and WA scores, however, seem minimal, and the results are encouraging. Both treatments had a clear advantage over the IN condition. While in most cases, the learners were able to utilize contextual information and come up with guesses which belonged to the same grammatical class as the original words and shared at least some of their semantic properties, the process of recording these semantic specifications in the lexical entry seems to require a longer time period.

The explanation for the findings obtained may lie in the nature of vocabulary learning and different learning mechanisms that are activated under each condition. Knowing a word is never an either–or situation, but rather a process during which individual words gradually move from a status of being unknown to being partially known and eventually integrated into the mental lexicon. Not all words are integrated to the same extent. The mental lexicon consists of numerous layers of vocabulary knowledge: core vocabulary, which includes the words that are well-known, and several layers of peripheral vocabulary consisting of words that are known to varying degrees. Vocabulary learning involves both assimilation of new entries in the lexicon and strengthening the connections between the core and peripheral vocabulary. The distribution of words between different layers is unstable. The vocabularies of the learners were found to show a high degree of flux and change, with words constantly moving in and out of different states, particularly where less frequent items were concerned (Meara & Rodriguez Sanchez, 1993).

Vocabulary instruction can therefore be viewed as a form of external stimulation provided to facilitate the transition of a particular item from one state to another. The three learning conditions discussed in this experiment present three different channels through which lexical networks can be enlarged and restructured. It is believed that observed variation in the effectiveness of the treatments reflects the activation of different elements in a lexical entry during the conversion process. It seems reasonable to assume that at the time of the post-tests, the 60 target words examined in this study were at various stages of development, and each of the learning conditions facilitated integration of semantic, syntactic and morpho-orthographic information in a different way.

As discussed before, in the Explicit Definition condition the link between the meaning and the form is developed by listing the core semantic properties of the concept. The Word Association treatment encourages learners to explore the semantic and syntactic properties (i.e. the lemma structure) of the target words. The learner acquires lemma information by examining other L2 entries, which share semantic or functional properties with the target word. In the process of inferring word meaning from context the learner fills in an empty lemma structure with syntactic information from surrounding context and semantic information from existing concepts (de Bot *et al.*, 1997). A fact that should not be overlooked is that the results for the ED and WA treatments were close with the scores being only slightly higher in the ED condition. The mechanisms that operate behind word integration in these two conditions, however, are different, and there are strong reasons to believe that they result in different forms of lexical representation and development of L2 entries with instruction through WA offering potentially some long-term benefits. As all target words were only perceptually, not conceptually unfamiliar items, the list of their semantic properties, although provided in L2, is likely to activate the corresponding L1 lemmas. To the extent that the properties of L1 and L2 lemmas are the same, this is not a problem. Copying of the L1 lemma information into the L2 lexical entry means a reduction in conscious recollection of L2–L1 links in productive use of L2 words, which in turn increases automaticity in production (Jiang, 2000).

The difficulties, however, occur when the properties of the corresponding lemmas are different. As two different languages rarely share identical semantic or syntactic specifications, information from L1 lemmas can weaken connections between L2 words and their conceptual representations resulting in interference errors even in very advanced learners, and in some cases, lexical fossilization. The WA treatment takes into account the fact that the L2 learner already has a semantic system in L1, which only partially overlaps with the semantic system of L2, and that growing lexical competence in L2 requires further differentiating of the two meaning systems. Instruction through word associations helps the learners focus not only on the meaning of the new word, but also strengthens the links between the target words and other words in the mental lexicon. The advantage of the WA strategy is that it encourages conceptual mediation rather than the lexical association of 'corresponding' L1 and L2 items. Word association tasks where the learners are asked to select the appropriate paradigmatic/syntagmatic responses highlight the semantic and syntactic properties of the target words, strengthen the links between the items in L2 mental lexicon, and help build new concepts for L2 lemmas.

On the basis of the different mechanisms behind the creation of a lexical entry and with no significant differences in the retention rate between the ED and WA treatments, it is possible to conclude that different types of vocabulary treatment may be suitable for different categories of words. While ED treatment may be the most efficient way of matching the core meaning with the form, it can be applied safely only on the words which either do not have counterparts in L1 or the words which have a high degree of semantic overlap in the two languages. It also seems that instruction through explicit definitions may be more suitable for lower levels of lexical proficiency when L2 vocabulary is limited and L1 lemma information may assist L2 use. On the contrary, instruction through word association may be the most effective way to deal with *'false friends'* – words which have L1 translations, but do not share a high degree of semantic overlap.

Underlying mechanisms that characterize inferencing from context share more similarities with the WA condition than instruction through explicit definitions and seem to provide good conditions for the development of lexical competence at a native-like proficiency level. Inferring word meaning from context assumes contextualized input, and therefore reduces the danger of L1 mediation. An empty L2 lemma structure is filled in with syntactic information from the text and semantic information from the existing concepts in the learner's conceptual system, and gradually integrated into the lexical entry. However, due to the limited exposure to contextualized input that most learners have, a new entry is often added to the lexicon with inadequate or even misleading semantic and syntactic specifications resulting in lower retention rate and more production errors as reflected by the results of the post-tests. The results suggest that compared to the ED and WA conditions, the Inferencing strategy, may require more time and repetition for integration and internalization of word forms and their lemmatic characteristics and, therefore, may not be suitable for learners who have limited exposure to the target language.

Conclusion

The present study set to examine how different approaches to vocabulary instruction influence the effectiveness and patterns of L2 vocabulary acquisition. To the extent that this sample is representative of advanced learners with limited exposure to L2, instruction through definitions and associations seems to be a more effective way of approaching L2 vocabulary. Inferring word meaning from context was behind the other two strategies in both productive and receptive uses of the target words, with the impact in productive use being more pronounced. Based on the findings that emerged, it seems that identifying word meaning from written context is a difficult task even for the students who have attained solid lexical knowledge of the target language. While each engagement with an unfamiliar word encountered in a text represents a potential opportunity for learners to expand their vocabulary, limited contact with the target language means that construction of word meaning from context can become a very slow and error-prone process. Therefore, it can be concluded that relying solely on incidental vocabulary learning may not be sufficient, and that advanced learners who have a limited contact with the target language benefit from explicit vocabulary instruction.

While the explicit definition condition produced the best results on both the translation and usage post-tests, the differences between the gains in the ED and WA treatments were not significant, and some findings from the research on the mechanisms of vocabulary learning in L2 indicate that instruction through word associations may have major long-term benefits. Word association task where the learners are asked to select the appropriate paradigmatic/syntagmatic responses highlights the semantic and syntactic properties of the target words, strengthens the links between the items in L2 mental lexicon, and helps build new concepts for L2 lemmas, consequently resulting in a greater degree of automaticity and accuracy in production. Another advantage of the Word Association approach is that it minimizes learners' reliance on the L1. Equivalent words in the L1 and L2 are likely to share only the core meaning and other semantic properties are likely to be language specific. Therefore, reliance on L1 can potentially lead to incomplete semantic development of the items in the L2 lexicon and lexical fossilization. Unlike the Explicit Definition approach where learners acquire the basic meaning of the word, instruction through word associations goes beyond the simple meaning definitions. It helps learners build links between the words that belong to the same semantic field and acquire knowledge of collocations specific to L2, consequently reducing the frequency of output errors. This is especially important in the case of adult learners who already have a fully developed semantic system in their L1.

While the sample size and the relatively short duration of the experiment make it difficult to make generalizations, the results of this study suggest that instruction through word associations may offer some significant benefits over other strategies for vocabulary teaching. It is hoped that the findings of this study will be of interest to instructors in similar instructional settings and prompt them to evaluate the existing practices and experiment with new approaches to vocabulary teaching. It is also hoped that the results of this study will stimulate further research in vocabulary teaching and word associations in L2.

Appendix I

Target Words			
Nouns (23)	*Verbs (20)*	*Adjectives (16)*	*Adverbs (1)*
statistics	to flee	enduring	terminally
foetus	to spark	foul	
brood	to pinpoint	bewitched	
culprit	to rescind	grubby	
surplus	to inject	eligible	
necromancy	to overturn	vague	
spell	to ingest	creepy	
compound	to assent	emboldened	
euthanasia	to bar	impaired	
dose	to proliferate	abject	
foe	to inflate	rampant	
apologist	to exploit	gleaming	
instigator	to dilute	prestigious	
privilege	to gravitate	sullied	
ego	to backfire	debased	
peer	to cohabit	intertwined	
proportion	to intervene		
persuasion	to reverse		
pronouncement	to publicise		
league	to dither		
welfare			
attainment			
incentive			

Appendix II

Practice Test Samples
a. *Explicit Definitions*
Directions: Read the definitions below and circle the one that best describes the meaning of the target word.
statistics means:

(a) materials for writing;
(b) a collection of information shown in numbers;
(c) a sum of money given to somebody in return for something dishonest;
(d) a germ that causes food poisoning.

b. *Word Associations*
Directions: For each of the words **in bold** circle the words that either have a similar meaning or can go together in a sentence.
Note: For each word there are FOUR associates.
inject
remove   ease   insert   suffer   drugs   pain-killer   arm   pain

c. *Inferencing from Context*
Directions: Read the following excerpts from the article 'All shall have prizes' and try to guess the meaning of the words **in bold**.

For years fashionable educators have been arguing that the worst thing you can do to young people is to damage their sensitive **egos** with criticism. 'If a child lives with criticism, he learns to condemn', goes a popular screed handed out to the parents of preschoolers. 'If a child lives with praise, he learns to appreciate; if a child lives with approval, he learns to like himself'.

What does *egos* probably mean? _____

References

Acklam, R. (1994) The role of the coursebook. *Practical English Teaching* 14, 12–14.
Adolphs, S. and Schmitt, N. (2003) Lexical coverage of spoken discourse. *Applied Linguistics* 24, 425–438.
Aghbar, A.A. (1990) Fixed expressions in written texts: Implications for assessing writing sophistication. Paper presented at a Meeting of the English Association of Pennsylvania State System Universities.
Aghbar, A.A. and Tang, H. (1991) Partial credit scoring of cloze-type items. Paper presented at 1991 Language Testing Research Colloquium, Educational Testing Service, Princeton, N.J.
Aitchinson, J. (1994) *Words in the Mind: An Introduction to the Mental Lexicon*. Oxford: Blackwell.
Allan, R. (2006) *Data-driven learning and vocabulary: Investigating the use of concordances with advanced learners of English*. CLCS Occasional Paper No. 66. Dublin: Trinity College.
Allwright, D. and Bailey, K. (1991) *Focus on the Language Classroom*. Cambridge: Cambridge University Press.
Al-Seghayer, K. (2001) The effects of multimedia annotation modes on L2 vocabulary acquisition: A comparative study. *Language Learning and Technology* 51, 202–232.
Alternberg, B. and Granger, S. (2001) The grammatical and lexical patterning of MAKE in native and non-native student writing. *Applied Linguistics* 22, 173–195.
Ames, W. (1966) The development of a classification scheme of contextual aids. *Reading Research Quarterly* 2, 57–82.
Anderson, J. (1982) Acquisition of cognitive skill. *Psychological Review* 89, 369–406.
Anderson, J.P. and Jordan, A.M. (1928) Learning and retention of Latin words and phrases. *Journal of Educational Psychology* 19, 485–496.
Ard, J. and Holmburg, T. (1983) Verification of language transfer. In S. Gass and L. Selinker (eds) *Language Transfer in Second Language Learning* (pp. 157–176). Rowley, MA: Newbury House.
Ariew, R. (1982) The textbook as curriculum. In T. Higgs (ed.) *Curriculum, Competence and the Foreign Language Teacher* (pp. 11–34). Illinois: National Textbook Company, The Pennsylvania State University.
Arnaud, P.J.L. and Savignon, S.S. (1997) Rare words, complex lexical units and the advanced learner. In J. Coady and T. Huckin (eds) *Second Language Vocabulary Acquisition: A Rationale for Pedagogy* (pp. 157–173). Cambridge: Cambridge University Press.
Arnold, W. and Rixon, S. (2008) Materials for teaching English to young learners. In B. Tomlinson (ed.) *English Language Learning Materials* (pp. 38–58). London: Continuum International Publishing Group.
Baddeley, A. (1990) *Human Memory: Theory and Practice*. Needham Heights, MA: Allyn and Bacon.

Baddeley, A. (1997) *Human Memory: Theory and Practice* (revised edition). Hove: Psychology Press.

Bahns, J. and Eldaw, M. (1993) Should we teach EFL students collocations? *System* 21, 101–114.

Barcroft, J. (2007) Effects of opportunities for word retrieval during second language vocabulary learning. *Language Learning* 57, 35–56.

Barrow, J., Nakashimi, Y. and Ishino, H. (1999) Assessing Japanese college students' vocabulary knowledge with a self-checking familiarity survey. *System* 27, 223–247.

Bates, E., Dale, P.S. and Thal, D. (1995) Individual differences and their implications for theories of language development. In P. Fletcher and B. MacWhinney (eds) *Handbook of Child Language* (pp. 1–42). Oxford: Basil Blackwell.

Bauer, L. and Nation, I.S.P. (1993) Word families. *International Journal of Lexicography* 6, 253–279.

Beglar, D. and Hunt, A. (1999) Revising and validating the 2000 Word Level and University Word Level vocabulary tests. *Language Testing* 16, 131–162.

Bengeleil, N. and Paribakht, T.S. (2004) L2 reading proficiency and lexical inferencing by university EFL learners. *The Canadian Modern Language Review* 61, 225–249.

Benson, P. (2000) Autonomy and information technology in the educational discourse of the information age. *ILEC Conference*, University of Hong Kong, December 2000. On WWW at http://ec.hku.hk/macomp/readings.htm. Accessed 4.4.2009.

Benson, M., Benson, E. and Ilson, R. (1986) *The BBI Combinatory Dictionary of English. A Guide to Word Combinations*. Amsterdam: Benjamins.

Benson, P. and Voller, P. (1997) *Autonomy and Independence in Language Learning*. London: Longman.

Bensoussan, M. and Laufer, B. (1984) Lexical guessing in context in EFL reading comprehension. *Journal of Research in Reading* 7, 15–32.

Bertenthal, B.I. (1999) Variation and selection in the development of perception and action. In G. Savelsbergh, H. van der Maas and P. van Geert (eds) *Non-Linear Developmental Processes* (pp. 105–121). Amsterdam: Koninklijke Nederlandse Academie van Wetenschappen.

Bjork, R.A. (1988) Retrieval practice and the maintenance of knowledge. In M.M. Grueneberg, P.E. Morris and R.S. Sykes (eds) *Practical Aspects of Memory: Current Research and Issues* (pp. 396–401). Chichester: Wiley.

Bley-Vroman, R. (1988) The fundamental character of foreign language learning. In W. Rutherford and M. Sharwood-Smith (eds) *Grammar and Second Language Teaching: A Book of Readings* (pp. 19–30). New York: Newbury House.

Bloem, I. and La Heij, W. (2003) Semantic facilitation and semantic interference in word translation: Implications for models of lexical access in language production. *Journal of Memory and Language* 48, 468–488.

Bloem, I., van der Boogard, W. and La Heij, W. (2004) Semantic facilitation and semantic interference in word translation: Further evidence for the conceptual selection model of lexical access. *Journal of Memory and Language* 51, 307–323.

Bogaards, P. and Laufer, B. (eds) (2004) *Vocabulary in a Second Language*. Amsterdam: John Benjamins.

Bowles, M.S. (2004) *Relearning to E-Learn*. Carlton: Melbourne University Press.

Braidi, S.M. (2002) Reexamining the role of recasts in native-speaker/nonnative-speaker interactions. *Language Learning* 52, 1–42.

Brennan, R., McFadden, M. and Law, E. (2001) *All that Glitters is Not Gold: Online Delivery of Education and Training*. Leabrook: NCVER. On WWW at http://www.ncver.edu.au/publications/662.html. Accessed 5.4.2000.

Brett, P. (1998) Using multimedia: A descriptive investigation of incidental language learning. *Computer Assisted Language Learning* 112, 179–200.

British National Corpus, version 2 (BNC World) (2001) Distributed by Oxford University Computing Services on behalf of the BNC Consortium. On WWW at http://www.natcorp.ox.ac.uk/.

Brown, C. (1993) Factors affecting the acquisition of vocabulary: Frequency and saliency of words. In T. Huckin, M. Haynes and J. Coady (eds) *Second Language Reading and Vocabulary Learning* (pp. 263–286). Norwood, NJ: Ablex.

Brown, D.F. (1974) Advanced vocabulary teaching: The problem. *RELC Journal* 5, 1–11.

Bruton, A. (1997) In what ways do we want EFL coursebooks to differ? *System* 25, 275–284.

Burt, M. (1975) Error analysis in the adult EFL classroom. *TESOL Quarterly* 9, 53–63.

Caramazza, A. (1997) How many levels of processing are there in lexical access? *Cognitive Neuropsychology* 14, 177–208.

Carroll, J.B. and Sapon, S. (1958) *Modern Language Aptitude Test*. New York: Psychological Corporation.

Carton, A. (1971) Inferencing: A process in using and learning language. In P. Pimsleur and T. Quinn (eds) *The Psychology of Second Language Learning* (pp. 45–58). Cambridge: Cambridge University Press.

Castillo Carballo, M.A. (2001) Colocaciones léxicas y variación lingüística: Implicaciones didácticas. *Lingüística Española Actual* XXIII, 108–133.

Cervero, M.J. and Pichardo Castro, F. (2000) *Aprender y enseñar vocabulario*. Madrid: Edelsa.

Chacón Beltrán, R. (2001) La enseñaza de vocabulario en inglés como L2: El efecto del énfasis en la forma lingüística en el aprendizaje de cognados falsos. Doctoral dissertation, University of Seville. On WWW at http://fondosdigitales.us.es/thesis/thesis_view?oid=458.

Chamot, A.U. (1987) The learning strategies of ESL students. In A. Wenden and J. Rubin (eds) *Learner Strategies in Language Learning* (pp. 71–83). New York: Prentice-Hall.

Channell, J. (1981) Applying semantic theory to vocabulary teaching. *English Language Teaching Journal* 35, 115–122.

Channell, J. (1988) Psycholinguistic considerations in the study of L2 vocabulary acquisition. In R. Carter and M. McCarthy (eds) *Vocabulary and Language Teaching* (pp. 83–96). New York: Longman.

Chapelle, C.A. (1997) CALL in the year 2000: Still in search of research paradigms? *Language Learning Technology* 11, 19–43.

Chikamatsu, N. (1996) The effects of L1 orthography on L2 word recognition: A study of American and Chinese learners of Japanese. *Studies in Second Language Acquisition* 18, 403–432.

Cho, K-S. and Krashen, S. (1994) Acquisition of vocabulary from the Sweet Valley Kids Series: Adult ESL acquisition. *Journal of Reading* 37, 662–667.

Chun, D. and Plass, J. (1996) Effects of multimedia annotations on vocabulary acquisition. *The Modern Language Journal* 80, 183–199.

Coady, J. (1993) Research on ESL/EFL vocabulary acquisition: Putting it in context. In T. Huckin, M. Haynes and J. Coady (eds) *Second Language Reading and Vocabulary Learning* (pp. 3–23). Norwood, NJ: Ablex.

Coady, J. (1997) L2 vocabulary acquisition through extensive reading. In J. Coady and T. Huckin (eds) *Second Language Vocabulary Acquisition* (pp. 225–237). Cambridge: Cambridge University Press.

Coady, J. and Huckin, T. (eds) (1997) *Second Language Vocabulary Acquisition*. Cambridge: Cambridge University Press.
Coady, J., Magoto, J., Hubbard, P., Graney, J. and Mokhtari, K. (1993) High frequency vocabulary and reading proficiency in ESL readers. In T. Huckin, M. Haynes and J. Coady (eds) *Second Language Reading and Vocabulary Learning* (pp. 217–228). New Jersey: Ablex.
Cobb, T. (1997) Is there any measurable learning from hands-on concordancing? *System* 25, 301–315.
Collins Cobuild English Dictionary (1995) J. Sinclair (editor in chief) London and Glasgow: Harper Collins.
Coltheart, M. and Rastle, K. (1994) Serial processing in reading aloud: Evidence for Dual-Route models in reading. *Journal of Experimental Psychology* 20, 1197–1211.
Corpas Pastor, G. (1996) *Manual de fraseología española*. Madrid: Gredos.
Costa, A., Caramazza, A. and Sebastián-Gallés, N. (2000) The cognate facilitation effect: Implications for the models of lexical access. *Journal of Experimental Psychology: Learning, Memory and Cognition* 26, 1283–1296.
Costa, A., Santesteban, M. and Caño, A. (2005) On the facilitatory effects of cognate words in bilingual speech production. *Brain and Language* 94, 94–103.
Council of Europe (2001) *A Common European Framework of Reference for Languages*. Cambridge: Cambridge University Press.
Cowie, A.P. (1978) The place of illustrative material and collocations in the design of a learner's dictionary. In P. Strevens (ed.) *In Honour of A. S. Hornby* (pp. 127–139). Oxford: Oxford University Press.
Coxhead, A. (2000) A new academic word list. *TESOL Quarterly* 34, 213–238.
Craik, F.I.M. and Lockhart, R.S. (1972) Levels of processing: A framework for memory research. *Journal of Verbal Learning and Verbal Behavior* 11, 671–684.
Craik, F.I.M. and Tulving, E. (1975) Depth of processing and the retention of words in episodic memory. *Journal of Experimental Psychology* 104, 268–294.
Cutting, J.C. and Ferreira, V.S. (1999) Semantic and phonological information flow in the production lexicon. *Journal of Experimental Psychology: Learning, Memory, and Cognition* 25, 318–344.
Damian, M.F. and Bowers, J.S. (2003) Locus of semantic interference in picture-word interference tasks. *Psychonomic Bulletin & Review* 10, 111–117.
Dat, B. (2008) ELT materials used in Southeast Asia. In B. Tomlinson (ed.) *English Language Learning Materials* (pp. 263–280). London: Continuum International Publishing Group.
Day, R.R. and Bamford, J. (1998) *Extensive Reading in a Second Language Classroom*. Cambridge: Cambridge University Press.
Day, R.R., Omura, C. and Hiramatsu, M. (1991) Incidental EFL vocabulary learning and reading. *Reading in a Foreign Language* 8, 689–696.
de Bot, K., Lowie, W.M. and Verspoor, M.H. (2007) A dynamic systems theory approach to second language acquisition. *Bilingualism: Language and Cognition* 10, 7–21.
de Bot, K., Paribakht, T. and Wesche, M. (1997) Toward a lexical processing model for the study of second language acquisition. *Studies in Second Language Acquisition* 19, 309–329.
De la Fuente, M.J. (2002) Negotiation and oral acquisition of L2 vocabulary. The roles of input and output in the receptive and productive acquisition of words. *Studies in Second Language Acquisition* 24, 81–112.
Deighton, L.C. (1959) *Vocabulary Development in the Classroom*. New York: Teacher's College Press, Columbia University.

DeKeyser, R.M. (1998) Beyond focus on form: Cognitive perspective on learning and practical second language grammar. In C. Doughty and J. Williams (eds) *Focus on Form in Classroom Second Language Acquisition* (pp. 42–63). Cambridge: Cambridge University Press.

Dell, G.S. (1986) A spreading-activation theory of retrieval in sentence production. *Psychological Review* 93, 283–321.

Dell, G.S., Schwartz, M.F. and Martin, N. (1997) Lexical access in aphasic and nonaphasic speakers. *Psychological Review* 104, 801–838.

Dominicis, M.C. and Reynolds, J.J. (1987) *Repase y escriba: Curso avanzado de gramática y composición*. New York: Wiley.

Doughty, C. and Varela, E. (1998) Communicative focus on form. In C. Doughty and J. Williams (eds) *Focus on Form in Classroom Second Language Acquisition* (pp. 114–138). Cambridge: Cambridge University Press.

Driscoll, M. (1994) *Psychology of Learning for Instruction*. Allyn and Bacon: MA, USA.

Drum, P.A. and Konopak, B.C. (1987) Learning word meanings from written context. In M.G. McKeown and M.E. Curtis (eds) *The Nature of Vocabulary Acquisition* (pp. 73–87). Hillsdale, NJ: Lawrence Erlbaum Associates.

Dubin, F. and Olshtain, E. (1993) Predicting word meanings from contextual clues: Evidence from L1 readers. In T. Huckin, M. Haynes and J. Coady (eds) *Second Language Reading and Vocabulary Learning* (pp. 181–202). Norwood, NJ: Ablex Publishing Co.

Dupuy, B. and Krashen, S. (1993) Incidental vocabulary acquisition in French as a foreign language. *Applied Language Learning* 4, 55–63.

Elley, W.B. (1991) Acquiring literacy in a second language: The effect of book-based programs. *Language Learning* 41, 375–411.

Ellis, N.C. (1994) Vocabulary acquisition: The implicit ins and outs of explicit cognitive mediation. In N.C. Ellis (ed.) *Implicit and Explicit Learning of Languages* (pp. 211–282). London: Academic Press Limited.

Ellis, N.C. (1997) Vocabulary acquisition: Word structure, collocation, word-class, and meaning. In N. Schmitt and M. McCarthy (eds) *Vocabulary: Description, Acquisition, and Pedagogy* (pp. 122–139). Cambridge: Cambridge University Press.

Ellis, R. (ed.) (2001) Form-focused instruction and second language learning. *A Supplement to Language Learning* (pp. 1–46). 51: supplement 1.

Ellis, R., Basturkmen, H. and Loewen, S. (2002) Doing focus-on-form. *System* 30, 419–432.

Ellis, R. and He, X. (1999) The roles of modified input and output in the incidental acquisition of word meanings. *Studies in Second Language Acquisition* 21, 285–301.

Ellis, R., Tanaka, Y. and Yamazaki, A. (1994) Classroom interaction, comprehension and the acquisition of L2 word meanings. *Language Learning* 44, 449–491.

Elman, J.L. (1995) Language as a dynamical system. In R. Port and T. van Gelder (eds) *Mind as Motion: Dynamical Perspectives on Behavior and Cognition* (pp. 195–225). Cambridge: MIT Press.

Elman, J.L. (2004) An alternative view of the mental lexicon. *Trends in Cognitive Sciences* 8, 301–306.

Fayez-Hussein, R. (1990) Collocations: The missing link in vocabulary acquisition amongst EFL learners. In J. Fisiak (ed.) *Papers and Studies in Contrastive Linguistics: The Polish English Contrastive Project* 26 (pp. 123–136). Poznan: Adam Mickiewicz University.

Folse, K. (1999) The effect of type of written practice activity on second language vocabulary retention. Unpublished doctoral dissertation, University of South Florida, Tampa.

Folse, K. (2004) *Vocabulary Myths*. Ann Arbor: The University of Michigan Press.
Folse, K. (2006) The effect of type of written exercise on L2 vocabulary retention. *TESOL Quarterly* 40, 273–293.
Fountain, R.L. and Nation, I.S.P. (2000) A vocabulary-based graded dictation test. *RELC Journal* 31, 29–44.
Frantzen, D. (1998) The value of one type of previous exposure for foreign language vocabulary learning. *Spanish Applied Linguistics* 2, 107–136.
Frantzen, D. (2003) Factors affecting how second language Spanish students derive meaning from context. *The Modern Language Journal* 87, 168–199.
Fraser, C. (1999) Lexical processing strategy use and vocabulary learning through reading. *Studies in Second Language Acquisition* 21, 225–241.
Freebairn, I. (2000) The coursebook – future continuous or past? *English Teaching Professional* 15, 3–5.
Gabrys-Biskup, D. (1992) L1 influence on learners' renderings of English collocation: A Polish/German empirical study. In P.J.L. Arnaud and H. Bejoint (eds) *Vocabulary and Applied Linguistics* (pp. 85–93). London: MacMillan.
Gairns, R. and Redman, S. (1986) *Working with Words*. Cambridge: Cambridge University Press.
Ganger, J. and Brent, M.R. (2004) Reexamining the vocabulary spurt. *Developmental Psychology* 40, 621–632.
Gavioli, L. and Aston, G. (2001) Enriching reality: Language corpora in language pedagogy. *ELT Journal* 55, 238–246.
Ghadessy, M. (1989) The use of vocabulary and collocations in the writing of primary school students in Singapore. In P. Nation and R. Carter (eds) *Vocabulary Acquisition* (pp. 110–117). *AILA Review*, No. 6.
Ghahremani-Ghajar, S. and Masny, D. (1999) Making sense in second orthography. *ITL Review of Applied Linguistics* 125–126, 229–251.
Gholamain, M. and Geva, E. (1999) The concurrent development of word recognition skills in English and Persian. *Language Learning* 49, 183–218.
Gitsaki, C. (1996) The development of ESL collocational knowledge. Doctoral dissertation, The University of Queensland, Brisbane, Australia.
Goldinger, S.D. (1998) Echoes of echoes? An episodic theory of lexical access. *Psychological Review* 105, 251–279.
Gómez Molina, J.R. (2004) Los contenidos léxico-semánticos. In J. Sánchez Lobato and I. Santos Gargallo (eds) *Vademécum para la formación de profesores. Enseñar español como segunda lengua (L2)/lengua extranjera (LE)* (pp. 789–810). Madrid: SGEL.
Goodfellow, R. (1994) A computer-based strategy for foreign-language vocabulary learning. Unpublished doctoral dissertation, Open University, UK.
Goodfellow, R. (1995) A review of the types of CALL programmes for vocabulary instruction. *Computer Assisted Language Learning* 2, 205–226.
Goulden, R., Nation, I.S.P. and Read, J. (1990) How large can a receptive vocabulary be? *Applied Linguistics* 11, 341–363.
Grace, C. (1998) Retention of word meanings inferred from context and sentence-level translations: Implications for the design of beginning-level CALL software. *The Modern Language Journal* 82, 533–544.
Granger, S. (1998) Prefabricated patterns in advanced EFL writing: Collocations and formulae. In A.P. Cowie (ed.) *Phraseology: Theory, Analysis and Applications* (pp. 145–160). Oxford: Clarendon Press.
Greenall, S. (1984) The coursebook credibility gap. *The EFL Gazette* 53, 14.
Greidanus, T., Bogaards, P., van der Linden, E., Nienhuis, L. and de Wolf, T. (2004) The construction and validation of a deep word knowledge test for advanced learners of French. In P. Bogaards and B. Laufer (eds) *Vocabulary in a Second Language* (pp. 191–208). Amsterdam: John Benjamins.

Griffin, G.F. (1992) Aspects of the psychology of second language vocabulary list learning. Unpublished doctoral dissertation, University of Warwick.
Griffin, Z.M. and Bock, K. (1998) Constraint, word frequency, and the relationship between lexical processing levels in spoken word production. *Journal of Memory and Language* 38, 313–338.
Groot, P.J.M. (2000) Computer assisted second language vocabulary acquisition. *Language Learning and Technology* 4, 60–81.
Gross, S. (2004) A modest proposal: Explaining language attrition in the context of contact linguistics. In M.S. Schmid, B. Köpke, M. Keijzer and L. Weilemar (eds) *First Language Attrition: Interdisciplinary Perspectives on Methodological Issues* (pp. 281–297). Amsterdam: John Benjamins.
Haastrup, K. (1991) *Lexical Inferencing Procedures or Talking About Words: Receptive Procedures in Foreign Language Learning with Special Reference to English*. Tübingen: Gunter Narr Verlag.
Hancin-Bhatt, B. and Nagy, W. (1994) Lexical transfer and second language morphological development. *Applied Linguistics* 15, 289–310.
Hansen, L. (2001) Language attrition: The fate of the start. *Annual Review of Applied Linguistics* 21, 60–73.
Harley, T.A. (1993) Phonological activation of semantic competitors during lexical access in speech production. *Language and Cognitive Processes* 8, 291–309.
Haynes, M. (1984) Patterns and perils of guessing in second language reading. In J. Handscombe, R.A. Orem and B.P. Taylor (eds) *On TESOL '83: The Question of Control* (pp. 163–176). Washington, DC: TESOL.
Haynes, M. and Baker, I. (1993) American and Chinese readers learning from lexical familiarization in English texts. In T. Huckin, M. Haynes and J. Coady (eds) *Second Language Reading and Vocabulary Acquisition* (pp. 130–152). Norwood, NJ: Ablex.
Hazenberg, S. and Hulstijn, J.H. (1996) Defining a minimal receptive second-language vocabulary for non-native university students: An empirical investigation. *Applied Linguistics* 17, 145–163.
Healey, D. (2002) *Learner autonomy with technology: What do language learners need to be successful?* On WWW at http://oregonstate.edu/~healey/tesol2002/autonomy/press–withbibliog.doc. Accessed 4.8.2003.
Henriksen, B. (1999) Three dimensions of vocabulary development. *Studies in Second Language Acquisition* 21, 303–317.
Herman, P.A., Anderson, R.C., Pearson, P.D. and Nagy, W.E. (1987) Incidental acquisition of word meaning from expositions with varied text features. *Reading Research Quarterly* 22, 263–284.
Higa, M. (1963) Interference effects of intralist word relationships in verbal learning. *Journal of Verbal Learning and Verbal Behavior* 2, 170–175.
Higa, M. (1965) The psycholinguistic concept of 'difficulty' in the teaching of foreign language vocabulary. *Language Learning* XV, 167–79.
Higueras, M. (1997) Las unidades léxicas y la enseñanza del léxico a extranjeros. *REALE*, 8, 35–49.
Higueras, M. (2004) La enseñanza-aprendizaje de las colocaciones en el desarrollo de la competencia léxica en el español como lengua extranjera. Unpublished doctoral dissertation, Universidad Complutense de Madrid, Madrid.
Higueras, M. (2007) *Estudio de las colocaciones léxicas y su enseñanza en español como lengua extranjera*. Málaga: ASELE.
Hilborn, R.C. (2004) Sea gulls, butterflies, and grasshoppers: A brief history of the butterfly effect in non-linear dynamics. *American Journal of Physics* 72, 425–427.

Hill, J. (1999) Collocational competence. *English Teaching Professional* 11, 3–7.
Hill, J. (2000) Revising priorities: From grammatical failure to collocational success. In M. Lewis (ed.) *Teaching Collocation. Further Developments in the Lexical Approach* (pp. 47–69). London: Language Teaching Publications.
Hill, M.M. and Laufer, B. (2003) Type of task, time-on-task and electronic dictionaries in incidental vocabulary acquisition. *International Review of Applied Linguistics* 41, 87–106.
Hilton, C. and Hyder, M. (1995) *Getting to Grips with Vocabulary*. London: BBP Letts Educational Ltd.
Hindmarsh, R. (1980) *Cambridge English Lexicon*. Cambridge: Cambridge University Press.
Holec, H. (1981) *Autonomy and Foreign Language Learning*. Oxford: Pergamon.
Holec, H. (ed.) (1988) *Autonomy and Self-Directed Learning: Present Fields of Application*. Strasbourg: Council of Europe.
Hornby, A.S., Ashby, M., Wehmeier, S. and McIntosh, C. (2005) *Oxford Advanced Learner's Dictionary* (7th Edition). Oxford: Oxford University Press.
Horst, M., Cobb, T. and Meara, P. (1998) Beyond a clockwork orange: Acquiring second language vocabulary through reading. *Reading in a Foreign Language* 11, 207–223.
Horst, M., Cobb, T. and Nicolae, H. (2005) Expanding academic vocabulary with an interactive on-line database. *Language Learning and Technology* 9, 90–110.
Horst, M. and Meara, P. (1999) Test of a model for predicting second language lexical growth through reading. *Canadian Modern Language Review* 56, 308–328.
Horwitz, E.K. (1988) The beliefs about language learning of beginning university foreign language students. *The Modern Language Journal* 72, 283–294.
Howarth, P. (1996) *Phraseology in English Academic Writing. Some Implications for Language Learning and Dictionary Making*. Tubingen: Niemeyer.
Hu, M. and Nation, P. (2000) Vocabulary density and reading comprehension. *Reading in a Foreign Language* 13, 403–430.
Huckin, T. and Bloch, J. (1993) Strategies for inferring word-meanings in context: A cognitive model. In T. Huckin, M. Haynes and J. Coady (eds) *Second Language Reading and Vocabulary Learning* (pp. 153–176). Norwood, NJ: Ablex.
Huckin, T. and Coady, J. (1999) Incidental vocabulary acquisition in a second language: A review. *Studies in Second Language Acquisition* 21, 181–193.
Hulstijn, J. (1992) Retention of inferred and given word meanings: Experiments in incidental vocabulary learning. In P. Arnaud and H. Bejoint (eds) *Vocabulary in Applied Linguistics* (pp. 113–125). London: Macmillan Academic and Professional Limited.
Hulstijn, J. (1993) When do foreign-language readers look up the meaning of unfamiliar words? The influence of task and learner variables. *The Modern Language Journal* 77, 139–147.
Hulstijn, J. (1997) Mnemonic methods in foreign language vocabulary learning: Theoretical considerations and pedagogical implications. In J. Coady and T. Huckin (eds) *Second Language Vocabulary Acquisition* (pp. 203–224). Cambridge: Cambridge University Press.
Hulstijn, J. (1998) There is no learning without attention. Paper presented at the annual meeting of the American Association of Applied Linguistics (AAAL), Seattle, WA.
Hulstijn, J. (2000) The use of computer technology in experimental studies of second language acquisition: A survey of some techniques and some ongoing studies. *Language Learning and Technology* 32, 32–43.

Hulstijn, J. (2001) Intentional and incidental second-language vocabulary learning: A reappraisal of elaboration, rehearsal and automaticity. In P. Robinson (ed.) *Cognition and Second Language Instruction* (pp. 258–286). Cambridge: Cambridge University Press.

Hulstijn, J., Hollander, M. and Greidanus, T. (1996) Incidental vocabulary learning by advanced foreign language students: The influence of marginal glosses, dictionary use, and reoccurrence of unknown words. *The Modern Language Journal* 80, 327–339.

Hulstijn, J. and Laufer, B. (2001) Some empirical evidence for the Involvement Load Hypothesis in vocabulary acquisition. *Language Learning* 51, 539–558.

Hussein, R.F. (1990) Collocations, the missing link in vocabulary acquisition amongst EFL learners. *Papers and Studies in Contrastive Linguistics* 26, 123–136.

Hutchinson, T. and Torres, E. (1994) The textbook as agent of change. *ELT Journal* 48, 315–328.

Jacquet, M. and French, R.M. (2002) The BIA++: Extending the BIA+ to a dynamical distributed connectionist framework. *Bilingualism* 5, 202–205.

Jasinski, M. (1998) Pedagogical issues emerging from this project. In M. Jasinski (ed.) *Teaching and Learning Styles that Facilitate Online Learning*. On WWW at http://www.tafe.sa.edu.au/lsrsc/one/natproj/tal/pedissues/pedaiss.htm. Accessed 20.1.2002.

Jenkins, J.R. and Dixon, R. (1983) Vocabulary learning. *Contemporary Educational Psychology* 8, 237–260.

Jiang, N. (2000) Lexical representation and development in a second language. *Applied Linguistics* 21, 47–77.

Jiang, N. (2004) Semantic transfer and development in adult L2 vocabulary acquisition. In P. Bogaards and B. Laufer (eds) *Vocabulary in a Second Language* (pp. 101–126). Amsterdam: John Benjamins Publishing Company.

Jiménez Catalán, C. (2002) El concepto de competencia léxica en los estudios de aprendizaje y enseñanza de segundas lenguas. *Atlantis* 24, 149–156.

Jiménez-Catalán, R.M. and Terrazas-Gallego, M. (2005–2008) The receptive vocabulary of English Foreign Language young learners. *Journal of English Studies* 5–6, 173–191.

Johns, T. (1988) Whence and whither classroom concordancing? In T. Bongaerts, T. van Els and H. Wekker (eds) *Computer Applications in Language Learning* (pp. 9–27). Dordrecht: Foris.

Johns, T. (1991) Should you be persuaded: Two examples of data-driven learning. In T.F. Johns and P. King (eds) *Classroom Concordancing* (pp. 1–13). Birmingham: ELR.

Johns, T. (1994) From printout to handout: Grammar and vocabulary teaching in the context of data-driven learning. In T. Odlin (ed.) *Perspectives in Pedagogical Grammar* (pp. 293–313). Cambridge: Cambridge University Press.

Jonassen, D., Mayes, T. and McAleese, R. (1993) A manifesto for a constructivist approach to uses of technology in higher education. In T. Duffy, J. Lowyck and D. Jonassen (eds) *Designing Environments for Constructivist Learning* (pp. 231–247). Berlin Heidelberg: Springer-Verlag.

Jung, U. (1988) Evaluating microcomputer software: The state of the art. In L. Legenhausen and D. Wolff (eds) *Computer Assisted Learning and Innovative EFL Methodology* (pp. 27–43). Augsburg: Augsburger I and I-Schriften.

Kachroo, J.N. (1962) Report on an investigation into the teaching of vocabulary in the first year of English. *Bulletin of the Central Institute of English* 2, 67–72.

Kaszubski, P. (2000) Selected aspects of lexicon, phraseology and style in the writing of Polish advanced learners of English: A contrastive, corpus-based approach. Unpublished doctoral dissertation, Adam Mickiewicz University, Poznan.˙ On WWW at http://main.amu.edu.pl/-przemka/research.html. Accessed November 2007.

Kearsley, G. and Shneiderman, B. (1999) *Engagement Theory: A Framework for Technology-Based Teaching and Learning*. On WWW at http://home.sprynet.com/~gkearsley/engage.html. Accessed 20.1.2000.

Kellerman, E. (1977) Towards a characterization of the strategy of transfer in second language learning. *Interlanguage Studies Bulletin* 21, 58–145.

Kellerman, E. (1978) Giving learners a break: Native language intuitions about transferability. *Working Papers in Bilingualism* 15, 309–315.

Kelly, P. (1990) Guessing: No substitute for systematic learning of lexis. *System* 18, 199–208.

Khalil, A. (1985) Communicative error evaluations: Native speakers' evaluation and interpretation of written errors of Arab EFL learners. *TESOL Quarterly* 19, 225–351.

Kitajima, R. (2001) The effects of instructional conditions on students' vocabulary retention. *Foreign Language Annals* 34, 470–482.

Knight, S. (1994) Dictionary use while reading: The effects on comprehension and vocabulary acquisition for students of different verbal abilities. *The Modern Language Journal* 78, 285–299.

Knupfer, P.B. (1993) *From Text to Television: Hermeneutic Textualism and the Challenge of Teaching of History*. Summer seminar of the International Visual Literacy Association, Delphi, Greece, June 19.

Koda, K. (1989) The effects of transferred vocabulary knowledge on the development of L2 reading proficiency. *Foreign Language Annals* 22, 529–540.

Koda, K., Takahashi, E. and Fender, M. (1998) Effects of L1 processing experience on L2 morphological awareness. *Ilha do Desterro* 35, 59–87.

Koike, K. (2001) *Colocaciones léxicas en el español actual: Estudio formal y léxico-semántico*. Madrid: Universidad de Alcalá and Universidad de Takushoku.

Koosha, M. and Jafarpour, A. (2006) Data-driven learning and teaching collocation of prepositions: The case of Iranian EFL adult learners. *Asian EFL Journal* 8, 1–13.

Krashen, S. (1989) We acquire vocabulary and spelling by reading: Additional evidence for the input hypothesis. *The Modern Language Journal* 73, 440–464.

Krashen, S. (1993) The case for free vocabulary reading. *The Canadian Modern Language Review* 50, 72–82.

Landauer, T.K. and Bjork, R.A. (1978) Optimum rehearsal patterns and name learning. In M.M. Gruneberg, P.E. Morris and R.N. Sykes (eds) *Practical Aspects of Memory* (pp. 625–632). London: Academic Press.

Lao, C.Y. and Krashen, S. (2000) The impact of popular literature study on literacy development in EFL: More evidence for the power of reading. *System* 28, 261–270.

Larsen-Freeman, D. (1997) Chaos/complexity science and second language acquisition. *Applied Linguistics* 18, 141–165.

Larsen-Freeman, D. (2006) The emergence of complexity, fluency and accuracy in the oral and written production of five Chinese learners of English. *Applied Linguistics* 27, 560–619.

Laufer, B. (1986) Possible changes in attitude towards vocabulary acquisition research. *IRAL* 24, 69–75.

Laufer, B. (1988) The concept of 'synforms' (similar lexical forms) in L2 learning. *Language and Education* 2, 113–132.

Laufer, B. (1991) Some properties of the foreign language learner's lexicon as evidenced by lexical confusions. *IRAL* 29, 317–330.

Laufer, B. (1992) How much lexis is necessary for reading comprehension? In P.J.L. Arnaud and H. Béjoint (eds) *Vocabulary and Applied Linguistics* (pp. 126–132). London: Macmillan.

Laufer, B. (1997) The lexical plight in second language reading. In J. Coady and T. Huckin (eds) *Second Language Vocabulary Acquisition: A Rationale for Pedagogy* (pp. 20–34). NY: Cambridge University Press.

Laufer, B. (1998) The development of passive and active vocabulary in a second language: Same or different? *Applied Linguistics* 19, 255–271.

Laufer, B. (2000) Electronic dictionaries and incidental vocabulary acquisition: Does technology make a difference? In U. Heid, S. Evert, E. Lehmann and C. Rohrer (eds) *Proceedings of EURALEX 2000* (pp. 849–854). Stuttgart University: EURALEX.

Laufer, B. (2003) Vocabulary acquisition in a second language: Do learners really acquire most vocabulary by reading? *The Canadian Modern Language Review* 59, 565–585.

Laufer, B. (2005a) Instructed second language vocabulary learning: The fault in the 'default hypothesis'. In A. Housen and M. Pierrard (eds) *Investigations in Instructed Second Language Acquisition* (pp. 311–329). Berlin and New York: Mouton de Gruyter.

Laufer, B. (2005b) Focus on form in second language vocabulary acquisition. In S.H. Foster-Cohen, M.P. Garcia-Mayo and J. Cenoz (eds) *EUROSLA Yearbook 5* (pp. 223–250). Amsterdam: John Benjamins.

Laufer, B. (2006) Comparing focus on form and focus on formS in second language vocabulary learning. *The Canadian Modern Language Review* 63, 149–166.

Laufer, B., Elder, C., Hill, K. and Congdon, P. (2004) Size and strength: Do we need both to measure vocabulary knowledge? *Language Testing* 21, 202–226.

Laufer, B. and Girsai, N. (2008) The use of native language for improving second language vocabulary: An exploratory study. In A. Stavans and I. Kupferberg (eds) *Studies in Language and Language Education* (pp. 261–275). Jerusalem: The Hebrew University Magnes Press.

Laufer, B. and Hill, M. (2000) What lexical information do L2 learners select in a CALL dictionary and how does it affect word retention? *Language Learning and Technology* 32, 58–76.

Laufer, B. and Hulstijn, J. (1998) *What leads to better incidental vocabulary learning: Comprehensible input or comprehensible output?* Paper presented at the Pacific Second Language Research Form (PacSLRF), Tokyo.

Laufer, B. and Hulstijn, J. (2001) Incidental vocabulary acquisition in a second language: The construct of task-induced involvement. *Applied Linguistics* 22, 1–26.

Laufer, B. and Levitzky-Aviad, T. (2003) Look up behaviour and word retention as a function of task type and word relevance. *AsiaLEX Proceedings*, Tokyo, Japan.

Laufer, B. and Nation, I.S.P. (1995) Vocabulary size and use: Lexical richness in L2 written production. *Applied Linguistics* 16, 307–322.

Laufer, B. and Nation, I.S.P. (1999) A vocabulary-size test of controlled productive ability. *Language Testing* 16, 33–51.

Laufer, B. and Paribakht, T.S. (1998) The relationship between passive and active vocabularies: Effects of language learning context. *Language Learning* 48, 365–391.

Laufer, B. and Shmueli, K. (1997) Memorizing new words: Does teaching have anything to do with it? *RELC Journal* 28, 89–108.

Laufer, B. and Sim, D.D. (1985) Reading and explaining the reading threshold needed for English for academic purposes texts. *Foreign Language Annals* 18, 405–411.

Lawley, J. (1996) *Vocabulary Builders: Book 1*. London and Glasgow: Collins.
Lawley, J. (2000) Muchos libros de inglés dan más problemas que soluciones. *El País*, p. 6.
Leech, G. (1974) *Semantics*. Baltimore: Penguin Books.
Levelt, W.J.M. (1989) *Speaking: From Intention to Articulation*. Cambridge, MA: The MIT Press.
Levelt, W.J.M. (2001) Spoken word production: A theory of lexical access. *Proceedings of the National Academy of Sciences of the United States of America* 98, 13464–13471.
Levelt, W., Roelofs, A. and Meyer, A. (1999) A theory of lexical access in speech production. *Behavioral and Brain Sciences* 22, 1–75.
Levenston, E.A. (1979) Second language acquisition: Issues and problems. *Interlanguage Studies Bulletin-Utrecht* 4, 147–160.
Levy, M. (1997) *Computer-Assisted Language Learning: Context and Conceptualization*. Oxford: Oxford University Press.
Lewis, M. (1993) *The Lexical Approach. The State of ELT and the Way Forward*. London: Language Teaching Publications.
Lewis, M. (1997a) *Implementing the Lexical Approach*. London: Language Teaching Publications.
Lewis, M. (1997b) Pedagogical implications of the Lexical Approach. In J. Coady and T. Huckin (eds) *Second Language Vocabulary Acquisition* (pp. 255–270). Cambridge: Cambridge University Press,
Lewis, M. (2000) There is nothing as practical as a good theory. In M. Lewis (ed.) *Teaching Collocation. Further Developments in the Lexical Approach* (pp. 10–27). London: Language Teaching Publications.
Lewis, M. and Hill, J. (1985) *Practical Techniques for Language Teaching*. London: Language Teaching Publications.
Li, X. (1988) Effects of contextual cues on inferring and remembering meanings of new words. *Applied Linguistics* 9, 402–413.
Little, D. (1996) Freedom to learn and compulsion to interact: Promoting learner autonomy through the use of information systems and information technologies. In R. Pemberton, E.S.L. Li, W.W.F. Or and H.D. Pierson (eds) *Taking Control: Autonomy in Language Learning* (pp. 203–218). Hong Kong: Hong Kong University Press.
Long, M. (1991) Focus on form: A design feature in language teaching methodology. In K. de Bot, R. Ginsberg and C. Kramsh (eds) *Foreign Language Research in Cross-Cultural Perspective* (pp. 39–52). Amsterdam: John Benjamins.
Lorenz, E.N. (1963) The predictability of hydrodynamic flow. *Transactions of the New York Academy of Sciences* 25, 409–432.
Lorenzo-Dus, N. and Meara, P. (2005) Examiner support strategies and test-taker vocabulary. *International Review of Applied Linguistics in Language Teaching* 43, 239–258.
Lotto, L. and de Groot, A. (1998) Effects of learning method and word type on acquiring vocabulary in an unfamiliar language. *Language Learning* 48, 31–69.
Luce, P.A. and Pisoni, D.B. (1998) Recognizing spoken words: The neighborhood activation model. *Ear and Hearing* 19, 1–36.
Luppescu, S. and Day, R. (1993) Reading, dictionaries, and vocabulary learning. *Language Learning* 43, 263–287.
Ma, K. and Kelly, P. (2006) Computer assisted vocabulary learning: Design and evaluation. *Computer Assisted Language Learning* 19, 15–45.
Mackin, R. (1978) On collocations: Words shall be known by the company they keep. In P. Strevens (ed.) *In Honour of A. S. Hornby* (pp. 149–165). Oxford: Oxford University Press.

Martin, M. (1984) Advanced vocabulary teaching: The problem of synonyms. *The Modern Language Journal* 68, 130–136.
Maruyama, F. (1995) Expanding vocabulary through reading. *Forum* 33, 36–39.
McCarthy, M. (1990) *Vocabulary*. Oxford: Oxford University Press.
McCarthy, M. and O'Dell, F. (2005) *English Collocations in Use*. Cambridge: Cambridge University Press.
McLoughlin, C. and Marshall, L. (2000) Scaffolding: A model for learner support in an online teaching environment. In A. Herrmann and M.M. Kulski (eds) Flexible futures in tertiary teaching. *Proceedings of the 9th Annual Teaching and Learning Forum 2000*. Perth: Curtin University of Technology. On WWW at http://lsn.curtin.edu.au/tlf/tlf2000/mcloughlin2.html. Accessed 20.11.2002.
Meara, P. (1990) A note on passive vocabulary. *Second Language Research* 6, 150–154.
Meara, P. (1995) The importance of an early emphasis on L2 vocabulary. *The Language Teacher* 19, 8–11.
Meara, P. (1997) Towards a new approach to modelling vocabulary. In N. Schmitt and M. McCarthy (eds) *Vocabulary: Description, Acquisition, and Pedagogy* (pp. 109–121). Cambridge: Cambridge University Press.
Meara, P. (2005) Reactivating a dormant vocabulary. *EUROSLA Yearbook* 5, 269–280.
Meara, P. and Babi, A. (2001) Just a few words: How assessors evaluate minimal texts. *International Review of Applied Linguistics in Language Teaching* 39, 75–83.
Meara, P. and Buxton, B. (1987) An alternative to multiple choice vocabulary tests. *Language Testing* 4, 142–151.
Meara, P. and Jones, G. (1990) *Eurocentres Vocabulary Size Test* (version E1.1/K10,MSDOS). Zurich: Eurocentres Learning Service.
Meara, P. and Milton, J. (2003) *X_Lex, The Swansea Levels Test*. Newbury: Express.
Meara, P. and Rodriguez Sanchez, I. (1993) Matrix models of vocabulary acquisition: An empirical assessment. In M. Wesche and T.S. Paribakht (eds) *Symposium on Vocabulary Research* (pp. 24–26). Ottawa: CREAL.
Milton, J. and Hopkins, N. (2005) *Aural Lex*. Swansea: Swansea University.
Milton, J. and Hopkins, N. (2006) Comparing phonological and orthographic vocabulary size: Do vocabulary tests underestimate the knowledge of some learners. *The Canadian Modern Language Review* 63, 127–147.
Milton, J. and Riordan, O. (2006) Level and script effects in the phonological and orthographic vocabulary size of Arabic and Farsi speakers. In P. Davidson, C. Coombe, D. Lloyd and D. Palfreyman (eds) *Teaching and Learning Vocabulary in Another Language* (pp. 122–133). UAE: TESOL Arabia.
Miralpeix, I. (2007) *Testing receptive vocabulary size: X_Lex and Y_Lex*. Paper presented at the 29th Language Testing Research Colloquium, Barcelona.
Mishan, F. (2004) Authenticating corpora for language learning: A problem and its resolution. *ELT Journal* 58, 219–227.
Mitchell, T.F. (1971) Linguistic 'going on': Collocations and other lexical matters arising on the syntagmatic record. *Archivum Linguisticum* 2, 35–69.
Mondria, J.A. (2003) The effects of inferring, verifying, and memorizing on the retention of L2 word meanings. *Studies in Second Language Acquisition* 25, 473–499.
Mondria, J.A. and Wiersma, B. (2004) Receptive, productive, and receptive + productive L2 vocabulary learning: What difference does it make? In P. Bogaards and B. Laufer (eds) *Vocabulary in a Second Language: Selection, Acquisition, and Testing* (pp. 79–100). Amsterdam/Philadelphia: John Benjamins.
Mondria, J.R. and Wit-de Boer, M. (1991) The effects of contextual richness on the guessability and the retention of words in a foreign language. *Applied Linguistics* 12, 249–267.

Morante, R. (2005) Modelos de actividades didácticas para el desarrollo léxico [online] REDELE, New Zealand. On WWW at http://www.sgci.mec.es/redele/revista4/morante.shtml.
Morsella, E. and Miozzo, M. (2002) Evidence for a cascade model of lexical access in speech production. *Journal of Experimental Psychology: Learning, Memory, and Cognition* 28, 555–563.
Morton, J. (1969) Interaction of information in word recognition. *Psychological Review* 76, 165–178.
Motteram, G. (1997) Learner autonomy and the Web. In V. Darleguy *et al.* (eds) *Educational Technology in Language Learning: Theoretical Considerations and Practical Applications* (pp. 17–24). Lyons: INSA (National Institute of Applied Science).
Na, L. and Nation, I.S.P. (1985) Factors affecting guessing vocabulary in context. *RELC Journal* 16, 33–42.
Nagy, W.E. (1997) The role of context in first- and second-language vocabulary learning. In N. Schmitt and M. McCarthy (eds) *Vocabulary: Description, Acquisition, and Pedagogy* (pp. 64–83). Cambridge: Cambridge University Press.
Nagy, W.E. and Herman, P.A. (1987) Breadth and depth of vocabulary knowledge: Implications for acquisition and instruction. In M.G. McKeown and M.E. Curtis (eds) *The Nature of Vocabulary Acquisition* (pp. 19–35). NJ: Lawrence Erlbaum.
Nagy, W.E., Herman, P.A. and Anderson, P.C. (1985) Learning words from context. *Reading Research Quarterly* 20, 233–253.
Nagy, W.E., McClure, E.F. and Mir, M. (1997) Linguistic transfer and the use of context by Spanish–English bilinguals. *Applied Psycholinguistics* 18, 431–452.
Nassaji, H. (2004) The relationship between depth of vocabulary knowledge and L2 learners' lexical inferencing strategy use and success. *The Canadian Modern Language Review* 61, 107–134.
Nation, I.S.P. (ed.) (1984) *Vocabulary Lists: Words, Affixes, and Stems.* English University of Wellington, New Zealand: English Language Institute.
Nation, I.S.P. (1990) *Teaching and Learning Vocabulary.* Boston: Heinle and Heinle.
Nation, I.S.P. (1993) Measuring readiness for simplified material: A test of the first 1,000 words of English. In M. Tickoo (ed.) *Simplification: Theory and Application* (pp. 193–202). Singapore: RELC.
Nation, I.S.P. (2001) *Learning Vocabulary in Another Language.* Cambridge: Cambridge University Press.
Nation, I.S.P. (2006) How large a vocabulary is needed for reading and listening? *The Canadian Modern Language Review* 63, 59–82.
Nation, I.S.P. (2007) Fundamental issues in modelling and assessing vocabulary knowledge. In H. Daller, J. Milton and J. Treffers-Daller (eds) *Modelling and Assessing Vocabulary Knowledge* (pp. 33–43). Cambridge: Cambridge University Press.
Nation, I.S.P. *Vocabulary Profiler*. On WWW at http://www.er.uqam.ca/nobel/r21270/cgibin/webfreques/web_vp.html.
Nation, I.S.P. and Meara, P. (2002) Vocabulary. In N. Schmitt (ed.) *An Introduction to Applied Linguistics* (pp. 35–54). London: Arnold.
Nation, I.S.P. and Newton, P. (1997) Teaching vocabulary. In J. Coady and T. Huckin (eds) *Second Language Vocabulary Acquisition* (pp. 238–54). Cambridge: Cambridge University Press.
Navarrete, N. and Costa, A. (2005) Phonological activation of ignored pictures: Further evidence for a cascade model of lexical access. *Journal of Memory and Language* 53, 359–377.

Nelson, T.H. (1987) *Computer lib/dream machines*. Rev. Ed. of Computer Lib of 1974. Redmond. Wash: Tempus Books of Microsoft Press.

Nesselhauf, N. (2003) The use of collocations by advanced learners of English and some implications for teaching. *Applied Linguistics* 24, 223–242.

Newton, J. (1993) Task based instruction among adult learners of English and its role in second language development. Unpublished doctoral dissertation, Victoria University, NZ.

Nicolova, O.R. (2002) Effects of students' participation in authoring of multimedia materials on student acquisition of vocabulary. *Language Learning and Technology* 6, 100–122.

Nurweni, A. and Read, J. (1999) The English vocabulary knowledge of Indonesian university students. *English for Specific Purposes* 18, 161–175.

O'Dell, F. (1997) Incorporating vocabulary into the syllabus. In N. Schmitt and M. McCarthy (eds) *Vocabulary: Description, Acquisition, and Pedagogy* (pp. 258–278). Cambridge: Cambridge University Press.

O'Neill, R. (1982) Why use textbooks? *ELT Journal* 36, 104–111.

Ooi, D. and Lee Kim-Seoh, J. (1996) Vocabulary teaching: Looking behind the word. *ELT Journal* 50, 52–59.

Oxford, R.L. and Scarcella, R.C. (1994) Second language vocabulary learning among adults: State of the art in vocabulary instruction. *System* 22, 231–243.

Paivio, A. (1986) *Mental Representations: A Dual Cognitive Approach*. New York: Oxford University Press.

Paribakht, T.S. (1985) Strategic competence and language proficiency. *Applied Linguistics* 6, 132–146.

Paribakht, T.S. (2005) The influence of first language lexicalization on second language lexical inferencing: A study of Persian-speaking learners of English as a foreign language. *Language Learning* 55, 701–748.

Paribakht, T.S. and Wesche, M. (1993) Reading comprehension and second language development in a comprehension-based ESL programme. *TESL Canada Journal* 11, 9–27.

Paribakht, T.S. and Wesche, M. (1997) Vocabulary enhancement activities and reading for meaning in second language vocabulary acquisition. In J. Coady and T. Huckin (eds) *Second Language Vocabulary Acquisition: A Rationale for Pedagogy* (pp. 174–200). Cambridge: Cambridge University Press.

Paribakht, T.S. and Wesche, M. (1998) "Incidental" and instructed L2 vocabulary acquisition: Different contexts, common processes. In D. Albrechtsen, B. Henriksen, I. M. Mees and E. Poulsen (eds) *Pespectives on Foreign and Second Language Pedagogy* (pp. 203–220). Odense: Odense University Press.

Paribakht, T.S. and Wesche, M. (1999) "Incidental" vocabulary acquisition through reading: An introspective study. *Studies in Second Language Acquisition* 21, 203–220.

Parry, K. (1993) Too many words: Learning the vocabulary of an academic subject. In T. Huckin, M. Haynes and J. Coady (eds) *Second Language Reading and Vocabulary Learning* (pp. 109–127). Norwood, NJ: Ablex.

Pérez Basanta, C. (1996) La integración de los contenidos léxicos en los métodos comunicativos: una cuestión pendiente. In J.D. Luque Durán and A. Pamies Bertrán (eds) *Segundas jornadas sobre estudio y enseñanza del léxico* (pp. 299–310). Granada: Método Ediciones.

Pérez Basanta, C. (1999) La enseñanza del vocabulario desde una perspectiva lingüística y pedagógica. In S. Salaberri (ed.) *Lingüística aplicada a las lenguas extranjeras* (pp. 262–307). Almería: Universidad de Almería.

Pérez Basanta, C. (2003a) Psycholinguistics and second language vocabulary teaching. *Indian Journal of Applied Linguistics* 29, 35–47.

Pérez Basanta, C. (Coord.) (2003b) ADELEX: Un programa para la evaluación y el desarrollo de la competencia léxica del inglés en un entorno virtual WEBCT para la Enseñanza universitaria. *Sello europeo a la innovación en la enseñanza y aprendizaje de lenguas extranjeras. Premios 2003* (pp. 111–143). Madrid: Ministerio Educación, Cultura y Deporte.

Pérez Basanta, C. (2004) Pedagogic aspects of the design and content of an online course for the development of lexical competence: ADELEX. *ReCALL* 16, 129–149.

Pérez Basanta, C. (2005) Assessing the receptive vocabulary of Spanish students of English philology: An empirical investigation. In J.M. Martínez-Dueñas Espejo, N. Mclaren, C. Pérez Basanta and L. Quereda Rodríguez-Navarro (eds) *Towards an Understanding of the English Language: Studies in Honour of Fernando Serrano* (pp. 456–477). Granada: Universidad de Granada.

Pérez Basanta, C. (2006a) Using technology for pre-service second language teacher education through WebCT. *International Journal of Technology, Knowledge, and Society* 2, 101–118.

Pérez Basanta, C. (2006b) ADELEX: Un programa virtual para la evaluación y desarrollo de la competencia léxica a través de las nuevas tecnologías. In C. Pérez Basanta (ed.) *Fundamentos teóricos y prácticos de ADELEX: Una investigación sobre la evaluación y el desarrollo de la competencia léxica a través de las nuevas tecnologías* (pp. 11–49). Granada: Comares.

Peters, E. (2007) Manipulating L2 learners' online dictionary use and its effect on L2 word retention. *Language Learning, and Technology* 11, 36–58.

Pigada, M. and Schmitt, N. (2006) Vocabulary acquisition from extensive reading: A case study. *Reading in a Foreign Language* 18, 1–28.

Pimsleur, P. (1967) A memory schedule. *The Modern Language Journal* 51, 73–75.

Pitts, M., White, H. and Krashen, S. (1989) Acquiring second language vocabulary through reading: A replication of the Clockwork Orange study using second language acquirers. *Reading in a Foreign Language* 5, 271–275.

Plas, J.J. (1998) Design and evaluation of the user interface of foreign language multimedia software: A cognitive approach. *Language Learning, and Technology* 2, 35–45.

Poel, K. and Swanepoel, P. (2003) Theoretical and methodological pluralism in designing effective lexical support for CALL. *Computer Assisted Language Learning* 16, 173–211.

Postman, L. and Keppel, G. (1970) *Norms of Word Associations*. New York: Academic Press.

Pressley, M., Levin, J.R. and McDaniels, M.A. (1987) Remembering versus inferring what a word means: Mnemonic and contextual approaches. In M.G. McKeown and M.E. Curtis (eds) *The Nature of Vocabulary Acquisition* (pp. 107–123). Hillsdale, NJ: Lawrence Erlbaum.

Prince, P. (1996) Second language vocabulary learning: The role of context versus translation as a function of proficiency. *The Modern Language Journal* 80, 478–493.

Qian, D.D. (1996) ESL vocabulary acquisition: Contextualization and decontextualization. *The Canadian Modern Language Review* 53, 120–142.

Qian, D.D. (2004) Second language lexical inferencing: Preferences, perceptions and practices. In P. Bogaards and B. Laufer (eds) *Vocabulary in a Second Language* (pp. 155–169). Amsterdam: John Benjamins Publishing Company.

Qian, D.D. and Schedl, M. (2004) Evaluation of an in-depth vocabulary knowledge measure for assessing reading performance. *Language Testing* 21, 28–52.

Rapp, B. and Goldrick, M. (2000) Discreteness and interactivity in spoken word production. *Psychological Review* 107, 460–499.

Read, J. (1993) The development of a new measure of L2 vocabulary knowledge. *Language Testing* 10, 355–371.

Read, J. (1998) Validating a test to measure depth of vocabulary knowledge. In A. Kunnan (ed.) *Validation in Language Assessment* (pp. 41–57). Mahwah, NJ: Lawrence Erlbaum.

Read, J. (2000) *Assessing Vocabulary*. Cambridge: Cambridge University Press.

Read, J. (2004) Plumbing the depths: How should the construct of vocabulary knowledge be defined? In P. Bogaards and B. Laufer (eds) *Vocabulary in a Second Language* (pp. 209–227). Amsterdam: John Benjamins.

Richards, J.C. (1976) The role of vocabulary teaching. *TESOL Quarterly* 10, 77–89.

Richards, J.C. (1993) Beyond the textbook: The role of commercial materials in language teaching. *RELC Journal* 24, 1–14.

Richards, J.E. (1976) The role of vocabulary teaching. *TESOL Quarterly* 10, 77–89.

Richards, B.J. and Malvern, D.D. (2007) Validity and threats to the validity of vocabulary measurement. In H. Daller, J. Milton and J. Treffers-Daller (eds) *Modelling and Assessing Vocabulary Knowledge* (pp. 79–92). Cambridge: Cambridge University Press.

Richards, J.C. and Schmidt, R. (2002) *Longman Dictionary of Language Teaching and Applied Linguistics*. London: Pearson Education Limited.

Rittershofer, J.S. (1987) The nominal reference system in the interlanguage of Japanese students writing in English: A discourse analysis. Doctoral dissertation, Columbia University Teachers College.

Robinson, B.F. and Mervis, C.B. (1998) Disentangling early language development: Modeling lexical and grammatical acquisition using an extension of case-study methodology. *Developmental Psychology* 34, 363–375.

Rosszell, R. (2003) *Combining extensive reading and intensive vocabulary study*. Paper presented at AAAL conference, Arlington.

Ruhland, H.G. (1998) *Going the Distance: A Non-Linear Approach to Change in Language Development*. Rijksuniversiteit: Groningen.

Russell, P. (1979) *The Brain Book*. London: Routledge and Kegan Paul.

Salling, A. (1959) What can frequency counts teach the language teacher? *Contact* 3, 24–29.

Saragi, T., Nation, I.S.P. and Meister, G.F. (1978) Vocabulary learning and reading. *System* 6, 72–78.

Schatz, E. and Baldwin, R. (1986) Context clues are unreliable predictors of word meanings. *Reading Research Quarterly* 21, 439–453.

Schmidt, R. (1990) The role of consciousness in second language learning. *Applied Linguistics* 11, 17–45.

Schmidt, R. (1994) Deconstructing consciousness in search of useful definitions for applied linguistics. *AILA Review* 11, 11–26.

Schmidt, R. (2001) Attention. In P. Robinson (ed.) *Cognition and Second Language Instruction* (pp. 3–33). New York: Cambridge University Press.

Schmitt, N. (1995) The word on words: An interview with Paul Nation. *The Language Teacher* 19, 5–7.

Schmitt, N. (1997) Vocabulary learning strategies. In N. Schmitt and M. McCarthy (eds) *Vocabulary: Description, Acquisition, and Pedagogy* (pp. 199–227). Cambridge: Cambridge University Press.

Schmitt, N. (1998) Tracking the incremental acquisition of second language vocabulary: A longitudinal study. *Language Learning* 48, 281–317.

Schmitt, N. (2000) *Vocabulary in Language Teaching*. Cambridge: Cambridge University Press.

Schmitt, N. (2008) Instructed second language vocabulary learning. *Language Teaching Research* 12, 329–363.

Schmitt, N. and Marsden, R. (2006) *Why is English Like That? Historical Answers to Hard ELT Questions.* Ann Arbor: Universty of Michigan Press.

Schmitt, N. and McCarthy, M. (eds) (1997) *Vocabulary: Description, Acquisition, and Pedagogy.* Cambridge: Cambridge University Press.

Schmitt, N. and Meara, P. (1997) Researching vocabulary through a word knowledge framework: Word associations and verbal suffixes. *Studies in Second Language Acquisition* 19, 17–36.

Schmitt, N. and Zimmerman, C.B. (2002) Derivative word forms: What do learners know? *TESOL Quarterly* 36, 145–171.

Schonell, F.J., Meddleton, I.G. and Shaw, B.A. (1956) *A Study of the Oral Vocabulary of Adults.* Brisbane: University of Queensland Press.

Schouten-van Parreren, C. (1991) *Psychological aspects of vocabulary learning in a foreign language.* Paper presented at the Vocabulary Acquisition in L2 Symposium, Malaga.

Sciarone, A. and Meijer, P. (1995) Does practice make perfect? On the effect of exercises on second/foreign language acquisition. *ITL* 107–108, 35–57.

Segler, T.M. (2001) *Second language vocabulary acquisition and learning strategies in ICALL environments.* On WWW at http://homepages.inf.ed.ac.uk/s9808690/newprop.pdf 30.4.2006. Accessed 3.8.2003.

Seibert, L.C. (1927) An experiment in learning French vocabulary. *Journal of Educational Psychology* 18, 294–309.

Seibert, L.C. (1930) An experiment on the relative efficiency of studying French vocabulary in associated pairs versus studying French vocabulary in context. *Journal of Educational Psychology* 21, 297–314.

Serrano van der Laan, M. (2008) Vocabulary for lower-level IELTS academic module candidates: An evaluation of a set of 14 IELTS glossaries. Unpublished doctoral research paper, UNED, Madrid.

Sheehan, R. (2005) Language as topic: Learner–teacher investigation of concordances. In C. Edwards and J. Willis (eds) *Teachers Exploring Task* (pp. 50–57). Basingstoke: Palgrave Macmillan.

Sheldon, L.E. (1987) Introduction. In L.E. Sheldon (ed.) *ELT Textbooks and Materials: Problems in Evaluating and Development* (pp. 1–10). London: Modern English Publications and the British Council.

Sheldon, L.E. (1988) Evaluating ELT textbooks and materials. *ELT Journal* 42, 237–246.

Sheorey, R. (1986) Error perceptions of native-speaking and non-native speaking teachers of ESL. *ELT Journal* 40, 306–312.

Shillaw, J. (1995) Using a word list as a focus for vocabulary learning. *The Language Teacher* 19, 58–59.

Sinclair, J. McH. (1991) *Corpus, Concordance, Collocation.* Oxford: Oxford University Press.

Sinclair, J. McH. and Renouf, A. (1988) A lexical syllabus for language learning. In R. Carter and M. McCarthy (eds) *Vocabulary and Language Teaching* (pp. 140–160). London and New York: Longman.

Singleton, D. (1999) *Exploring the Second Language Lexicon.* Cambridge: Cambridge University Press.

Skehan, P. (1993) Foreign language learning ability: Cognitive or linguistic? *Thames Valley University Working Papers in English Language Teaching* 2, 151–191.

Snellings, P., van Gelderen, A. and de Glopper, K. (2002) Lexical retrieval: An aspect of fluent second language production that can be enhanced. *Language Learning* 52, 723–754.

Sökmen, A.J. (2000) Current trends in teaching second language vocabulary. In N. Schmitt and M. McCarthy (eds) *Vocabulary: Description, Acquisition, and Pedagogy* (pp. 237–257). Cambridge: Cambridge University Press.
Sparks, R. and Ganschow, L. (2001) Aptitude for learning a foreign language. *Annual Review of Applied Linguistics* 21, 90–111.
Stæhr, L.S. (2008) Vocabulary size and the skills of listening, reading and writing. *Language Learning Journal* 36, 139–152.
Stahl, S.A. and Fairbanks, M.M. (1986) The effects of vocabulary instruction: A model-based meta-analysis. *Review of Educational Research* 56, 72–110.
Starreveld, P.A. and La Heij, W. (1995) Semantic interference, orthographic facilitation and their interaction in naming tasks. *Journal of Experimental Psychology: Learning, Memory, and Cognition* 21, 686–698.
Sternberg, R.J. (1987) Most vocabulary is learnt from context. In M.G. McKeown and M.E. Curtis (eds) *The Nature of Vocabulary Acquisition* (pp. 89–105). Hillsdale, NJ: Erlbaum.
Studolsky, S. (1989) Is teaching really by the book? In P.W. Jackson and S. Haroutunian-Gordon (eds) *From Socrates to Software: The Teacher as Text and the Text as Teacher. Eighty-Ninth Yearbook of the National Society for the Study of Education*, Part 1 (pp. 159–84). Chicago: University of Chicago Press.
Swain, M. (1985) Communicative competence: Some roles of comprehensible input and comprehensible output in its development. In S. Gass and C. Madden (eds) *Input in Second Language Acquisition* (pp. 235–253). New York: Newbury House.
Swain, M. and Lapkin, S. (1995) Problems in output and the cognitive processes they generate: A step towards second language learning. *Applied Linguistics* 16, 371–391.
Swan, M. (1992) The textbook: Bridge or wall? *Linguistics and Language Teaching* 2, 32–35.
Tarone, E. (1980) Communication strategies, foreigner talk, and repair in interlanguage. *Language Learning* 30, 417–431.
Thelen, E. and Smith, L.B. (1994) *A Dynamic Systems Approach to the Development of Cognition and Action*. Cambridge, MA: MIT Press.
Thornbury, S. (2002) *How to Teach Vocabulary*. Essex: Longman.
Thorne, A. and Thorne, C. (2000) Building bridges on the Web: Using the Internet for cultural studies. In P. Brett and G. Motteram (eds) *A Special Interest in Computers: Learning and Teaching With Information and Communications Technologies* (pp. 59–73). Whitsable, Kent: IATEFL.
Tice, J. (1991) The textbook straitjacket. *Practical English Teaching* 3, 23.
Tinkham, T. (1993) The effect of semantic clustering on the learning of second language vocabulary. *System* 21, 371–380.
Tinkham, T. (1997) The effects of semantic and thematic clustering on the learning of second language vocabulary. *Second Language Research* 13, 138–163.
Tomiyana, M. (1980) Grammatical errors and communication breakdown. *TESOL Quarterly* 14, 71–79.
Tomlinson, B. (2008) *English Language Learning Materials*. London: Continuum International Publishing Group.
Tréville, M.C. (1996) Lexical learning and reading in L2 at the beginner level: The advantage of cognates. *The Canadian Modern Language Review* 53, 173–189.
Tribble, C. (1997) Improvising corpora for ELT: Quick-and-dirty ways of developing corpora for language teaching. On WWW at http://www.ctribble.co.uk/text/Palc.htm.
van Dijk, M.W.G. (2003) Child language cuts capers: Variability and ambiguity in early child development. Doctoral dissertation, University of Groningen.

van Geert, P. (1991) A dynamic systems theory model of cognitive and language growth. *Psychological Review* 98, 3–53.
van Geert, P. (2008) The dynamic systems approach in the study of L1 and L2 acquisition: An introduction. *The Modern Language Journal* 92 (2), 179–199.
van Geert, P. and van Dijk, M. (2002) Focus on variability, new tools to study intra-individual variability in developmental data. *Infant Behavior and Development* 25, 340–374.
Van Patten, B. (1990) Attending to content and form in the input: An experiment in consciousness. *Studies in Second Language Acquisition* 12, 287–301.
Vermeer, A. (1992) Exploring the second language learner lexicon. In L. Verhoeven and J.H.A.L. De Jong (eds) *The Construct of Language Proficiency: Applications of Psychological Models to Language Assessment* (pp. 147–171). Amsterdam: John Benjamins.
Verspoor, M., de Bot, K. and Lowie, W. (2004) Dynamic systems theory and variation: A case study in L2 writing. In H. Aertsen, M. Hannay and R. Lyall (eds) *Words in Their Places: A Festschrift for J. Lachlan Mackenzie* (pp. 407–421). Amsterdam: Free University Press.
Verspoor, M.H., Lowie, W.M. and van Dijk, M. (2008) Variability in L2 development from a dynamic systems perspective. *The Modern Language Journal* 92, 214–231.
Vitevich, M.S., Luce, P.A., Pisoni, D.B. and Auer, E.A. (1999) Phonotactics, neighborhood activation, and lexical access for spoken words. *Brain and Language* 68, 306–311.
Waring, R. (1997) The negative effects of learning words in semantic sets: A replication. *System* 25, 261–274.
Waring, R. (2003) At what rate do learners learn and retain new vocabulary from reading a graded reader? *Reading in a Foreign Language* 15, 130–163.
Warschauer, M. (1996) Motivational aspects of using computers for writing and communication. In M. Warschauer (ed.) *Telecollaboration in Foreign Language Learning* (pp. 29–46). Honolulu, USA: University of Hawai'i Second Language Teaching and Curriculum Center.
Watts, N. (1997) A learner-based design model for interactive multimedia language learning packages. *System* 25, 1–18.
Webb, C. (1996) Hypertext and the construction of individual narratives: implications for socially constructed curriculum in primary schools. On WWW at http://ausweb.scu.edu.au/aw96/educn/webb/paper.htm. Accessed 6.5.2006.
Webb, S. (2005) Receptive and productive vocabulary learning: The effects of reading and writing on word knowledge. *Studies in Second Language Acquisition* 27, 33–52.
West, M. (1953) *A General Service List of English Words*. London: Longman.
White, R.V. (1995) *The ELT Curriculum*. Oxford: Blackwell.
Widdowson, H.G. (1978) *Teaching Language as Communication*. Oxford: Oxford University Press.
Wilkins, D. (1972) *Linguistics in Language Teaching*. London: Edward Arnold.
Willis, D. (1990) *The Lexical Syllabus*. London and Glasgow: Collins.
Willis, J. and Willis, D. (1988) *Collins COBUILD English Course*. London and Glasgow: Collins.
Woolard, G. (2000) Collocation: Encouraging learning independence. In M. Lewis (ed.) *Teaching Collocation. Further Developments in the Lexical Approach* (pp. 28–46). London: Language Teaching Publications.
Wotjak, G. (1999) ¿Qué puede aportar la lexicografía a la enseñanza de lenguas extranjeras? In J.M. Becerra Hiraldo *et al.* (eds) *La enseñanza de segundas lenguas* (pp. 17–42). Granada: Universidad de Granada.
Xue, G. and Nation, I.S.P. (1984) A university word list. *Language Learning and Communication* 3, 215–229.

Young, D. (1993) Processing strategies of foreign language readers: Authentic and edited input. *Foreign Language Annals* 26, 451–468.

Zahar, R., Spada, N. and Cobb, T. (2001) Acquiring vocabulary through reading: Effects of frequency and contextual richness. *Canadian Modern Language Review* 57, 541–572.

Zahorik, J.A. (1995) *Constructivist Teaching*. Bloomington, IN: Phi Delta Kappa Educational Foundation.

Zhang, X. (1993) English collocations and their effect on the writing of native and non-native college freshmen. Unpublished doctoral dissertation, Indiana University of Pennsylvania.

Zimmerman, C.B. (1997) Historical trends in second language vocabulary instruction. In J. Coady and T. Huckin (eds) *Second Language Vocabulary Acquisition: A Rationale for Pedagogy* (pp. 5–19). Cambridge: Cambridge University Press.

Zuluaga, A. (2002) Los enlaces frecuentes de María Moliner. Observaciones sobre las llamadas colocaciones. *Lingüística Española Actual* XXIV, 97–114.

Index

Academic Word List 49, 191
active
 – knowledge 8, 21, 23, 24, 41, 47, 49, 54, 56
 – vocabulary 47. 48, 56
antonym 36, 39, 158
Arabic 86, 88, 90, 92, 93
AuralLex 85, 86, 88, 93, 95
aural vocabulary 87
authentic language 17, 18, 20, 113
autonomy 5, 164, 165, 173, 178, 181, 182

bilingual 2, 46, 63, 64, 108, 194
 – context 76
 – dictionary 162, 173
 – glossary 10
 – lexicon 46
 – word list 10, 21, 153-155, 161
breadth of vocabulary 112, 124
British National Corpus 114, 115

Cambridge International Corpus 146, 166
Chinese 84, 86, 88, 90, 177
classroom 104, 109, 112, 115, 116, 121, 123, 126, 150-152, 154, 161, 171, 173, 180, 183
 – activity 174
 – context 16, 24, 26
 – EFL 109, 110
 – instruction 26, 198
 – language 6
 – materials 6
 – resources 6
 – time 6
classroom-based study 126
cloze test 9, 118, 120
COBUILD Corpus 145-149
cognate 62, 77, 82
 – language 3
 – word 3
collocation 9, 23, 24, 31, 37, 38, 46, 64, 66, 70, 72, 75, 77, 80, 81, 109, 112, 113, 116-118, 120, 122, 161, 165, 167, 168, 177, 178, 187, 189, 192, 195, 203
 – lexical 11, 160, 162-164, 168, 172, 173
 – grammatical 174
Common European Framework 113, 115
communication skills 87
communicative 1, 8, 21, 26, 92, 93, 94, 174, 189
 – ability 92

 – activity 17, 18, 20, 166, 167, 172
 – approach 7, 161, 173, 189
 – competence 162, 175, 178, 185
 – situation 1
 – skill 8, 94, 98
 – task 7, 17, 21, 95
 – teaching 23, 26, 174
 – textbook 152
computational linguistics 3, 178
computer-assisted language learning (CALL) 11, 21, 176, 175-185
concordance 9, 21, 112, 113-124, 176
Constructivism 11, 178, 179, 181-185
context availability hypothesis 11, 179, 180
controlled production 47-57
core vocabulary 112, 200
corpus 11, 29, 113-115, 117, 122-124, 145, 146, 166, 176-178
 – linguistics 11, 177, 178
 – spoken 83,
 – written 83,
crossassociation 36, 37
cross-sectional 3, 47, 51, 57

data-driven learning 112, 113-115, 117
declarative knowledge 26
default hypothesis 15, 16, 26
depth of knowledge 3, 61, 112, 117, 118
depth of processing 11, 25, 113, 159, 160, 180
 – hypothesis 180
dictionary 4, 5, 9, 16, 19, 21-23, 25, 29, 45, 50, 63, 112, 113, 115, 123, 125, 146, 161, 162, 173, 193
 – bilingual 161, 162
 – definition 47, 116
 – electronic 20, 22
 – online 21, 176, 177
Discrete Model 100, 101, 105, 108
distance learning 182, 183
dual-coding theory 179

EFL 15, 44, 47, 75, 77, 102, 103, 106, 107, 113, 145, 146, 148, 153, 175
 – classroom 109, 119, 152, 171, 190
 – learner 75, 106, 146
English 7-10, 15, 23, 24, 28-32, 40, 42, 44, 49-51, 53, 55, 56, 62-64, 66, 73, 75-78, 82, 83, 86, 88, 95, 97, 102-104, 107, 108, 112-119, 127, 130, 131-135, 139-142, 145,

227

155, 158, 163, 165, 167-171, 177, 178, 187, 190-195
English as a Foreign Language 8, 10, 15, 83, 97, 99, 127
ESL context 48, 77
Eurocentres Vocabulary Size Test 83, 84
evaluation 25, 79
explicit
– approaches 5, 112
– vocabulary learning 3, 4, 123, 166
– teaching 6, 12, 32, 112
extensive reading 4, 6, 33

false friend 202
Farsee 86
focus on form 7, 17, 18, 19, 20, 21, 23, 24, 26, 27
focus on forms 7, 17, 18, 20, 21, 23, 24, 26, 27
foreign language 4, 8, 16, 24, 83-87, 89, 92, 96,127, 135, 145, 153, 157, 171, 187, 189
foreign language context 4, 24
fossilization 43, 188, 189, 201, 203
free production 8, 41, 47-57
French 8, 46, 62-82
frequency bands 49, 88, 191

grammar
– rules 1
– teaching 1
Grammar Translation Method 189
Greek 86

Hebrew 24
high frequency word 10, 112, 145-47, 153
hypertext 21, 176, 178, 181, 182, 184, 185
hypertextuality 178, 181, 182, 184, 185

imaginability hypothesis 11, 179
implicit vocabulary learning 3, 186
incidental 7, 18, 19, 21, 22, 128
– acquisition 9, 17, 126
– approaches 5
– focus on form 7, 17, 19, 26
– focus on forms 7, 20, 26
– learning 4-6, 18, 20, 22, 24, 26, 33, 39-41, 117, 203
– word acquisition 7, 26
incremental learning 10, 127, 129-132
Indo-European language 76
instruction 6, 11, 12, 15, 23-25, 27, 38, 61, 62, 110, 176, 179, 180, 181, 183, 186, 187-189, 192, 193, 195-203
– classroom 26
– form-focused 7, 15, 17, 18, 24, 26
– grammar 76
– word-focused 8, 17, 18
intentional 16, 18, 21-23, 180
– focus on form 7

– focus on forms 7, 21, 23, 26
– learning 6, 12, 18, 22, 39, 40, 147
interaction 2, 3, 7, 8, 17, 19, 41, 42-44, 46-48, 51-57, 126, 156, 178, 182, 183, 184, 187, 207, 210, 219, 224
involvement
– hypothesis 25
– load hypothesis 24-27
isolated word 108, 127, 131, 172

Keyword Approach 35, 39
Keyword Method 33

L2
– input 11, 25
– lexical knowledge 41, 54, 57
– reading 11, 33, 61, 62, 77, 186
language assessment 3
learner autonomy 164, 165, 173, 178, 181, 182
Levels Test 50, 58, 83-85
lexeme 162, 188
lexical
– acquisition 2, 3, 157, 179, 180, 188, 189
– competence 2, 11, 111, 175, 176-178, 185, 189, 201, 202, 221
– depth 97
– development 8, 41, 43, 47, 48, 61, 188, 189, 200
– family 103, 109, 110
– inferencing 8, 61, 62, 65, 67, 73, 75-77, 192
– item 9,15, 17, 23, 24, 26, 46, 47, 62, 99, 100, 102, 103, 108, 110, 166, 167, 172, 173, 177, 179, 187, 188
– learning 3, 5, 11, 48, 113
– representation 99, 100, 108, 188, 201
– retrieval 107-110
– syllabus 10, 148, 149, 151
Lexical Approach 175
lexical unit 5, 7, 10, 157, 160-162, 164, 165-168, 171, 172
– *one*-word 160, 165-168, 171, 172
– *multi*-word 160
lexicalization pattern 62, 77
lexicography 11, 177
lexicology 11, 177
lexicon 2, 46, 47, 56, 57, 83, 92, 94, 112, 160, 161, 163, 164, 200, 202
– bilingual 46
– L1 46, 75
– L2 8, 46-48, 57, 75, 158, 203
– learner 3, 87
– mental 11, 35, 45-47, 57, 83, 85, 93, 97, 164, 178, 180, 185, 187, 188, 200, 201, 203
lexis 3, 93, 174, 176, 185, 192
loanwords 30
longitudinal 3, 45, 47, 49, 50, 56, 116, 118

Index

mapping 93
materials 6, 7, 10, 26, 29, 49, 103, 106, 109, 143, 148, 152, 154, 156, 157, 176, 178-183, 190, 205
mental processing 3, 5
minimal pair 102
Modern Language Aptitude Test 85
mother-tongue 3, 147
multiword unit 17

non-communicative task 7, 17, 20
noticing 4, 24, 25, 27, 165, 177

online
 – learning 11, 184, 185,
 – resources 181
oral fluency 87
orthographic vocabulary 8, 84, 86-88, 92-98
orthography 75-77, 84, 95

paradigmatic association 109, 118, 192, 201, 203
passive
 – knowledge 8, 23, 41, 47-49, 52, 56
 – vocabulary 25, 47, 48, 54, 56-58, 158
pedagogical implications 118, 133, 135
phonological
 – form 84-86, 92, 93, 97, 108
 – representation 92, 99, 101
 – vocabulary 8, 9, 84, 86-88, 92-97
polysemous meaning 133
polysemy 31, 37, 118, 132-135
procedural knowledge 26
production
 – controlled 47-57
 – free 8, 41, 47-56
productive vocabulary 198
pronunciation 108, 110, 112, 135
psycholinguistics 3, 11, 178, 179
pushed output hypothesis 25, 27

qualitative 3, 43, 64, 123, 160
quantitative 3, 67, 75, 119, 160

reading 3-6, 8, 11, 15, 16, 18-21, 40, 61-63, 73, 75-77, 82-84, 86-88, 91-98, 99, 109, 126-128, 130, 149, 150, 154, 159, 161, 162, 166, 176, 186, 187, 190-192
receptive vocabulary 5
recycling 6, 7, 34, 36, 38, 40, 147, 148, 157, 161, 170
 – vocabulary 10, 34, 156, 160, 165, 172, 172
register 2, 19, 31, 37, 38, 70, 87, 112, 115, 164
rhythmical pattern 102

scaffolding 182, 184
self-study 152
semantic
 – association 187
 – family 109, 110
 – network 5, 103, 108, 109, 187, 189
sentence grammar 65, 66, 73, 76, 80, 81
Spanish 9, 10, 15, 62, 103, 105-107, 110, 126, 127, 129-135, 141, 147, 148, 153, 163, 165, 167-185
speech production 99, 102, 108-110
spelling 36, 105, 107, 110, 112, 135, 140, 195
 – mistake 105
spoken language 19, 86, 93, 190
strategy(-ies) 3-7, 10, 32, 33, 39, 45, 61, 75, 76, 86, 112, 130, 132, 135, 157, 161, 165, 169, 170, 172, 173, 177, 178, 182, 186, 187, 193
stress pattern 104
structuralism 2
synforms 130, 131
synformy 32, 33, 37
synonym 9, 20, 30, 36, 39, 51, 73, 118-120, 122, 158, 193
syntagmatic association 109, 118, 192, 201, 203

target language 2, 8, 11, 28, 44, 65, 77, 103, 158, 171, 187, 189, 197, 202, 203
task-based
 – approach 113, 183
 – material 151
 – methodology 151
 – syllabus 151
testing 50, 57, 88, 95, 107, 111, 118, 119, 126, 135, 176
think aloud protocol 64
translation 20, 22-24, 82, 130, 131, 135, 157-159, 194, 195-203
 – L1 10, 17, 157-159, 161, 162, 165, 171, 173, 188, 189
t-test 90, 119, 195

University Word List 49

validity 102, 106, 194
 – construct 84
 – content 84
vocabulary
 – acquisition 2, 4-7, 9, 11, 12, 38, 99, 126, 134, 173, 176, 177, 179, 180, 185, 190, 202
 – attrition 45
 – instruction 11, 17, 25, 27, 62, 179, 186, 187, 189, 192, 196, 197, 200, 202, 203
 – L2 7, 9, 11, 15, 16, 26, 41, 42, 45, 46, 57, 109, 126, 130, 132, 134, 159, 160, 161, 163, 173, 188, 202
 – size 8, 9, 15, 16, 29, 30, 38, 47, 48, 50, 83, 84, 86-88, 90-94, 96-98, 186
Vocabulary Levels Test 83, 84
vocalic segment 104

web-based pedagogy 181

word
- association 11, 64, 65, 70, 71, 76, 77, 80, 81, 177, 186, 205
- collocation 64-66, 70, 71, 75, 77, 80, 81
- focused instruction 7, 17-19, 24, 26-27
- frequency 6, 8, 41, 47, 48, 88
- knowledge 6, 7, 9, 11, 26, 28, 30-32, 34, 36, 38, 40, 41, 41, 46, 50, 84, 85, 112, 113, 117, 118, 123, 126, 155, 164, 177, 178, 194, 196
- morphology 65, 70, 71, 73, 76, 80, 81
- recall 8, 41, 49, 50, 51, 56
written language 19, 93

X_Lex 83, 86-91, 93-95

For Product Safety Concerns and Information please contact our EU Authorised Representative:

Easy Access System Europe

Mustamäe tee 50

10621 Tallinn

Estonia

gpsr.requests@easproject.com